The Castles of Wales

The
Castles
of Wales

Lindsay Evans

BARNES
&NOBLE
BOOKS
NEW YORK

IN MEMORY OF MY PARENTS

Contents

List of Illustrations   ix

Acknowledgements   xi

Preface   1

Introduction   3

THE CASTLES   29

Appendix I: Genealogies   230

Appendix II: Who, what, when and where   237

Appendix III: A castle building glossary   255

Appendix IV: A Welsh place name glossary   261

Bibliography   270

List of Illustrations

Giler Gate House (*Author's Collection*)
Glynllifon, Fort Williamsburg (*Author's Collection*)
Pembroke Castle by Paul Sandby (*National Library of Wales*)
Dolbadarn Castle by Richard Wilson (*National Museum of Wales*)
Dolbadarn Castle by J.M.W. Turner (*Royal Academy of Arts*)
Aberystwyth Castle (*Wales Tourist Board*)
Beaumaris Castle (*Wales Tourist Board*)
Beaupre Porch (from window) (*Author's Collection*)
Bodelwyddan Castle (*Author's Collection*)
Bronllys Castle (*Author's Collection*)
Caergwrle Castle (*Author's Collection*)
Caernarfon Castle (*Wales Tourist Board*)
Caernarfon Castle (*Author's Collection*)
Caerphilly Castle (*Author's Collection*)
Cardiff Castle (*Wales Tourist Board*)
Cardiff Castle, chimney breast of banqueting hall (*Author's Collection*)
Carew Castle (*Wales Tourist Board*)
Carew Castle (*Author's Collection*)
Castell y Bere (*Author's Collection*)
Castell Coch, washstand (*Author's Collection*)
Chepstow Castle (*Wales Tourist Board*)
Chirk Castle (*National Trust*)
Chirk Castle (*Author's Collection*)
Coity Castle (*Wales Tourist Board*)
Conwy Castle by Julius Caesar Ibbetson (*National Library of Wales*)
Conwy Castle (*Author's Collection*)

Cricieth Castle (*Author's Collection*)
Cyfarthfa Castle (*Author's Collection*)
Denbeigh Castle (*Wales Tourist Board*)
Dinefwr Castle (*Author's Collection*)
Dolforwyn Castle (*Cadw*)
Flint Castle (*Author's Collection*)
Grosmont Castle (*Wales Tourist Board*)
Gwrych Castle (*Author's Collection*)
Harlech Castle (*Michael Fairfax Rawlings*)
Harlech Castle, rear view (*Michael Fairfax Rawlings*)
Hawarden Castle (*Author's Collection*)
Hay Castle (*Author's Collection*)
Kidwelly Castle (*Wales Tourist Board*)
Llansteffan Castle (*Wales Tourist Board*)
Llawhaden Castle (*Wales Tourist Board*)
Manorbier Castle (*Wales Tourist Board*)
Ogmore Castle (*Wales Tourist Board*)
Pembroke Castle (*Wales Tourist Board*)
Pembroke Castle by John 'Warwick' Smith (*National Library of Wales*)
Penrhyn Castle (*National Trust*)
Powis Castle (*Author's Collection*)
Raglan Castle (*Wales Tourist Board*)
Rhuddlan Castle (*Wales Tourist Board*)
Skenfrith Castle (*National Trust*)
St Donats Castle (*Author's Collection*)
Tretower Castle (*Wales Tourist Board*)
Tretower Court (*Author's Collection*)
Weobley Castle (*Cadw*)
White Castle (*Wales Tourist Board*)

Acknowledgements

I should like to offer my warmest thanks to Constable's commissioning editor, Carol O'Brien for her constructive interest and her constant encouragement, and to Tara Lawrence, her assistant, for her kindness and patience in dealing with matters of detail. Margaret Body, the copy editor, was the embodiment of tact and good humour, and made a number of valuable suggestions.

Christine Kenyon and Alexandria Quinlan of Cadw and Sian Newton of Wales Tourist Board went out of their way to be helpful, and their assistance is greatly appreciated.

I should also like to thank Michael Fairfax-Rawlings, Sir William Gladstone, and Richard Keen of the National Trust in Wales. As well as being an excellent typist with impeccable Welsh, Meinir Jones was a wonderful listener and became a real friend in need.

Valerie, who has had the great fortune of living at various times close to three of the best castles of Wales, was a constant companion, and added enormously to the enjoyment of the enterprise.

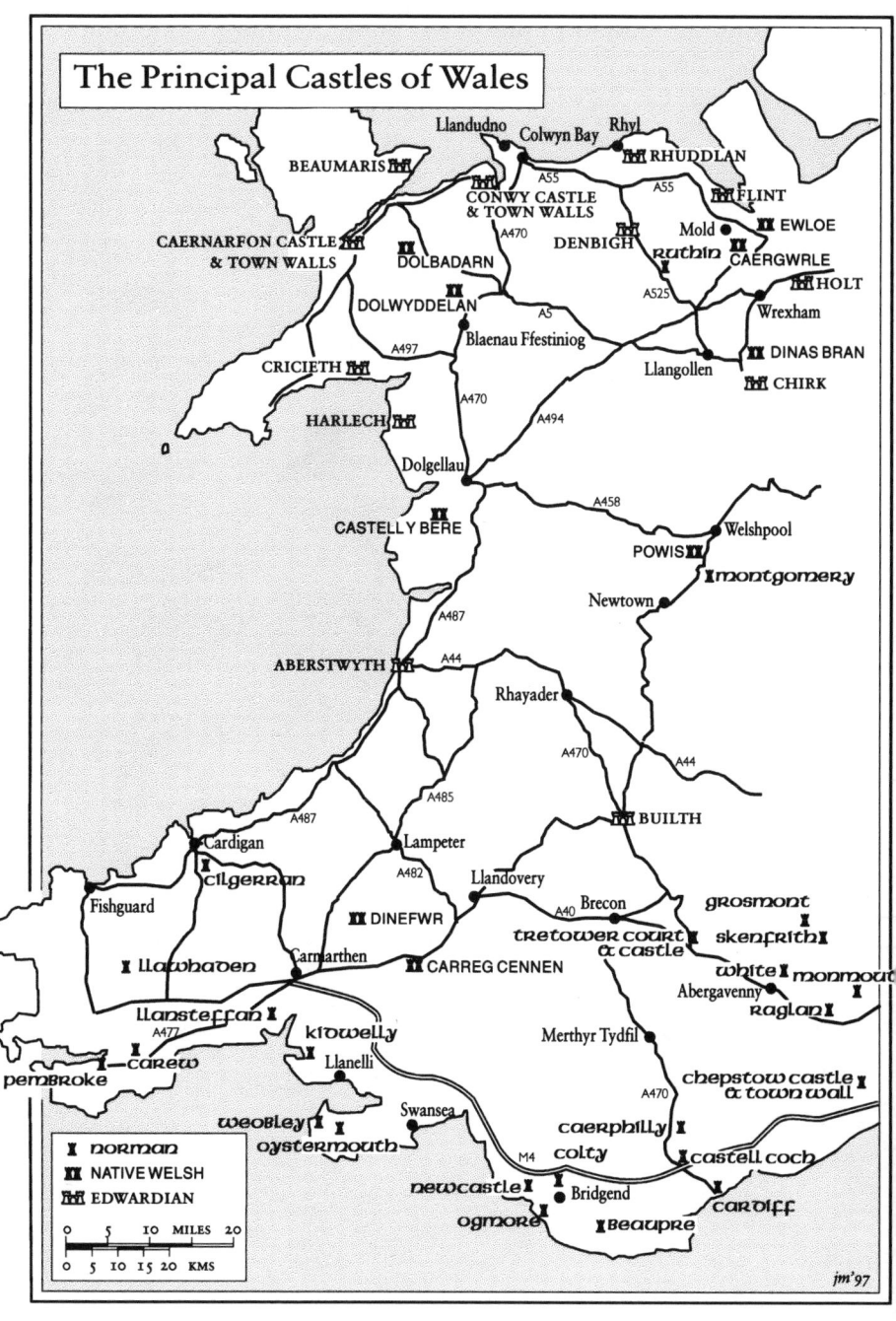

The Principal Castles of Wales

Llandudno
Colwyn Bay
Rhyl
RHUDDLAN
BEAUMARIS
A55
CONWY CASTLE
& TOWN WALLS
A55
FLINT
A470
EWLOE
CAERNARFON CASTLE
& TOWN WALLS
DOLBADARN
DENBIGH
Mold
Ruthin
CAERGWRLE
A525
HOLT
DOLWYDDELAN
A5
Wrexham
Blaenau Ffestiniog
A497
CRICIETH
Llangollen
DINAS BRAN
A470
CHIRK
HARLECH
A494
Dolgellau
A458
Welshpool
CASTELL Y BERE
POWIS
Montgomery
A487
Newtown
ABERSTWYTH
A44
Rhayader
A470
A44
BUILTH
A485
Cardigan
Lampeter
CILGERRAN
A482
Llandovery
Fishguard
DINEFWR
A40
Brecon
GROSMONT
Carmarthen
Tretower court
& castle
Skenfrith
Llawhaden
CARREG CENNEN
White
monmout
Abergavenny
Llansteffan
A477
Kidwelly
Raglan
carew
Llanelli
Merthyr Tydfil
pembroke
chepstow castle
& town wall
A470
Weobley
Swansea
caerphilly
oystermouth
M4
colty
castell coch
newcastle
Bridgend
cardiff
ogmore
Beaupre

I	norman
II	NATIVE WELSH
𝕳	EDWARDIAN

0 5 10 MILES 20
0 5 10 15 20 KMS

jm '97

Preface

It is not intended that this book should be read from cover to cover, but that the individual entries should provide sufficient preliminary background information on the castles the reader proposes to visit. In most cases, further historical and architectural details may be gleaned from guide books available on site.

The castles are listed alphabetically. Four of them are designated World Heritage Sites by Unesco and the World Heritage Convention of 1972.

Opening hours vary, but standard Cadw hours, when referred to on the heading, generally mean:

> Summer: 09.30–18.30 Mondays–Sundays (Late March–Late Oct. BST)
> Winter: 09.30–16.00 Mondays–Saturdays (GMT)
>   14.00–16.00 Sundays* (Late Oct.–Late March GMT)
> * Beaumaris, Caernarfon, Caerphilly, Castell Coch, Chepstow, Conwy, Harlech, Kidwelly and Raglan are open from 11.00–16.00 on Sundays in winter.

Cadw admission charges, where applicable, range from £1.70 to £3.80.

The county names are those in use after the local government reorganisation of 1996.

At the end of the book the four appendices are intended to fill in the genealogical and historical background, explain the terminology of castle building and provide a Welsh glossary. The bibliography offers suggestions for further reading.

An encouraging note on pronunciation

Welsh, unlike Scottish or Irish Gaelic, is entirely phonetic. It sounds as it looks. So just have the strength of your convictions and do your best with *ll* and *ch*, which are a lot less trouble than the faint-hearted make out.

Just remember seven points:

1 Vowels are shorter, dare one say purer, less drawled than in English.
2 The stress comes on the last syllable but one.
3 *ff* = f and *f* = *v*
4 *c* and *g* are hard, as in 'conger'
5 *dd* = th, as in 'then' and *th* = th, as in 'thin'
6 *w* is a vowel = oo
7 *y* is a vowel = u, as in 'hut' when alone or anywhere except the final syllable
= i, as in 'hit' in a final syllable
Mynydd (mountain), pronounced munith, with the th of 'then', illustrates the two *y* sounds. Get *mynydd* right and Welsh-speakers will know you are trying.

Introduction

The hundreds of miles of Welsh coastline have exerted a great attraction for thousands of years. Invaders, up to the present day, have explored and exploited the estuaries, shores and inlets, with varying degrees of curiosity and ruthlessness, from plundering and colonising, to hard industrialisation and persuasive commercialism, each bringing its own particular brand of pollution.

Many of the early invaders, however, discovered that, easy as their initial conquest might have been, the prospect of making substantial inroads was far more daunting, and any real progress was thwarted by mountains. In fact, the mountains of Wales have played as important a part in the history of the country as the sea. If the latter introduced new habits, customs, fashions and vocabulary, the former safeguarded all that was indigenous, all that was Welsh.

The mountains of Snowdonia are the strongholds of her nationhood; for anybody travelling through Snowdonia, *Cadernid Gwynedd* (The Might of Gwynedd) is a resonantly apt description. Nobody can see those ranges without realising that they are the natural defences of a country whose official independence was eventually lost over 200 years after England had kow-towed to Norman rule. They were the mountains which impeded Roman progress westwards to Ireland; they were the mountains which caused Edward I to embark on his vast programme of castle building, involving state enterprise on such a level that the Crown's debts to Italian merchant bankers were severe and serious. £100,000 was expended on a show of subjection.

Commandeering the coastal plain of South Wales presented no such obstacles for the Romans. The rivers Usk, Wye and

Severn offered favourable means of communication, with the latter advantageously having access to the Bristol Channel.

Having established themselves in Wales at *Venta Silurum* (Caerwent), they made their westward advance to *Isca* (Caerleon), where their legionary fortress became the centre of a road system, linking it inland with *Burrium* (Usk) to the north and *Gobannium* (Abergavenny), to the north-west, leading westwards on to Llandovery. Following the coastal plain westwards, the road led to Caerdydd (Caer-dyf – the fort on the Taff – hence Cardiff), thence to *Nidum* (Castell Nedd; Neath), and onwards through *Leucarium* (Casllwchwr; Loughor), to *Maridunum* (Caerfyrddin; Carmarthen), on the banks of the tidal river Tywi. It was a route which, having been opened, greatly facilitated the westward advance of the Normans a thousand years later, who established strongholds on the site of Roman forts and settlements.

In North Wales, the Romans made their regional centre at *Segontium* (within walking distance of the town and Edwardian castle of Caernarfon), which was easily accessible by sea. However, their plans for an effective road network were considerably hampered by the mountains of Snowdonia, although placenames like Caerhun and Caerllugwy clearly indicate that they managed to assert their authority, however localised it might have been. Their presence at Segontium was not only physically impressive, but was to play a significant role in early medieval Welsh literature, and ultimately affect the building of Edward I's great fortress palace at Caernarfon.

It was through their language that the Romans made the greatest impact on Wales. In addition to those words dealing with fortifications, such as *caer*, *cas*, and *castell*, there are place names starting with *pont* (bridge), and *ystrad-* (L. *strata* = vale). *Ffenestr* (window), and *mur* (wall), are domestic, *melin* (L. *molina* = mill), more communal, and *eglwys* religious from the Roman adoption of Greek, *ecclesia* (church). The days of the week in Welsh are based on Roman and not Norse gods.

Subsequent invaders, the Norsemen, confined themselves to coastal regions and established no settlements in Wales comparable to those in England, Scotland and Ireland. Nevertheless, they stayed here long enough to imprint their presence not only on individual place names, such as Sweinesei (Swansea), but on islands, as in Anglesey, Bardsey, Caldey and Ramsey, Skokholm, Grassholm, Priestholm, Flat Holm, Steep Holm, and Skomer. Two of the most frequented of these Norse settlements are Great and Little Orme's Head, near Llandudno in Gwynedd.

It was, of course, the next invasion of these islands which resulted not only in conquest, but in the introduction of a new civilisation. The success of that conquest and the continued subjugation of the conquered depended on many factors: the most visible of them was the castle.

Conquest and Castle

The train journey from Chester to Cardiff is one of the most fertile in Britain, following as it does the frontier between England and Wales, the March. Yet it has never been called the March or Marcher Line, which would have indicated, *en passant*, its historical significance. Apart from the starting point, Chester, two important towns on the route, Shrewsbury and Hereford, feature as major contributory factors to the Norman Conquest of Wales, while Ludlow, with the outline of its fine castle and church rising from the lush river plains of the Shropshire–Herefordshire border, also adds to the appreciation of this journey, skirting the once uncompromisingly hostile division between invader and invaded, England and Wales.

After 1066, Chester, Shrewsbury and Hereford were established as Marcher lordships, each governed by an ally of the Conqueror, and each becoming a palatine earldom: William's nephew, Hugh Lupus, 'The Fat', of Avranches at Chester; Roger de Montgomery at Shrewsbury, and William FitzOsbern at Hereford. Each one was expected to achieve the same objective: to move westwards and control the territory which had been 'acquired' by whatever means were expedient.

Hugh Lupus relied on his cousin, Robert of Rhuddlan, to make effective inroads towards and beyond the river Clwyd, which traditionally denoted the boundary of North Wales, and had therefore been an area of constant struggle. Having thrown up a motte-and-bailey in 1073, known as Twthill, two years later he marked his westwards advance by asserting his hold of Degannwy, a strategically placed site on the Conwy estuary, and one which had been appreciated for its defensive strength centuries earlier.

The forward thrust was continued after Robert of Rhuddlan's death in 1088 by Hugh Lupus himself, who built a castle at Aberlleiniog, near Penmon in Anglesey, and at Caernarfon, where he took advantage of the site, which almost a hundred years later, proved so important to Edward I. Both castles represented the short-lived victory of Hugh, earl of Chester over Gruffudd ap Cynan, in whose *maerdrefi* the motte-and-bailey defences were established.

At Shrewsbury, Roger de Montgomery was able to gain control of Powys without much effort, giving his name to the former settlement called Baldwin. The Welsh equivalent, Maldwyn became the native form of Trefaldwyn for the town and Sir Faldwyn for the county. The territory between Hereford and the Bristol Channel was put in the care of another kinsman of the Conqueror, William FitzOsbern to whom the very nature of the lowlands of Gwent and the coastal plain presented no major challenge.

The first Norman defences were statements marking newly gained territory, and consisted of an earthwork and timber compound, comprising, in its simplest form, a mound and an enclosure. Additional defence was provided by a deep ditch surrounding the enclosure, or bailey, thus forming a motte-and-bailey.

Further westward in the Vale of Glamorgan, and on the Gower Peninsula, the principal characteristic of a defensive site was recognised not by the mound or the motte but only by an enclosure, probably far more severely ditched and classed as a 'ringwork'.

The most notable exception to the Norman earth-and-timber stronghold was FitzOsbern's castle at Chepstow, being the first stone-built fortress in the newly conquered area west of the Wye. It was a building of enormous significance, for it established Wales as being a land of castles, representing as it did, the *Marchia Wallie* – 'the March of Wales'.

The advantage of the motte-and-bailey fortifications was three-fold: they could be put up quickly, they were cheap in terms of labour and material, and they made their presence known in no uncertain terms. Those whose sites were chosen initially for their military impact, but which gradually developed in administrative and social importance, were refortified in masonry.

The Norman advances of *Marchia Wallie* did not go unheeded by the native Welsh, who attempted to reclaim their hold of the property west of the March. In retaliation, the representatives of *Pura Wallia* (the non-Norman, and therefore the pure Welsh) also began to build castles, the first probably being the stronghold at Trallwng, near the later fortress of Powis, at Welshpool. This was built by Cadwgan ap Bleddyn in 1111, whose territory was for generations, if not centuries, under threat not so much from the English, but from the Welsh themselves, and particularly from the powerful House of Gwynedd.

More Welsh castles gradually appeared, such as those at Dryslwyn, Carreg Cennen, and at Dinefwr, the seat of the rulers of Deheubarth, but although chieftains and princes now had a common enemy, the Normans, they could not easily settle the consistent animosity among themselves, a national trait which was to debilitate every effort at forming a united front against the invader and conqueror, not only William of Normandy, but subsequent English kings and, most dramatically and traumatically, against Edward I. The final military crisis arose in 1282, not only because of the Anglo-Welsh hostility, innate and passionate though it was by tradition, nor because of internecine strife between one Welsh chieftain and his neighbours, but because of genetic flaws in two brothers which blurred the perception of their own worth, making their relationship an impossibility and thereby creating a series of situations which led to a national tragedy.

The period between the Norman infiltration into Wales and the Statute of Wales in 1284, produced hundreds of castles, most of which did not survive the motte-and-bailey stage, though those that are still visible give ample testimony to their former strength and presence. Those that were refortified in masonry bear equal testimony not only to man's manipulation of materials, but to his military sophistication. The fact that so many of them, almost a thousand years later, are still standing, in whatever state of dilapidation, considering the ravages

Organisation of Labour for Edward I's Castle Building in Wales

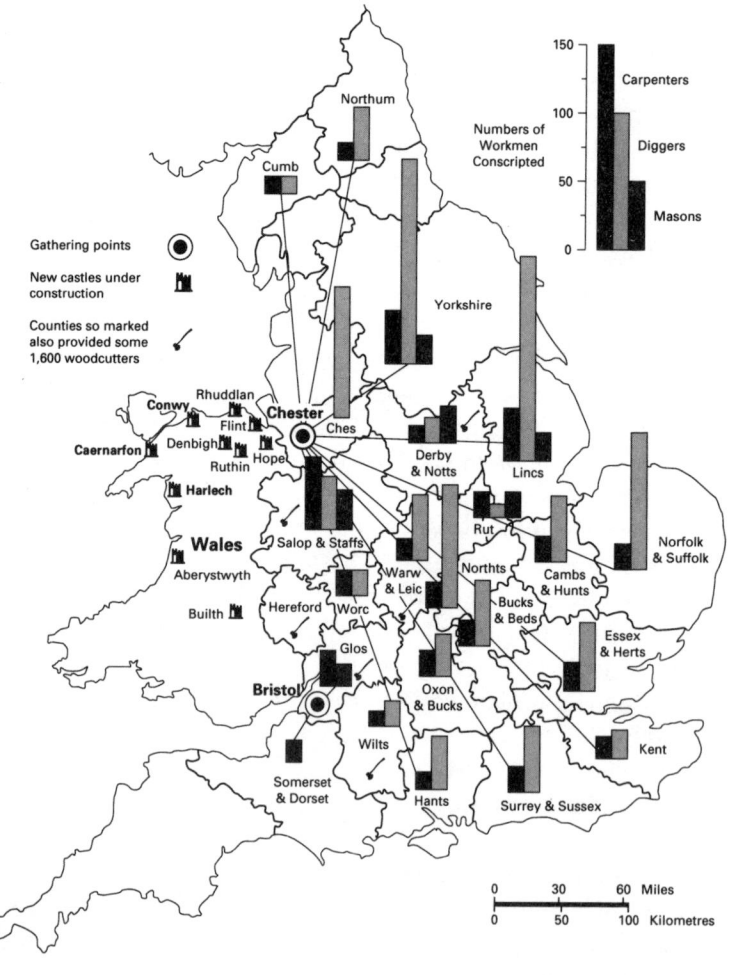

of rebellions, a civil war and sheer neglect, is eloquent testimony of the mason's mastery of his materials.

Fortunately, enough remains of the Norman, Welsh and Edwardian castles for people to see them now in a detached way as statements of defensive architecture, giving valuable indications of prevailing techniques. Whatever the achievements of the Normans and the native princes, it was the highly wrought sophistication of the partnership between Edward I and Master James of St George that brought to Wales a standard of military architecture that can proudly compete with the best in Europe and the Middle East, the source of so much of the inspiration.

After 1284: from fortress to mansion

Wales has a number of medieval castles which developed from fortified strongholds into great residences of considerable opulence and splendour. The two outstanding examples are those at Chirk and Powis, though the much smaller Picton (Pembrokeshire) and Penhow (Gwent) also have their fascination, the latter probably qualifying more as a tower-house. As such, it represents a building type rare in Wales: the small fortified dwelling, so common in south-west Ireland, and on the English and Scottish border, in particular, but which surprisingly rarely appeared on the borders between England and Wales, considering the traditional animosity between the two countries.

One possible explanation for this absence is the fact that the loss of Welsh independence, formalised by the Statute of Wales in 1284, brought in its wake a period of conformity and compromise, its equanimity fractured, nevertheless, by the revolt led by Rhys ap Maredudd, the only descendant of the Lord Rhys, in 1287, and that led by Madog ap Llywelyn in 1294. The uprising of Owain Glyndŵr during the first decade of the fifteenth century was to cause the refortification of many of the Norman and Edwardian castles and also bring about the irrevocable end of many of them.

Weobley Castle in Gower, West Glamorgan is an example of a building which was breaking out of its strictly defensive character. In Breconshire there is Scethrog on the banks of the Usk and clearly visible from the A40 near Llansantffraed, though the original defensive tower has been embodied in domestic extensions over the centuries. The tower at Talgarth, not far away, is now a house and shop in the village street.

More substantial is the Tower at Broncoed, near Mold in Flintshire. This three-storeyed square structure was built in 1445 by Rheinallt ap Gruffudd ap Bleddyn who reputedly hanged the mayor of Chester from a staple in the principal room of his home, a relic which is a source of considerable interest to visitors to the house. An early drawing by Moses Griffith (1747–1819) depicts the tower without its additions.

Pembrokeshire has some interesting examples of the tower-house, the most prominent being Roch Castle, so called after its Norman founder Adam de Roche, members of whose family were supporters of Richard Strongbow, earl of Pembroke, when he invaded Ireland in 1167. They forged strong links with the country and became lords of Fermoy. Standing proudly in its village of Roch on the A487 near Newgale, it changed hands at least twice during the Civil War, but seems never to have had a settled history since. Its present appearance is the result of the extensive refurbishment carried out in the first years of this century to the orders of John Wynford Philipps, created viscount St David's in 1918.

Also belonging to the Roch family was the smaller scale Benton Castle standing on guard above the river Cleddau near Milford Haven. It was in the possession of Sir John Perrot of Carew Castle in Tudor times, and after standing ruinous for centuries was rebuilt in the 1930s by Ernest Pegge, a man of similar energetic zeal to J.R. Cobb who did so much renovation work at two other Pembrokeshire castles: at Pembroke itself and at Manorbier. Benton is in private ownership.

Like Benton, Upton stands close to tidal water, in this case on the river Carew. On the death of the male line of the Malefant family, whose ancestors built the castle in the thirteenth century, the property went to a daughter who married Owen ap Gruffudd ap Nicolas of Dinefwr, whose descendants lived there until the second half of the eighteenth century. Though the castle is privately owned, the grounds are in the care of the

Pembrokeshire Coast National Park Authority and are open to the public occasionally.

Two of the other defensive structures in Pembrokeshire which fall into the category of the tower-house, but which have not been improved or converted into comfortable houses, are Eastington at Rhoscrowther, with its crenellated wall-walk and turret, and the robust Tower at Angle, its machicolations and loopholes giving it an uncompromising military appearance.

A type of fortified building which falls into neither the category of the castle nor the tower-house is the adaptation of the motte-and-bailey, where the buildings, though not fortified, were rebuilt in timber, and where greater emphasis was given to the moat. The most historic of these is Sycharth, the home of Owain Glyndŵr, and a subject of endless fascination and speculation. It was destroyed by Henry IV's men in 1403 during the uprising, and it subsequently reverted to its original appearance as a motte-and-bailey site, which dates back to the late eleventh or early twelfth century.

One of the gentry poets, Iolo Goch (c. 1320–c. 1398) wrote about Sycharth in what has turned out to be the most extended and detailed description of a medieval residence in Welsh literature. Owain's home was almost completely self-sufficient – the best beer was brought from Shrewsbury – and would have had many of the features of the baronial estates which were emerging from the confines of ward and curtain wall into more open ground. Though Iolo Goch often lists, rather than describes the appurtenances of Owain's court, the over-all effect is an almost magical evocation of medieval social life and conditions among the gentry. The following paraphrase of the middle section of the *cywydd* describes the life beyond the bright girdle of water, and through the gate that leads to the elevated timber buildings on the summit of a green hill, so that the *llys* seems nearer to heaven: in addition to a church, there are chapels with fine windows, and in the grounds themselves, a vineyard as well as an orchard; a mill fed by ample water, and a stone-built dovecote; a pond well stocked with pike and sewin; peacocks and herons on terraces, and beyond, cornfields, and ploughs drawn by powerful horses. A rabbit park, and a deer park complete this remarkable word-picture of which the scenes in the duc de

Berry's *Très Riches Heures* might be regarded as a pictorial equivalent.

Moated sites, in themselves, could be considered as defensive properties, though since they often tend to appear in clusters in low-lying areas, considerations of drainage might account for their particular layout. The moat was also a good source of fresh fish for the larder. Although the properties which they safeguarded have in most cases disappeared, those buildings that remained have been replaced or altered to such an extent that they bear no resemblance to their original character. So many of the moated sites, even without their original buildings are on private property and therefore inaccessible.

An exception is Doghill, near Dyffryn, in South Glamorgan. It once formed the centre of Worleton Manor held by the bishops of Llandaff, who also owned Hen Gwrt, the moated site near Llantilio Crossenny. Croesfoel, near Wrexham, is another well-preserved survivor in an area which could once boast several good examples.

The castle, as we understand the term, was to regain its former defensive importance during the Owain Glyndŵr uprising. Sudden as the eruption was, many castles and fortified towns had a modicum of warning in order to stengthen their structure and increase their garrisons. On the whole, whatever precautions and emergency actions were taken, they were inadequate to combat the ferocity of the attacks and assaults and, occasionally, the prolonged sieges.

This momentous threat to morale and social equilibrium forced people to look with fresher eyes at the worth of their castles. If some had been almost completely destroyed, many had put up a show of resilient resistance, particularly at Aberystwyth and Harlech, which eventually surrendered in 1409 to Henry of Monmouth, later Henry V, as a result of the English force's 'mynes and all manner of engins that were thought needful for the destruccion of them and there castle'.

Major revolts might have been subdued temporarily, but local squabbles leading to minor skirmishes could end up as serious confrontations, if not out-and-out warfare. Rebellion within one's own family and household was always a lurking possibility. Raglan is the product of such a fear of internecine intrigue, its great tower able to serve as a separate and self-contained defensive unit, should the need arise. Later additions by subsequent generations are full-blown manifestations of military architecture at its most ornate and sophisticated, fashions seen by the English and the Welsh who served abroad during the French Wars and who adopted or adapted, according to requirements – mostly for show. Like Bodiam and Herstmonceux in East Sussex, it was as much a status symbol as a fortification; like the owners of these two English castles, the builders of Raglan would have had to be granted a licence to crenellate.

The accession of Henry VII in 1485 and the beginning of the Tudor dynasty brought to an end the domestic unrest of the Wars of the Roses, a period of turmoil which had also occasioned the military use of many Welsh castles, though on no major scale. It was a time which caused sufficient concern to some of the squirearchy, such as a Vaughan of Tretower Court who in 1480 added a gatehouse and a battlemented wall-walk, giving his home the appearance of a fortified manor house. As such, it is the best example in Wales, and often referred to as the equivalent of the finest English surviving example, Stokesay in Shropshire, which its owner, Lawrence of Ludlow called a 'castle', a gesture of social success, rather than one of military clout.

One of the great supporters of young Henry Tudor in his bid for the Crown was Rhys ap Thomas, who subsequently was generously rewarded. Many castles in South-West Wales were granted to him, among them Carew and Weobley, where he made great improvements, the most significant being 'at Carew.

During the reign of Elizabeth, the lore of the castle and the power of possession for which it stood brought about an even more romanticised attitude towards the past than that typified by such 'chivalry' castles as Raglan. Those features which had been essential in strict defensive and functional terms were adapted: the inner ward would become the principal courtyard of a grand new Elizabethan house, with its large windows, generously and expensively glazed, facing outwards onto a peaceful landscape. The might of the tower, rarely, if ever crudely 'copied', would be suggested by more subtle means, as at Hardwick Hall, Derbyshire (1590–97) and at Wollaton Hall, Nottinghamshire (1580–85).

The social history and character of Wales changed dramatically after the Act of Union of 1536, and the attention of the Welsh squirearchy was drawn to the English court. The Seisyll family (Cecils) of Alltyrynys, on the Gwent and Herefordshire border, were progenitors of the builders of Burghley and Hatfield. A branch of the Herbert family acquired monastic property in Wiltshire, made Wilton into a great house and became Earls of Pembroke. What might have happened to the domestic architecture of Elizabethan Wales had they stayed here?

Grandeur is not all, however. Both Oxwich (West Glamorgan) and Beaupré (South Glamorgan) are fascinating hybrids, showing on the one hand, an awareness of Renaissance decoration, if not a complete appreciation of its subtlety, and on the other the reluctance to part with the time-honoured precautions of defence.

There was no such tussle between polite show and hard reality in the valleys, as opposed to the coastal plains, of Glamorgan. The former, since the Norman occupation, had been recognised as the *Welshry* because of their powerful and unpredictable resistance movements. The latter, on the other hand, had allied themselves far more readily with the incursion of a foreign force who found the low-lying terrain almost indicating a Welcome to Wales.

At Llancaiach Fawr (between Nelson and Treharris in Mid Glamorgan), near the Roman auxiliary fort of Gelligaer, it was a compromise between adequate domestic comfort and effective security. Almost the entire structure of this early sixteenth-century house was built in one single period, and it is an illuminating survivor of a Tudor gentry house of this area which has retained its character and integrity, thanks to that underrated chain of events and circumstances which, as far as the historical worth of a building is concerned, can lead to impoverishment, which leads to neglect, thereby avoiding those phases of relative prosperity which might result in irreparable 'improvements' to a building that was eloquent in its own original right. Llancaiach Fawr is now open to the public as a 'Museum of Living

Giler Gate House

History' and administered by Rhymney Valley District Council, who took over the property in 1987.

The gatehouse, whose military power was first introduced into Wales at Harlech, became a feature that was to supersede every other defensive building within the curtain walls of an Edwardian castle, combining as it did, forbidding might and residential convenience, amounting to palatial royal splendour as planned for Beaumaris. By Elizabethan times, its origins of aggressive defence had muted into gestures of welcome. The gatehouse now betokened success, serving no useful purpose, but imparting, often through its sturdy masonry, the notion that it was the entrance of a gentleman of consequence. The gatehouse at Tretower Court, as has already been mentioned, served a more serious purpose of semi-defence, but at Giler, off the A5 between Cerrig y Drudion and Pentrefoelas, the gatehouse fulfilled no such function. The most accessible is that at Plas Mawr (Great House) at Conwy, built towards the end of Elizabeth I's reign, and a suitably proclamatory statement of a successful man of his time and certainly a man-about-town – his own town. This, the best example of an Elizabethan town house in the British Isles, has been recently restored with great care by Cadw.

In the reign of James I, the idealisation of the castle typified by the tower-motif is illustrated by two examples in Wales. Just outside Newport, Gwent, stand the skeletal remains of Ruperra, a house of great distinction built in 1626 by Thomas Morgan, steward of the earl of Pembroke. Its similarity with Lulworth Castle in Dorset, also chivalric in evocation, has often been noted. Corner drum towers, and crenellated parapet evoked vividly the owner's awareness of the concept of the castle in romantic and pictorial terms.

In North Wales, near Mold in Flintshire, stands Plas Teg, dating from 1610, and the only Jacobean courtier house in Wales. Its extruded corner 'towers', each with ogival cupolas strongly resemble those at Hatfield (Hertfordshire) and Blickling (Norfolk). Even without castellation – the Flemish gables have taken decorative precedence – the general outline of the house conforms to the notion of the symmetrical fort in an idealised formal landscape with the one remaining gazebo indicating the boundaries of the outer ward, if not the moat.

The period of the Civil War introduced the last phase of the military and defensive use of the Welsh castles, or those that had not been too heavily raided during the Owain Glyndŵr uprising. The major strongholds among the survivors were refortified, some as at Conwy, by the private funds of an individual, in this case, John Williams, Archbishop of York, a native of the town, the remains of whose house are all too scant and neglected, but who 'repaired, victualed and supplied it with ammunition at mine own charges'. Henry Somerset, like the archbishop, a staunch Royalist, spent the sum of £40,000 supporting the garrison at Raglan which by the 1640s had developed into what was probably the greatest country house in Wales.

The havoc caused by the sustained sieges of the castles was made even worse by the Parliamentarian demolition that followed, making them incapable of further military use. Few castles were worth restoring after such relentless and deliberate

onslaughts. Most were abandoned and became prey to whole-
sale robbing, some retained enough of their integrity to be
restored and become useful homes again, before becoming
grand places of display, as at Chirk and Powis.

At Cardigan Castle, whose ruins are visible from the road,
a house (strictly private) was built on the remains of the keep.
The twin-towered gatehouse at Newport Castle (Pembrokeshire) became a house (strictly private), with the original
defensive curtain wall forming a splendid garden enclosure. A
private house was built within the defences of Manorbier
Castle, and also at Bronllys Castle.

Eighteenth-century architectural taste underwent more frenetic changes of aesthetic allegiance than its predecessors. The
cult of the 'Scottish castle', encouraged by Robert Adam, did
not go unnoticed in Wales. Although his fellow-Scot, the 1st
marquess of Bute commissioned him to design the modernisation of Cardiff Castle in the 1770s, Adam's ideas were not
executed. A few miles away, however, he worked on Wenvoe
Castle for a successful Yorkshireman, Peter Bird, for whom
a battlemented roofline epitomised lineage. The 'castle' was
demolished in the 1910s but the stables still stand, designed by
Henry Holland, the architect of Lord Bute's rebuilding of the
domestic nucleus of Cardiff Castle.

A drawing by Moses Griffith of 1776, depicts Plas Newydd
on Anglesey undergoing a transformation from a gabled
country house into castellated assertiveness for Sir Nicholas
Bayley, father of the 1st earl of Uxbridge and grandfather of
the 1st marquess of Anglesey. Emerging from this process of
aggrandisement, are three towers; an octagonal, a D-ended and
a rectangular, two of which have decorative and highly exaggerated arrow-loops. By 1800, the metamorphosis was complete,
the achievement of James Wyatt and his assistant Joseph Potter.
It bore, by then, only a scant resemblance to Moses Griffith's
delightfully naïve depiction. When the 5th marquess of Anglesey
lived there at the turn of the century, the crenellations had
obviously made such an impression on him that he changed
the name from Plas Newydd to Anglesey Castle.

Further westwards downstream, commanding the entrance
of the Menai Strait, is Fort Belan, built by Lord Newborough

in the late eighteenth century with the aim of defending North Wales against Napoleonic invasion. A few miles inland, in the grounds of Lord Newborough's country seat, Glynllifon, now a college of further education, is the minuscule Fort Williamsburg, which was supposedly intended to accommodate his family and 'garrison' should such an eventuality ever arise.

It was the nineteenth century, however, that was to bring into existence the full-blown revival of the 'castle', not merely variations on the theme of castellation. The new phenomenon was an extravagant medium not only for displaying vast new wealth, but for commissioning architects who could interpret the past according to the whims and eccentricities of their clients. For A.W. Pugin, the whole idea was monstrous.

> What could be more absurd than houses built in . . . the castellated style? Portcullises which will not lower down . . . drawbridges which will not draw up . . . turrets so small that the most diminutive sweep could not ascend them! . . . guard rooms without either weapons or guards; sally-ports, out of which a military man never did go out; donjon keeps which are nothing but drawing-rooms, boudoirs and elegant apartments; watch-towers, where the house-maids sleep, and a bastion where the butler keeps his plate; all is a mere mask, and the whole building an ill-conceived lie.

Among the first of them, though not on a virgin site, was the encasing of Broadlane at Hawarden in 1809, probably in a gesture of conformity with the genuine thirteenth-century castle in the park. A politely rational eighteenth-century country house of no great pretension was suddenly engulfed by medievalism. For an unashamedly extravagant show of mock chivalry, Wales has no better example than the Gwrych Castle (1815) on the A55 express road, near Abergele. Five years later, work was started on the incomparable Penrhyn Castle, near Bangor, sternly Normanesque in every detail. This in a dispirited way is the style of Bryn Bras Castle (c. 1830–35) at Llanrug, near Caernarfon, though there is no evidence that Thomas Hopper, the architect of Penrhyn, was also involved there.

In South Wales, Cyfarthfa Castle (1825), near Merthyr Tydfil,

Glynllifon, Fort Williamsburg

also had its followers. Though it incorporated an earlier house, the 'medieval' mantle of Hensol Castle (now a hospital) designed by T.H. Wyatt in 1835, is a far less oppressive composition than that of Maesllwch Castle (1841) between Brecon and Hay-on-Wye, and Robert Lugar's second attempt at 'castle' design in Wales, his first having been Cyfarthfa. After making a fortune in India, William Wilkins bought the Maesllwch estate, but finding the early eighteenth-century structure incommensurate with his new status, aggrandised it out of all recognition. Proud of his Norman stronghold, he restyled himself de Winton.

In the same county, bordering on West Glamorgan, at the head of the Swansea Valley, a house called Bryn Melin, designed by T.H. Wyatt in the 1840s for a local landowner, acquired a new identity in the 1880s when the world famous Italian diva, Adelina Patti, fell under its spell and bought it. With the addition of a castellated wing with turrets and mock machicolations, Bryn Melin (Mill Hill) became Craig-y-Nos Castle, taking the name of the nearby prominence, 'The Rock of the Night'. Here Madame Patti, 'The Queen of Song', built a private theatre of exquisite charm, where she sang with her husband, the tenor Ernesto Nicolini, for royalty, nobility and gentry. It is now used in the month of June every year by a local operatic society.

In so many cases, the term 'castle' was used as indiscriminately in Wales as the word *plas* (great house, mansion) as a means of denoting a residence whose size and location gave it a mark of distinctiveness, rather than one of distinction. Such pretensions, more social rather than architectural, have been known to be ludicrously misleading.

No such criticism can assail the last – or the latest – 'castle' built in Wales. Castell Gyrn (not to be confused with Gyrn Castle at Llanasa, Flintshire which assumed that title by the addition of a castellated tower during the last century) is a work of imaginative verve and scholarly care by its architect owner, John Taylor, whose father's land, with its incomparable views over Ruthin, the Vale of Clwyd and towards Gwynedd, was put to such imaginative use in the late 1970s. His great appetite for the past has led to an ongoing programming of ingenious, but relevant, additions. Though strictly private, Castell Gyrn is eminently visible, in true castle tradition, from most directions.

John Taylor's request for a licence to crenellate resulted in the following reply:

> It appears the issue of such licences did not rest on statute and became extinct after the reign of Edward IV [1483]. No possibility is seen of reviving the procedure and it is therefore regretted that no action can be taken on your client's petition.

The Castle and the Artist

The first delineations of Welsh castles were not intended to be in any way artistic expressions or impressions, but found themselves almost incidentally as part of town maps. William Marshall's forbidding stronghold at Pembroke was the first drawn, and in an intriguingly reticent way. It appeared in a manuscript by the Pembrokeshire historian, George Owen of Henllys (c. 1552–1613), and forms the background to a decorated version of the initial letter T, behind which the Norman donjon makes an immediate impact.

The approximate date of 1593 for this depiction is just over a decade before the appearance of John Speed's *The Theatre of the Empire of Great Britain* (1610). His map of Cardiff is interesting not only because of the appearance of the Norman castle, but because it is possible to see how the now capital city of Wales has retained the plan of the seventeenth-century town and its medieval forebear. Speed's Beaumaris is even more discernible today, simply because subsequent expansion was limited by its marine position.

In the latter decades of the seventeenth century, Francis Place, a young English gentleman of ample means, enjoyed a holiday in West Wales, during which he made drawings of Tenby and Pembroke castles. They were immediate and personal responses to what he had seen, and as such are of considerable topographical interest.

In 1684, the duke of Beaufort, in his capacity as Lord President of the Council in Wales, and the Lord Warden of the

Marches wrote the account of his *Official Progress through Wales*. His 'illustrator' was Thomas Dineley or Dingley, possibly the first of that breed of servant/artist/companion who was to become almost a conventional presence for so many gentlemen tourists in the eighteenth and nineteenth centuries. Dineley's were sketches more than drawings, often showing little grasp of perspective, but all of informative interest today, particularly those of Chirk, Picton, Powis and Hay, where the country houses have emerged out of their military shells.

Castles were attractive subjects for the print-makers of the eighteenth century, among whom a Dutchman, Jan Kip (1653–1722), was one of the first; and later to become one of the most prominent. In *Britannia Illustrata* of 1707 appeared the first published view of a Welsh castle, other than those which had already appeared on various maps. This was Kip's engraving of Chepstow, giving a bird's-eye view of the castle on its cliff above the river Wye, winding towards the Bristol Channel.

Two decades or so later, the brothers Samuel and Nathaniel Buck began on their energetic enterprise. Every year, from 1728–53, they toured England and Wales, producing panoramic views of great precision and detail of 'cities, seaports and capital towns'. To these should be added castles: among them Carmarthen and Haverfordwest are particularly interesting as they show the prominent positions which they still held at that date. With the depiction of Swansea, we not only see the castle before it was ruthlessly vandalised in the nineteenth century, but its Norman contemporary stronghold at Oystermouth vaunting itself on the eminence across the bay, and which was to receive separate attention in an individual study by the brothers Buck.

During the last quarter of the eighteenth century Paul Sandby (1725–1809), well known for his drawings of Windsor Castle, now in the Royal Collection at Windsor, worked extensively in Wales, producing sepia aquatints, among them a handsome composition of Cardiff Castle made in 1777. Earlier in the decade he had been employed by Sir Watkin Williams Wynn of Wynnstay, Denbighshire, and one of the foremost patrons of the eighteenth century, to make drawings of a tour through North and South Wales.

Contemporary with Sir Watkin was Thomas Pennant of

Pembroke Castle by Paul Sandby

Downing in Flintshire, who also took with him on his travels a servant-companion, Moses Griffith, who was capable of making illustrations, not considered to be of artistic merit then as much as of topographical worth, fulfilling the function of a series of pictorial records. His Dolwyddelan Castle is of particular interest because it shows the square tower before its restoration in the nineteenth century.

In 1777 also the indefatigable Swiss artist, Samuel Hieronymus Grimm (1733–94) undertook a tour of Wales with Henry Penruddock Wyndham, a scholar gentleman typical of his time who had already discovered the sights and beauties of Wales in 1774, after which he published *A Gentleman's Tour through Monmouthshire and Wales*, which was illustrated by Grimm in later editions.

Thomas Rowlandson (1756–1827), perhaps best known as a caricaturist and for his drawings of the *Tour of Dr Syntax*, made several topographical drawings of buildings in Wales, some of which were reproduced as etchings and used to illustrate Henry Wigstead's *Remarks on a Tour to North and South*

Wales in the Year 1797. Among them are a strikingly stark Caerphilly Castle and the incomparably sited Castell Dinas Brân.

The landscape painter also was attracted to castles, not only as a subject to be delineated in terms of a mere structure in a background but as a building worthy of imaginative interpretation through light and colour. Richard Wilson (1714–82) 'the father of British landscape painting' and, in fact, a Welshman brought up at Penegoes in Montgomeryshire, was greatly influenced by his sojourn in Rome, and by the work of Claude and Poussin. His depictions of the castles at Cilgerran, Caernarfon, Dolbadarn, Pembroke and Castell Dinas Brân are set not in Welsh light, but under the honeyed glow of Italian skies. J.M.W. Turner's (1775–1851) treatment of two of these, Cilgerran and Dolbadarn is dramatically different. Full of foreboding and suspicion, Dolbadarn's dark history, where Llewelyn ap Gruffudd, 'the Last', had imprisoned his own brother Owain, over a long period, appealed to Turner's sympathy which he conveyed in his own lines:

> How awful is the silence of the waste,
> Where nature lifts her mountains to the sky.
> Majestic solitude, behold the tower
> Where hopeless Owen, long imprison'd pin'd,
> And wrung his hands for liberty, in vain.

Turner's *Dolbadarn*, on which he worked between 1798 and 1800, was the painting which he chose to present to the Royal Academy in 1802 when he was elected as Academician. It has much of the Gothic ferocity of John Martin's *The Bard* (1817), depicting a mountainous landscape of Alpine dimensions, complete with jagged rocks above a swirling river into which a bearded demented old man with his harp, is about to throw himself.

The castle in Martin's middle ground is a work of copious inventiveness, imparting threatening hostility and combining the power and might of both Conwy and Harlech. The solitary figure represents the Bard, the subject of Thomas Gray's (1716–71) poem of that name, written in 1755.

Dolbadarn Castle by Richard Wilson

> On a rock, whose haughty brow
> Frowns o'er old Conwy's foaming flood,
> Rob'd in the sable garb of woe,
> With haggard eye the poet stood;
>
> Loose his beard and hoary hair
> Stream'd, like a meteor, to the troubled air;
> And with a master's hand, and prophet's fire,
> Struck the deep sorrows of his lyre.

The cause of the bard's despair is the conquest of his country by Edward I. His plight caught the imagination and sympathy of a number of artists, apart from John Martin. One of them was Thomas Jones (1742–1803), a pupil of Richard Wilson's. In his version of c. 1774, the bard is again about to throw himself into an abyss. There is no castle in evidence, but a

Dolbadarn Castle by J.M.W. Turner

number of bodies lie strewn upon the ground. In the background is a druidic stone circle, and frenzied birds fly around some gnarled trees bent by the wind.

One of the best known of the later interpretations of the theme of the Bard is by Philippe Jacques de Loutherbourg (1740–1812), which was used as the frontispiece of the publication *Musical and Poetical Relicks of the Welsh Bards*, produced in 1784. Though there is no castle in evidence, de Loutherbourg had depicted many Welsh strongholds, among them, Harlech and Conwy.

By the very nature of their sites and situations, most of the castles of Wales have attracted artists of a wide range of technical ability and interpretative imagination. To the names already mentioned can be added those of John Sell Cotman (1782–1842); David Cox Snr (1753–1859); David Cox Jnr (1809–85); Henry Gastineau (1791–1876); Thomas Girtin (1775–1802);

Julius Caesar Ibbetson (1759–1817); John Varley (1778–1842).

The castle, by the end of the First World War, had proved to be an interesting and historic phenomenon, worthy of being taken into state guardianship. Safety of existing structures was of paramount importance, and with it came the unpredictable demands and requirements of conservation and preservation. The untamed world which had surrounded the ruins, and which had appealed to the artistic imagination, was cleared away, leaving clean-cut outlines and crisp definitions. These were subjects for the accuracy and precision of the camera lens, not of the professional photographer, who could always convey his individual interpretation, but of the thousands of castle visitors who wished to keep a memento of place and occasion.

There was still scope for another approach, and that was by means of the imaginative reconstruction, a method of interpreting the former appearance of ruined buildings and a technique practised and perfected by Alan Sorrell (1904–76), whose illustrations, on display in so many castles, have enlivened curiosity as well as satisfied the queries of thousands of people attempting to make sense of our unroofed heritage, where sometimes only footings give any idea of the demarcation between one building and the next, let alone an indication of what the function of such buildings were.

Even so, some castles, whatever the state of their rescue, communicate a sense of their uncompromising grandeur by their position alone. One such is Carreg Cennen, on its forbidding craggy eminence, whose massive challenge has been admirably conveyed by the outstanding post-war Welsh artist, Kyffin Williams (b. 1918), who also depicted Harlech from an unconventional angle. Both are in the possession of the National Library of Wales. These were by no means the only Welsh castles which he has drawn or painted over the years, though most are now in private ownership.

William Selway, an artist from Caernarfon, has found a natural source of inspiration in that castle and in Conwy. His work shows great delicacy at the same time conveying the might of the Edwardian fortresses. In recent years Cadw itself commissioned a number of Welsh artists to convey their impressions of a castle of their choice.

Abergavenny, Y Fenni (Monmouthshire)
Near town centre, Open access, Admission free, Local Authority

The Romans recognised the importance of the point where the rivers Gavenny and Usk meet, and there built a fort which they called *Gobannium* c. 50AD. The Normans who were quick to take advantage of the site, as they were with so many other Roman establishments, adopted Gobannium and adapted it to their own needs.

It was Hamelin de Ballon who was responsible for the initial assertion of the invaders' occupation, which was consolidated by the founding of the town. The earth and timber stronghold was replaced by a masonry construction, and it maintained its prestige over many generations as the headquarters of the Norman lordship of Abergavenny, and proved suitable for entertaining royalty. When it passed into the hands of William de Braose, the castle took on the appalling character of a Greek tragedy, for in 1175 he invited Seisyllt ap Dyfnwal, the leader of the Welsh in Gwent Uwchcoed, together with his son, and other prominent Welshmen of the locality, to celebrate Christmas. Not only were all the guests murdered, but de Braose's men then set upon Seisyllt's Castell Arnallt, destroying it and murdering his wife and his young child. This attempt to debilitate the spirit of the Welsh did no more than to excite the men of Gwent to retaliate with unalloyed hostility. Abergavenny Castle was attacked by them under the command of Hywel ap Iorwerth who 'burnt the whole place down'. They then went in search of de Braose and his men but, although they succeeded in killing his sheriff, he himself escaped. A descendant, also a William, was hanged by Llywelyn ap Iorwerth for having a love affair with his wife, Joan, the daughter of King John. It is little wonder that the historian William Camden (1551–1623) wrote that Abergavenny 'has been oftner stained with infamy of treachery that any other castle in Wales'.

Effigies of subsequent holders of the castle, such as the Cantelupe and Hastings families, lie in St Mary's church, founded as a Benedictine priory by Hamelin de Ballon, the builder of the castle, which by the seventeenth century was in the hands of the

Nevill family, who took its name as the title for the marquessate which was created in 1876.

The scant remains of the thirteenth- and fourteenth-century castle consist of the fragments of two towers, while a third forms part of a house of unknown date which could have been built to take full advantage of both site and materials. Later buildings consist of a fifteenth-century gatehouse, possibly built at the time of the Owain Glyndŵr rebellion, and the nineteenth-century decorative tower built by the Nevill family. For all the lack of medieval remains, the strategic importance of the site is evident, though here, as in most castles, the visitor's attention is now drawn to the striking quality of the surrounding landscape, rather than to more hostile considerations. The combination of the river setting, and the backcloth of the four mountains: Ysgyryd Fawr, Ysgyryd Fach (the Skirrids), the Blorenge and Mynydd Pen-y-fâl (the Sugar Loaf) makes Abergavenny one of the most peaceful of locations, completely belying the gory details of the more horrific aspects of its past.

Aberystwyth (Cardiganshire)
On the promenade, Open access, Admission free, Local Authority

Considering its eminent position on the confluence of the Rheidol and the Ystwyth into Cardigan Bay, it is surprising that this was the first stronghold to be built on this spot. In fact it did not appear until 1277, when along with Builth, Flint and Rhuddlan it formed part of Edward I's first campaign to subject the Welsh. Its building was a matter of some urgency, for writs were sent to English sheriffs to send craftsmen to Aberystwyth, and the instructions in certain cases were quite specific: Devon, Gloucestershire and Hampshire were each to send sixty 'good' masons; Somerset and Dorset each to find 120 masons and 'good' carpenters. Edward's brother, Edmund Crouchback was given control of the castle.

The result was a concentric castle, roughly diamond-shaped, and as such, not unlike Rhuddlan. It shared characteristics with other Edwardian strongholds: it was near the sea – like Harlech, built during Edward's second campaign, on the west coast –

Aberystwyth Castle

and it was associated with a fortified town and, although the defences have disappeared, the original grid plan is clearly discernible, the nature of the settlement suggested by Eastgate and Great Darkgate Streets.

The castle costs amounted to £4,300, spread over four years, considerably more than the £1,650 spent at Builth, spread over five years. The sum, compared with Edward's castles at Flint and Rhuddlan, is modest; compared with the expensive outlay on the castles of the second campaign, it is paltry.

Aberystwyth's twin-towered Great Gatehouse had a feature which we see again at Harlech, though it was not repeated in any of Edward's other castles, because no other site required such a precaution, which took the form of an outer much smaller gatehouse, placed on a far lower level than the principal structure.

The castle was taken by Owain Glyndŵr in 1404, and it took the forces of Prince Henry – the future King Henry V – to regain it in 1408, after heavy artillery pounding. The Civil War put an end to any semblance of defensiveness in 1646, when it

Beaumaris Castle

was blown up by Colonel Rice Powell. Later in that century the Royal Mint was accommodated there.

The surroundings are remarkable, not only because of its marine situation, but because of the eccentric shape and architecture of the nearby college buildings, built originally as a hotel.

Beaumaris, Biwmaris (Anglesey)
In the town, Open: standard hours, Admission charge, Cadw, A WORLD HERITAGE SITE

For all the anti-Welsh fervour that went into their construction, the Edwardian castles have Welsh names that resonate with the nature and spirit of the sites on which they were built. The exception is Beaumaris, and in spite of the name's transliteration into Biwmaris on road signs, the place sounds resolutely foreign, though it was, like so many place names in Wales, a geographical or geological description of the area; in this case, *Beau Mareys*, the Norman-French for 'fair' or 'fine marsh'.

As in the other Edwardian castles, the lay-out was dictated by the terrain, so that here, the expansiveness of flat land on the Menai Strait allowed for a generous ground plan where the King's surveyor, James of St George, could put into operation the principles of the concentric fortress without being hampered by the restrictions of outcrop or ridge. He had utilised the combination of level coastland and water very effectively at Flint (1277), the first of his castles in Wales, and in the same year, at Rhuddlan, had taken advantage of a sufficiently rock-free area to introduce the idea of the principal castle buildings being surrounded by an outer wall protected by regularly spaced towers. During his second Welsh campaign, he returned with greater precision to the box-within-a-box plan at Harlech (1283), a precision thrust upon him by the very confines of that steep rocky site.

It was at Beaumaris (1295), however, that he was able to bring these principles of concentric planning to fruition, resulting in a castle renowned as much for the splendour of its architectural impact as for the subtlety of its defensive design.

The lay-out of the inner ward is perfectly symmetrical, and if a paper cut-out plan of it were to be folded in half, one side would perfectly match the other. The departure from this geometrical precision occurs in the curtain walls of the outer ward, and for specific tactical reasons, for the southern outer gatehouse, the Gate next the Sea, and its northern counterpart, Llanfaes Gate, are out of alignment with their inner gates, so that the assailant, even if he had gained access to the outer ward, would find himself in a confined space and having to decide on a quick change of direction while under attack from the archers on the battlements of the inner ward. This ingenuity of plan was accentuated at the South Gate by the addition of a barbican, which would further impede progress and put the enemy at even greater risk from the garrison. In addition, the castle was defended by the customary devices of portcullises, spyholes and machicolations.

The massive inner ward consisted of four corner drum towers

and one in the middle of the west and east ranges. The palatial gatehouses on the north and south ranges were originally planned to form a mirror image, although the inner facing section of the south gatehouse was never completed. Enough remains of its north twin, however, to indicate the steps that Master James had taken in refinement and sophistication since the ward-facing elevation of the gatehouse at Harlech, still far more assertive because of its greater state of preservation. Even in its incomplete state, it is obvious that the accommodation at Beaumaris was on a far more lavish scale, with three extensive suites of rooms, two in the gatehouses, and a third in the north-eastern end of the inner ward, a section containing the tower which housed the chapel, the best preserved part of the castle. It is an exquisite room, with five lancet windows lighting the upper part of the walls, while the lower part is decorated with trefoil-headed arcading, an arrangement which gives the chapel a feeling of loftiness, in keeping with its spiritual purpose.

The present height of the towers of the inner ward gives little indication of how they were originally intended to dwarf the curtain walls of the outer ward which is in the form of a very shallow octagonal, and protected by twelve angle towers and two gatehouses. Work on the castle was interrupted during the period of Edward's war against Scotland between 1300–6, but was resumed in 1306 and continued for at least a further twenty-four years, and into the reign of Edward III.

In spite of James of St George's genius, the crowning glory of his career was never finished and, as late as 1343, a survey of Beaumaris indicated that, although work on the defences had been completed and the castle was strong, the ambitious plans for the grand royal apartments had remained as plans.

During the Glyndŵr uprising, it succumbed to the Welsh force who held it for two years. The years that followed were uneventful in terms of its military – or any other – activity, and by 1543 the castle had 'scarcely a single chamber . . . where a man could be dry'. Even so, the fortress was not considered too damp to imprison the Catholic martyr, William Davies, for six months. A memorial to him, 'one of the most appealing of all the Welsh martyrs', was built in Beaumaris in 1909.

During the Civil War (1642–48), Beaumaris, like Chester, attained a position of crucial importance as a port for troops and supplies sailing from Ireland to support the Royalist cause in England and Wales, and Richard Bulkeley of Baron Hill, the head of the leading Royalist family in Anglesey, refortified the castle. In October 1648 it fell to the Parliamentarians who garrisoned it for several years after the war. It was not razed until the late 1650s, though it still remained the property of the Bulkeley family.

When Richard Fenton visited the castle in 1810, he noted in his diary that 'this is perhaps the most perfect specimen now existing of such a portion of an old Castle and perhaps the most elegant . . . Pity Lord Bulkely will not repair the slight defects that now exist, which might be done for less than £100, to preserve so very beautiful a Model.' It was a very optimistic estimate.

That such a meticulously planned military stronghold should have been put to the test of combat on only two occasions and after Edward's fighting machine was already out-of-date, is one of the many ironies relating to Beaumaris Castle.

Unlike the other great castles of Wales of both the Norman and Edwardian conquests, it is visible to the outside world only at the last moment. The corniche road from Menai Bridge leads to the town by way of stuccoed villas which give all the semblance of a polite watering town in the south of England. It is the straight main street that suggests the ancestry of the settlement. Even so, the castle itself does not come into view until the very last.

Beaumaris was created a borough in 1296 by Edward, when the Welsh inhabitants of Llanfaes were evicted to the opposite end of the island to form a settlement which was to become known as Newborough. It did not become a walled town, however, until 1414, when the turmoil created by the Owain Glyndŵr uprising had put the neighbourhood into a state of such anxiety that greater protection from the Welsh was considered essential.

Like Caerphilly, Beaumaris had no natural protection. Caerphilly's concentric design was a man-made safeguard, with vast water defences contrived to thwart the enemy further. Beaumaris, at sea-level, in addition to its elaborate provision of attacking and entrapping devices, could take full advantage of the tidal water of the Menai Strait. This resulted in its little dock, a unique feature in military architecture, capable of accommodating 40-ton sea-going vessels whose cargoes could be unloaded directly into the castle. An iron ring for tying up such vessels is visible on the eastern wall of the castle dock.

The site was chosen not in order that Master James could put into practice his most advanced and polished ideas of concentric architecture, but because it was crucially important to Edward in order to complete his plan to secure dominion over the whole of Gwynedd, an ambition which had been upset in September, 1294, when Madog ap Llywelyn, a kinsman of Llywelyn ap Gruffudd, led a force of men to sack the town of Caernarfon, attack its great castle, still in the process of being built, and hold it for six months. The king's original opinion that town and castle would be sufficiently powerful to control the Menai Strait was urgently revised. The north-east end of this important marine thoroughfare had to be sealed as well. Beaumaris was the favoured site.

The building programme on this, the last of Edward and James's castles in Wales, was begun in the summer of 1295, involving a labour force of 2,000 labourers, 400 masons working with Anglesey stone quarried at Penmon and Benllech, thirty smiths and carpenters. By September 1296, progress was advanced enough for a borough charter to be granted, and by 1298 the castle was said to be 'complete'; in other words, defensible rather than finished.

Views from the castle at Beaumaris are far more striking than the views of the castle itself. The moods of Snowdonia and the ever-changing colour and movement of the Strait are unforgettable, whereas Edward's fortress seems in a state of constant repose, its walls and low towers a subject of amateur sketches rather than firing the imagination of those artists like Cotman, Girtin, Sandby, Turner and Wilson who immortalised his other great statements of hostility. Through Sir Richard Williams-Bulkeley, Bt (1862–1942), a descendant of the Bulkeley who played a prominent part in the Civil War, the castle was placed in the guardianship of the Ministry of Public Buildings and Works in 1925.

Beaupré (South Glamorgan)
1m (1.6km) SW of St Hilary, near Cowbridge. 500m walk across fields. Open: standard hours, Admission free, Cadw

On a knoll above the river Thaw in the Vale of Glamorgan stands Beaupré Castle. The second part of the name is strictly incorrect because the building is not defensive, although its unyielding appearance might give the impression of owners who wished to keep a hostile outside world at bay, but the Norman element of the name is still eminently applicable, for it is indeed a beautiful pastoral spot.

In plan Beaupré, or Old Beaupré, as it is sometimes called, is not unlike a small Oxbridge college, one which has been strangely transported to this place of monastic seclusion. It owed this plan to sixteenth-century additions and improvements made to the early fourteenth-century house, the home of the Basset family whose name has been associated with this area right up until the second half of the nineteenth century when church registers last record the 'Bassets of Beaupré'. The person responsible for this metamorphosis was not a Basset, but a Basset son-in-law, Sir Rhys Mansel of Oxwich who had married James Basset's daughter and sole heir, Elinor. Although there were no children from this marriage, Mansel's daughter by his second wife married William Basset and, as a result, his interest and involvement in Beaupré continued until his death in 1559. The work instituted by Sir Rhys was continued by his son-in-law, and in turn, by his son, Richard Basset.

It was to this period that Beaupré owes its two most decorative features: the gatehouse, and the porch in the inner court. The first, of 1586, is an interesting hybrid, combining elements of medieval functionalism and sixteenth-century decoration. The doorway is surmounted by the arms of the Bassets and the letters RB and CB (Catherine Basset), Richard's first wife, and the date 1586. This panel, flanked with balusters set in niches, also contains the Welsh motto in somewhat eccentric spelling,

Beaupre Porch (from window)

Gwell Angay na Chwilydd (Better Death than Dishonour). The storey above has two three-light mullioned windows, and centrally placed above them a squatter version lighting the gable.

The second contribution of Richard Basset, however, shows far more assurance in the handling of decorative devices. This is the entrance to the hall, in a form of a three-storey porch, each storey displaying a different architectural order, so that the entrance is flanked by the Doric, the heraldic panel above by the Ionic, and the splendid window above that, now blocked, by the Corinthian. The date of this handsome structure is 1600, the year of its builder's sixty-fifth birthday. It is a gesture of the utmost confidence, and its sophistication in the middle of this remote and idyllic area takes the visitor completely by surprise. Though much less ornate than the entrance to the hall at Kirby Hall (Northamptonshire, c. 1570) and far less grand than the five-storey tower of the Bodleian Library at Oxford (1613–24) the porch at Beaupré is one of the most distinguished statements of Renaissance architecture in Wales.

Bodelwyddan (Flintshire)
Near St Asaph, off A55, Open: standard hours, Admission charge, National Portrait Gallery & Local Authority

The original Tudor Bodelwyddan underwent a range of stylistic guises before being castellated in the 1830s by J.A. Hansom, better known as the inventor of the cab, and his partner Edward Welch, who between them won the competition for Birmingham Town Hall in 1830.

The frequent towers and turrets and the vast expanse of crenellated curtain walling give the appearance of an establishment of gigantic dimensions, whereas the part of the house accommodating the grand rooms is that of a medium-sized country house, whose generous spaces lend themselves admirably to the building's function, which is as an outpost for the Victorian period of the National Portrait Gallery. Before that, between 1920–82, it had been a girls' boarding school, Lowther College.

Many of the ancillary buildings have been adapted for use as studios and boutiques which are either independent or satel-

Bodelwyddan Castle

lites of the hotel complex which has been discreetly built within the 'castle ward'.

From the A55, Bodelwyddan makes a swaggering chivalric statement, perhaps inspired by the presence of the nearby genuinely medieval fortress of Rhuddlan, or, ironically, by the recently erected Gwrych further along the same road. 'Castle' mania was rife, and the builder John Hay Williams, keenly aware of his ancestry, would not have turned his back on the current trends in domestic architecture and he would certainly have attempted to challenge, if not outshine, the newcomer at Gwrych.

Brecon, Aberhonddu (Powys)
Near town centre, External views only from the Castle Hotel, Privately owned

The English version of the town's name is derived from an early Welsh leader, Brychan. The county name, Brycheiniog, comes from the same root, whereas the name of the town, Aberhonddu, is a geographical description: the mouth of the Honddu. Its development is associated with the Norman occupation of the area, and in particular with Bernard de Neufmarché who ousted Rhys ap Tewdwr in 1093 and soon afterwards established his rule over the area with the raising of a motte-and-bailey on the confluence of the Honddu and the Usk, and at some distance from the Roman fort. Neufmarché founded the Benedictine priory, and its church, St John's in the first decade of the twelfth century.

In 1231 Llywelyn ap Iorwerth attacked both Hay and Brecon, burning the towns and destroying the castles. In a second campaign, two years later, he completely overran Brycheiniog, ruthlessly destroyed the castles, and 'plundering and pillaging every place'. Brecon Castle was besieged with catapults and engines for a month, while at the same time he 'turned the whole town into ashes'.

The castle was rebuilt in stone by Humphrey de Bohun in the early thirteenth century, and fragments of a twelfth-century round tower surmounting Bernard de Neufmarché's motte occupy a prominent place in the garden of the Bishop's Palace, and can be seen from the road below. Humphrey de Bohun's contribution is the great hall, which is a striking feature in the grounds of the Castle Hotel, and reputedly copied at the nearby castles of Bronllys and Crickhowell. There are few traces of the medieval town wall, but the street pattern indicates its existence.

Bronllys (Powys)
8m (12.8km) NE of Brecon on A497, Keep only, Open access, Admission free, Cadw

Bronllys's most significant feature is the round keep, a fashion which had been introduced into Gwent as well as Powys by the early thirteenth century. Similar structures can be seen at Tretower (Powys) and also at Skenfrith (Monmouthshire).

The origins of the stronghold were laid in about 1086 by Richard FitzPons, a follower of Bernard de Neufmarché whose

Bronllys Castle

name is closely associated with the Welsh Kingdom of Brycheiniog. The site which he chose was of great strategic importance,
since it rests not only above the confluence of the Dulais and
the Llynfi, but within a few miles of where the Lynfi flows into
the river Wye.

The early fortification would have consisted of wooden defences superimposed on earthworks, and it was this outline which dictated the later development of the castle in masonry. It was probably FitzPons's great-grandson, William Clifford III (1221–63) who was responsible for building the stone round keep on the original motte or mound.

Entry was at first-floor level, and the vaulted space beneath it, which was reached by means of a trap door, served as a store-room, and could, when necessary, also have been a prison. This lack of external access at ground level gave the first-floor entry a basic means of defence. It was an arrangement later adopted by the earlier fortified manor houses, and by the great Bishop's Palace at St David's.

The accommodation of the keep comprised a room on each floor, and originally there was only one storey above the first-floor which would have provided the principal domestic quarters. In the fourteenth century an upper storey was added and the evidence of fenestration, a fireplace and latrine suggests a far greater awareness and appreciation of comfort.

These improvements were the work of Rhys ap Hywel who had acquired Bronllys early in the fourteenth century, and by his son, Philip ap Rhys. They were probably responsible for building the great hall, whose walls form part of the stable block belonging to the eighteenth-century house built within the inner bailey.

Bronllys was beyond repair by 1521.

Builth, Llanfair-ym-Muallt (Powys)
Behind main street, Earthworks remain only, Open access, Admission free, Local Authority

Three features make Builth Castle different from the others built by Edward I. It was the smallest of them, it was inland, and its masonry disappeared centuries ago. The latter could well be a symbolic refusal of the Welsh people of these parts to accept the very existence of the English king, for it was at a spot nearby that his forces killed Llywelyn ap Gruffudd in 1282, thereby destroying every hope of an independent Wales.

The real motives for the removal of the stonework were far
less idealistic.

The origins of the site go back to the Norman invasion when
Philip de Braose, son of William de Braose, took possession of
the cantref of Buellt and in about 1100 threw up a motte-and-
bailey of formidable size at an extremely strategic crossing point
of the river Wye. Neither its appearance nor its strength went
unchallenged and after 1168 when Rhys ap Gruffudd, the Lord
Rhys, of Deheubarth destroyed the castle, it was rebuilt and
refortified on several occasions, as it was defended by the Anglo-
Normans and the Welsh in turn. In 1260, according to the *Brut*
('The Chronicle of the Welsh Princes'), 'Llywelyn's men, by a
night attack, without a single battle blow, took the castle of
Builth.' Such a successful raid leaves much to the imagination.

In 1277, the year of Edward I's first Welsh War, he began
refortifying Builth more powerfully than it had ever been before.
Temporary buildings to serve as hall, chamber, chapel, kitchen
and smithy for the garrison cost £5, but were soon replaced by
a new great hall, kitchen, brewhouse and stable. The building
was under the control, though probably from a distance, of
Master James of St George, who was to distinguish himself as
master of the king's works in Wales and one of the most brilliant
military architects of the Middle Ages. Even so, progress was
not straightforward, and from the first there were a number of
temporary halts because of lack of building funds. Eventually,
the castle that appeared consisted of a great tower on the motte,
and a masonry girdle which followed the Norman lay-out, and
which incorporated several smaller towers.

The castle withheld the siege of 1294 during the revolt against
Edward I led by Madog ap Llywelyn, but Owain Glyndŵr's
uprising over a hundred years later caused considerable damage.
Leland, in his *Itinerary in Wales* between 1536–39, nevertheless
referred to Builth as 'a fair castel of the Kinges'.

Ruthless dismantling by local landowners was commonly
found in castles that had outlived their use, as in the case of
the building of a manor house near Caerphilly with stones from
Gilbert de Clare's castle, and the construction of Eaton Hall
on the Cheshire border by Sir Thomas Grosvenor, with stones
from Holt Castle. The masonry at Builth was so fully exploited

Caergwrle Castle

that the castle resumed its original earthwork appearance by the end of Queen Elizabeth's reign. Only the name Castle Street gives the visitor any indication of its existence, but the earthwork is still remarkable for its strength and its powerful effect on the imagination.

Caergwrle (Flintshire)

4.5m (7.2km) from Wrexham on road to Mold (A541). Car park in middle of village. Path to castle near Post Office. Open access, Admission free, Local Authority

Since the early 1990s, due to Local Authority enterprise and enthusiastic support from the inhabitants of neighbouring towns and villages, this castle has come into prominence. Voluntary labour and expert supervision have fully revealed a defensive site dating from Roman times which might well have been an outpost of *Deva* (Chester).

What we see today are the scant remains of a castle built in 1277 by Dafydd ap Gruffudd, as a result of the Treaty of Aberconwy of that same year, by which Edward I rewarded him with the *cantrefi* of Rhufoniog and Dyffryn Clwyd, an area which boasted the strategic establishments of Denbigh and Ruthin, as well as Caergwrle itself (referred to in the English records as Hope, from an adjacent settlement of that name).

This regal largesse was in recognition of Dafydd's participation in the side of the English army which he had joined because of a dispute with his brother Llywelyn who had deprived him of much of his natural inheritance. The king's gift gave Dafydd the means to build not only the castle at Caergwrle, to which Edward had made a contribution of 100 marks, but also one at Denbigh.

It was the last native Welsh castle to be built, but one that was never completed. Caergwrle's design reflects the builder's Anglo-Welsh affinities, though the D-ended towers, of which little remains, indicate the influence of the distinct defensive architecture of his native country.

By 1282, Dafydd, whose earlier decision to ally himself with the English forces could only be interpreted as the action of a traitor, now changed his allegiance completely. He considered that his stronghold at Caergwrle, though unfinished, offered him enough power to attack the English castle at Hawarden. A night-raid on Palm Sunday of that year, followed by raids on Flint and Rhuddlan, had disastrous consequences as far as any hope of Welsh independence was concerned. Realising the repercussions of his attacks, Dafydd demolished Caergwrle before the English army could put it to effective military use.

Even in its debilitated state, Edward considered it worth refurbishment, and in 1283 set about repairing the structure so that he could make a gift of the castle to his queen, Eleanor of Castile. Within a year Caergwrle was on fire, while the royal couple were staying there. The castle was destroyed in the conflagration and, remaining unrepaired and abandoned, became an easily accessible quarry for centuries.

The general outlines of the remains have changed little since 1742 when Samuel and Nathaniel Buck depicted the castle. This leads one to speculate how many of the gentry houses of the surrounding countryside were constructed of the dressed stone as well as the basic masonry of Dafydd ap Gruffudd and Edward I's little known castle.

Caergwrle had a short life of a mere six-year span, and considering its significance in the struggle between English and Welsh supremacy, it has been sparsely interpreted and, until recently, little respected. However scant the remains of the built defences, the steep natural escarpment, and the particularly deep ditches, although suggesting a much earlier fortification, also point to considerable costly energy expended on this frontier post at a crucial time in the history of Wales.

The view from the castle spectacularly indicates its strategic importance as a military site, commanding views towards Shropshire, the Mersey and across to Chester and to the Cheshire Plain, which is dramatically interrupted by the gigantic outcrop of Beeston, crowned by the elaborate thirteenth-century defences of Ranulf, earl of Chester.

The castle and its grounds were presented to the locality by the earl of Derby in the 1960s, and are much appreciated by the inhabitants.

Caernarfon (Gwynedd)
In town centre, Open: standard hours, Admission charge, Cadw, A
WORLD HERITAGE SITE

Caernarfon Castle is incomparable. People have their favourites among the Edwardian castles of North Wales, some awe-struck by Harlech and its dominating position, others admiring the ingenious compactness of Conwy, and possibly a smaller number finding aesthetic satisfaction in the almost perfect symmetry of Beaumaris. What places Caernarfon in a separate category is that it is more than a castle: it is a symbol not only of Edward's conquest of Wales, but of the long and distinguished history of the site and its traditional connection with imperial Rome. Caernarfon has a precise meaning: the fort facing Môn, the Welsh name for Anglesey, coming direct from the Latin, *Mona*.

The *caer* is situated on a peninsula formed by the Menai Strait which divides the island from the mainland, and the river Seiont, the name which the Romans adopted from their auxíliary fort, Segontium, about half a mile away, established by Agricola in 78AD. Although there are no references to it in

Caernarfon Castle

historical documents, it features prominently in the Welsh native tale, *The Dream of Macsen*, the hero being based on Magnus Maximus, who held high military rank under Theodosius in the British wars of the 370s AD.

In this story from *The Mabinogion*, the setting is Caer Aber Seint, 'the fort on the mouth of the Seiont', which bears a striking resemblance to the site of Edward's castle. Macsen is disturbed by the vision of a woman of such beauty that he seeks the aid of wise men to whom he relates, in the greatest detail, the content of his dream, in which he had seen a great city at the mouth of the river, where he saw a great castle with many great towers of various colours. Thirteen men were sent from Rome to locate the beautiful woman, following the clues that Macsen had been able to provide. Their quest eventually brought them face to face with the maiden sitting in a chair of red gold. Kneeling down before her, they hailed her as Empress of Rome. In due course, Macsen himself arrives at Caer Aber Seint to claim Elen as his wife and empress. Although no record exists of either of them having been at Segontium, the legend is vibrant with associative resonances.

The presence of the Roman fort, nevertheless, was of enormous strategic importance which the Normans in 1090 were able to put to forceful effect, as, for example, they did at Cardiff, though their fortification was not raised on the site of Segontium itself but on that of the present Caernarfon Castle. The Norman fort was built by Hugh Lupus, earl of Chester, who in 1067 had been given land on the Welsh borders by William the Conqueror, with the aim of extending territorial power westwards. Within twenty-five years of the appearance of the motte-and-bailey at Caernarfon, the Normans lost their grip on North Wales, and their strongholds were claimed by the princes of Gwynedd.

Hugh's mound at Caernarfon became the centre of the *maerdref*, and was still in evidence when in 1283 Edward embarked on his ambitious enterprise in what the biographer of Gruffudd ap Cynan, King of Gwynedd, had described as 'the old city of the Emperor Constantine, son of Constans the Great'. Castle, town walls and quay were conceived as an integrated unit. In 1283 also a contemporary chronicler recorded the discovery of a body, reputedly that of Constantine, in Caernarfon, which 'was honourably reburied in a nearby church at the king's own orders'.

The identity of the corpse was not as important as the notion of its antiquity and its association with the Roman remains of Segontium. Edward was now not merely the conqueror of Gwynedd, he was heir to its imperial past. The castle that he now planned with Master James of St George was not only a fortress and a centre of regional administration; it was more, even, than a royal palace, fit for a king and his entourage who had usurped another country and deprived it of its independence. It was, above all, to reflect the glory of Rome and Edward's illustrious rôle in that radiant inheritance.

The hardened cynic Samuel Johnson, visiting Caernarfon Castle with his Welsh friend, Mrs Thrale, thought it 'an edifice of stupendous majesty and strength', remarking also 'I did not think there had been such buildings. It surpassed my ideas.' Both are the sort of comments that Edward himself might have wished to elicit when he set to work on his magnificent building programme.

It had features that were unique to Caernarfon, because of all his previous castle sites, Caernarfon was unique, in terms of its military history, but predominantly because of its mythological associations.

The highly conscious effort to set Caernarfon Castle apart from the king's other Welsh strongholds resulted in the coloured banded masonry, inspired by the walls of fifth-century Roman Constantinople. It was their polygonal towers which might also have made Edward and Master James choose this shape rather than the round or drum towers used in their other defensive collaborations. Dominating all of them is the formidable Eagle Tower, aptly named the *magna turis*, surmounted by three turrets, each designed to bear a stone eagle, the unmistakable symbol of Imperial Rome. Welsh people have always interpreted the sign of the eagle as standing for Eryri, or Snowdonia, the eagle's (*eryr* in Welsh) natural stronghold. By 1292, the town walls together with the south-facing castle walls with their distinctive banded masonry had been completed. There was still considerable work left to be done on the Eagle Tower, and the northern aspect of the castle was still only in the initial stages of being built. In the 1294 revolt, Madog ap Llywelyn was quick to take full advantage of the situation, and having breached the town walls, he was able to destroy the timber-framed buildings of the castle which had been raised ten years previously in order to accommodate Edward and his wife, Eleanor of Castile, while awaiting the birth of their second son.

No time was wasted in repairing the damage caused by the rebellion, and work on the north wall and the principal entrance, the King's Gate, was begun at the same time. The programme of building and reinforcement lasted for several decades and included the completion of the Eagle Tower, with the addition of the fourth storey and three turrets. During this period, the dismantled timber-framed Hall of Llywelyn, part of Llywelyn ap Gruffudd's residence at Conwy, was re-erected within the walls of Caernarfon Castle. The king's great design, however, remained uncompleted at the time of his son's death in 1327.

In 1403 the castle withstood a siege by Owain Glyndŵr and his French troops. Undeterred by his failure and the loss of 300 men, Owain attempted to take the castle again the following year, but was defeated by the resilience of a garrison of only twenty-eight.

During the Civil War (1642–48), Caernarfon was held for the king, by its constable John, Lord Byron who, having been besieged three times, eventually relinquished his hold and surrendered to Major-General Mytton in 1646. With the Restoration, a warrant for demolition in 1660 went unheeded, and during the next 150 years, the great Edwardian fortress palace was forsaken and became a rich quarry, as well as the haunt of painters and sketchers. It has probably challenged the ability of more artists than any other Welsh castle.

In 1840, the Commissioners of Woods and Forests on behalf of the Crown, which still owned the property, embarked on a comprehensive plan of restoration, with repairs to the external walls, under the direction of Anthony Salvin (1799–1881), a highly successful architect with a thriving fashionable country-house clientele, as well as considerable expertise in the restoration and alteration of historic defensive buildings. The renovation programme was continued under the direction of Sir Llewelyn Turner, the deputy constable of the castle.

From the south side, and certainly from Anglesey, there is little indication that the castle is not in a splendidly maintained condition and eminently habitable. It is only on going through the King's Gate and entering the upper ward that the extent of the incomplete state of the buildings becomes obvious.

In lay-out, there is a marked resemblance between Caernarfon and Conwy, both having two wards, with one leading longitudinally to the other, because there was insufficient ground area for a concentric design. The ground plan has been compared to a figure eight and to an hour-glass because of the 'waist' which divides the lower from the upper wards, both of which are far more extensive in area than those of Conwy, though this greater space in no way diminishes the processional character of Caernarfon.

The formidable strength and royal prestige of Edward's greatest statement of power are both conveyed physically as well as symbolically by the massive twin-towered principal entrance, the King's Gate. It was protected by no fewer than

Caernarfon Castle

five doors, six portcullises, arrow-loops, spyholes and murder-holes, a sequence of daunting barriers matched, if not surpassed, by those at Beaumaris twelve years later. A room above the main gate-passage accommodated a chapel; through its floor rose two of the portcullises on those infrequent occasions when the great gate was opened. A similar arrangement can be seen in the chapel at Harlech. Above the entrance, ironically delicate in its forbidding setting, stands the much eroded statue of Edward II in a decorated niche.

The Queen's Gate, looking out towards Castle Square, probably the bailey of the Norman stronghold, is also twin-towered and was originally reached by a stone ramp.

Of all the castle's towers, the most majestic and decorative is the Eagle Tower, with ample provision on each of its three floors above the basement antechamber for domestic comfort. It was in all probability designed to accommodate Sir Otto de Grandison, Edward's lieutenant, and first justiciar of North Wales. Traditionally, it was in this tower that the king and queen's second son, Edward, was born on the 25th April 1284, though the building was far from completed by that date. Nor is there any evidence to support the claim that Edward made a public pronouncement – an improbable gesture of appeasement – that the infant 'was borne in Wales and could speak never a word of English'. What is undeniable is that the young Edward of Caernarfon, now that his brother Alfonso, his senior by more than ten years had died, was heir to the throne.

In 1301 he was created the first Prince of Wales by his father who also granted him the royal lands in Wales. This title has been given to the eldest son of the reigning monarch ever since, although there was no regal or formal recognition of such a conferment until 1911, when David Lloyd George, who was not only MP for Caernarfon, and constable of the castle, but Chancellor of the Exchequer, choreographed a pageant of opulent spectacle for the investiture of the teenage Prince Edward, the son of George V and Queen Mary. Fifty-eight years later, the ceremony, with additional details, was repeated when his grand-nephew, Prince Charles, approaching his twenty-first birthday, undertook the principal rôle in this twentieth-century ritual.

The circular slate dais on which the queen invested her son stands very near to the centre of the Norman castle, a structure which dictated the layout of this upper ward of James of St George's scheme.

The ground floor of the Chamberlain Tower is laid out as it was for the 1969 Investiture when Prince Charles used it as his robing room, and in the Queen's Tower is the regimental museum of the Royal Welch Fusiliers. What was the main chamber of the first floor of the Eagle Tower is now equipped as a small viewing theatre, and adjacent to it is a well presented exhibition of the castle and its part in the Edwardian conquest.

Caerphilly, Caerffili (Caerphilly)
In town centre, Open: standard hours, Admission charge, Cadw

The *caer* in the name indicates the existence of a Roman fort 1200 years before Gilbert de Clare, the powerful Marcher lord, started building what was to be the largest non-royal castle in Britain. It is twice the size of the Tower of London with its outer walls, and its thirty acres can encompass Edward I's castles at Beaumaris, Caernarfon, Conwy, Harlech and Rhuddlan. Such was the might of the fortress of de Clare, who as well as being lord of Glamorgan, was earl of Gloucester, earl of Hertford and lord of Tonbridge in Kent, and of Clare in Suffolk, from where the family took its name.

Although the lowlands of Glamorgan had yielded to the Normans as early as 1090, the more hilly regions to the north of the county retained their independence for almost 200 years after the Conquest. After 1258 when he was accorded the title Prince of Wales by his fellow-Welsh rulers, Llywelyn ap Gruffudd's advance southwards from his Gwynedd base was seen as disconcertingly rapid and effective by the Anglo-Normans who realised that their Welsh acquisitions were under severe threat of being regained. It was Llywelyn's control over Breconshire that caused alarm to Gilbert de Clare, who realised that the low mountain ranges with their sturdy Welsh resistance would all too readily ally themselves with Llywelyn's southward advance, and soon take over the whole of the Glamorgan

Caerphilly Castle

coastal plain. He therefore moved northwards and usurped the territory of the native ruler, Gruffudd ap Rhys in 1267, the year in which by the Treaty of Montgomery Henry III himself recognised Llywelyn as 'Prince of Wales'. Unheeding, a year later and by now lord of Glamorgan de Clare started work on his castle. It was a futile demonstration of his recent control over the area, because Llywelyn ap Gruffudd invaded the district and demolished Gilbert's fortification. The king's death in 1272, and the ensuing strife between the new king, Edward I, and Llywelyn, deflected the Prince of Wales's interest from Caerphilly, and de Clare proceeded with his ambitious plans which absorbed his energy until his death in 1295. His son, also named Gilbert, who died at the Battle of Bannockburn in 1314, probably undertook those of his father's schemes that had not been completed at the time of his death.

Two years later, in 1316, by which time the castle had passed to Gilbert the Younger's sister, Eleanor, and her husband, Hugh le Despenser, King Edward II's favourite, Caerphilly was besieged by Llywelyn Bren, a local chieftain, in a show of resentment against the new royal administration which had followed de Clare's death. Llywelyn Bren was put to death by le Despenser in 1318, an act which was not to go unheeded by the neighbouring barons who were already alerted to the favourite's influence on King Edward II, and the effect such an alliance might have on their own properties. By 1321, their disgust was demonstrated not only by acts involving the destruction of much of the murderer's property in South Wales, but by making a powerful petition to the king, voicing their disapproval of the Despensers, father and son. As a result, Edward sent them both into exile, but only for a short time. On their return Hugh, the son, rebuilt the great hall at Caerphilly, which involved the expertise of the king's carpenter William de Hurley, and his master mason Thomas de la Bataille. Its restoration in recent years has succeeded in revealing its majestic medieval stature, and public events as well as private receptions give an opportunity for people to appreciate the magnificent fabric and dimensions of what is one of the grandest spaces in Britain still in use.

Caerphilly was nevertheless extremely vulnerable because of Despenser's relationship with the king, and during a visit to her native country in 1325, the queen, Isabella (the 'She Wolf of France'), enlisted the support of a number of noblemen, including Roger Mortimer, whose mistress she became, with the sole intent of freeing the king from the resolute grip of le Despenser.

By 1326 Despenser's fall was inevitable, because of the odds that were so heavily stacked against the king himself. Together they moved first to Chepstow which was virtually in the control of le Despenser, since the king had granted it to his own half-brother, Thomas de Brotherton. Their plans to escape from there to Ireland were thwarted by the tides and their forced landing in Cardiff resulted in Edward and his party making Caerphilly their base for a while before seeking refuge in other places in Glamorgan. When they were finally captured Hugh le Despenser was hanged and Edward was imprisoned at Berkeley Castle where he was mocked and shaved in cold water from the Severn. 'Whether you will or no, I have warm tears for my beard' was his submissive response. He was murdered with a ferocity which rivalled the most agonising of punishments in any Greek tragedy. Little wonder that Charles Lamb wrote of Christopher Marlowe's play *Edward II* that 'the death scene . . . moves pity and terror beyond any scene, ancient or modern, with which I am acquainted.'

Eleanor, le Despenser's widow, retrieved the lordship of Glamorgan in 1328, and Caerphilly remained in that family until the early fifteenth century when Isabel, the heiress, married Richard Beauchamp, earl of Worcester. Caerphilly ceased to be of great domestic importance from then onwards, since Beauchamp paid more attention to Cardiff Castle, which had also come to him through marriage. This shift of interest established a trend which was to be continued by Isabel's second husband, another Richard Beauchamp, the earl of Warwick and cousin to the earl of Worcester, and later by the Herbert family. It was during the tenure of Henry Herbert, 2nd earl of Pembroke, that Caerphilly was leased in 1583 to Thomas Lewis, a man of considerable status in Glamorgan society, having twice served as sheriff, as well as being a deputy lieutenant. He was given permission to make free and unlimited use of the castle stonework in order to aggrandise his ancestral home, Y Fan, noted by John Leland in the 1530s as 'a fair place caullid *Vanne*, wher Mr. Edward Lewys dwellith'. It was during the same visit that Leland described the castle itself 'sette emonge marisches, wher be ruinus waulles of a wonderful thiknes, and toure kept up for prisoners'. The 'ruinous walls' were to be reduced even further almost fifty years later by the dismantling of the original ashlar dressings by Lewis's son.

The castle played very little part in the Civil War, although earthwork defences were thrown up in order to protect the approaches. These occupied the site of the original Roman fort. The leaning tower – inclined at a sharper angle than that at Pisa – might be a casualty of the Civil War, or else subsidence; whatever the reason, its dramatic profile is always a good talking point.

In 1776, a wealthy Scottish landowner, John Stuart, the son of the 3rd earl of Bute, George III's prime minister, married Charlotte Windsor. As a descendant of the illustrious Herberts, she was heiress to vast estates in Glamorgan, including Cardiff,

Castell Coch and Caerphilly. Stuart became the first marquess of Bute, and while his grandson, the 2nd marquess (1794–1884), the 'creator' of Cardiff as the coal metropolis of the world, was not particularly interested in architecture, his son, the 3rd marquess (1847–1900), and to a lesser extent the 4th marquess (1881–1947), transformed the appearance of their South Wales castle inheritance. What the 3rd marquess had not completed at his early death, was continued with zest and expertise by his son who devoted many years to a major restoration of Caerphilly Castle. He also ordered the demolition of a street of small town houses, so that its great eastern front could be seen to better advantage.

With the death of the 4th marquess in 1947, the Butes lost hold on most of their estates in South Wales, and the castle was taken into guardianship a few years later. Father and son between them had re-roofed the magnificent hall, and had reinstated substantial sections of walls and towers. The dressed stone that had been 'robbed' by Thomas Lewis for Y Fan – sometimes referred to, ironically, as Castell Y Fan – was replaced by concrete. Y Fan itself was in a state of severe disrepair for well over a century and the building which bears its name, and which is visible from the ramparts, is a sadly inadequate reconstruction of the 1990s showing none of that awareness of the past that has contributed to the successful undertaking of the castle's care and maintenance by Cadw.

The site of Caerphilly Castle is surprisingly low-lying, so that the water defences are a compensation and substitute for height, the natural ally of any fortified site. It is not only its enormous size nor the fact that it is the first concentric castle in Britain that gives it such a mark of distinction; it is the intricacy of its water defences that sets it apart from any other castle, even though it might owe its inspiration to Kenilworth Castle, which was surrounded by what amounted to a lake, and which resisted attack for six months in 1266, when the son of Simon de Montfort held out against the Lord Edward, the future Edward I, a siege at which Gilbert de Clare was also present.

The castle itself, which is placed on a central island and protected by a surrounding curtain wall, consists of a rectangular inner ward, fortified by round towers at each angle, with a twin-towered gateway leading into the outer ward, and a formidable gatehouse (1270), based on one built only a few years previously at Tunbridge by Richard de Clare, Gilbert's father. Apart from the hall, this is the most complete part of the castle. It was designed to be capable of independent defence, and its tactical combination of keep and gatehouse, together with its indomitable aspect set it apart from any other contemporary fortification. It was not until Master James of St George's Edwardian castles at Harlech (1283–89) and Beaumaris (1295–96) that similar constructions appeared in Wales.

There are no remains of the medieval town at Caerphilly, nor the burgage pattern and walled defences which would be expected in so important a settlement. This very simple town, bereft of any architectural distinction, seems to keep a respectful distance from Gilbert de Clare's *tour de force*, whose monumental scale and complexity have been so expertly restored, thanks to the 3rd and 4th marquesses of Bute, and now to Cadw.

Caldicot (Monmouthshire)

5m (8km) SW of Chepstow off M4 at Junction 22, Open: standard hours, Admission charge, Local Authority

During the last twenty years, Caldicot has captured the popular imagination of South-East Wales and the South-West of England by being the setting for mock medieval banquets and this form of entertainment has tended to draw visitors' attention away from the long defensive history of the site, whose importance extends back to Roman times where their presence in this part of Gwent was very prominent.

The area yielded to the Normans soon after the Battle of Hastings and their advance westwards was greatly facilitated by following the routes established by the Romans and by the unchallenging terrain of the coastal plains. Caldicot's position, a mere two miles from the river Severn, is nothing like as dramatic a situation as its neighbour, Chepstow, but by the period of the replacing of the first earth-and-timber stronghold with masonry defences, Caldicot took on a far more menacing aspect, particularly by the appearance of the earliest of the improvements, the round keep which was built on the original motte some time during the first half of the thirteenth century. The builder was Humphrey de Bohun, earl of Hereford, and hereditary constable of England. The family, headed in each generation by a Humphrey, held the lordship and castle of Caldicot until 1373.

In type it very much resembles the round keeps at Skenfrith, also in Gwent, and at Bronllys and Tretower, both in Powys, but what sets Caldicot apart is the small semi-circular tower on the west side of the keep, which houses a chamber on its highest floor, and a dungeon in the basement, with a solid mass between these two vastly contrasting spaces. The tower keep itself is made up of four floors, each with a hooded fireplace, and connected by means of steps built into the thickness of the walls. The curtain wall was built soon after the keep and enclosed a polygonal area. The entrance to the castle was through an arched gateway at the side of the round tower in the middle of the wall, and protected by the greater height of the keep.

The third stage in the masonry development of the castle is represented by the first-floor great hall built along the south curtain wall. Only three windows set into the curtain wall remain to give some indication of its status.

On the death of the last Humphrey de Bohun in 1373, the castle passed to his two daughters. One of them, Eleanor, married Thomas of Woodstock, the youngest son of Edward III. Between 1384–89, vast sums were spent on the castle to make it worthy of a royal residence, and the result was the immensely imposing Great Gatehouse on the south wall, and the smaller gatehouse on the north wall. Thomas of Woodstock was murdered in 1397 for opposing the marriage of Richard II to Isabelle de Valois, and was 'by the direction of the Earl Marshal, smothered between two feather beds'.

Through the marriage of his daughter to the earl of Stafford, the castle eventually passed to the dukes of Buckingham, a hapless breed. They held several castles in Wales, including Brecon and Hay. The first duke was killed at the Battle of Northampton at the beginning of the Wars of the Roses in 1460; the 2nd duke was beheaded by Richard III and the 3rd by Henry VIII. Caldicot then passed to the Duchy of Lancaster, and it was not until the middle of the last century that it regained any semblance of a settled existence, when it was bought by J.R. Cobb (1821–97), a promoter of the Brecon and Merthyr Railway, and a castle enthusiast who also did some restoration work at Manorbier and Pembroke. At Caldicot he restored the Great Gatehouse, now the venue for those enjoyable fanciful recreations of the less military and hostile aspects of life in the Middle Ages.

Candleston (Vale of Glamorgan)
Near Merthyr Mawr, 2m (3.2km) SW of Bridgend, Open access, Admission free, Private ownership

This fortified manor house takes its name from its builder, William de Cantelupe, a follower of William the Conqueror. The two-storey tower, which probably replaced the original foundation, dates from the thirteenth century and consists of a chamber reached from the basement level by steps built into the thickness of the wall. A first-floor hall, added in the following century, has sufficient remains of a fireplace to display its ornate character and the status of the hall itself. A ruined wall encloses these two medieval structures as well as further additions, including early nineteenth-century stables which were probably built by John Nicholl, a successful lawyer who lived at Candleston between 1806–08 while his house, Merthyr Mawr, was being built. The estate village of Merthyr Mawr consists only of thatched cottages, probably the largest community of its kind in Wales and enormously appealing. Candleston Castle lies on the opposite side of the river Ogwr from the de Londres stronghold of Ogmore. Ewenni priory, only two miles away, is another building of interest in this Norman enclave of South Glamorgan.

Cardiff, Caerdydd (Cardiff)

Cardiff City centre, Open: standard hours, Admission charge, Local Authority

The wall that surrounds the castle in the very heart of the shopping centre is a handsome nineteenth-century structure maintained to a high standard and reflecting the unalloyed civic pride accorded to a capital city. A close look at a section of the structure will reveal the remains of a Roman wall which formed part of the fort that gave the settlement its name: Caerdyf: the fort of the Taf (river Taff) to become Cardiff, and the Welsh version that evolved from this, Caerdydd. The Normans in their conquest of Wales followed the same thrust westwards as the Romans had done, and in the case of Cardiff, set up a fortification within the earlier defences. As in previous Roman foothold-to-fort strategy, the proximity of easy river crossing, and hence sea access, together with the additional advantage of good land communication, were equally valued by the Normans, who in 1081, raised a motte whose height was not matched by any similar defence in Wales. Norman control in these parts was finally assured by the defeat in 1091 of Iestyn ap Gwrgan, the last independent ruler of Glamorgan. The usurper was Robert FitzHamon, earl of Gloucester, who built a timber keep on the earlier ditched motte. It was his son-in-law, Robert, earl of Gloucester, and the illegitimate son of Henry I, who was responsible for the next stage in the development of the castle: the building in masonry of a polygonal keep, probably a precaution taken against the Welsh uprising of 1136, which followed the death of Henry I the previous year, and which resulted in general civil discontent. The keep dominates the castle enclosure not only by its extraordinary height, but by its sheer size.

Apart from the put-log holes, it is a mass of masonry and a dauntingly formidable structure, or so it must have seemed to everybody who did not have the intense motivation and conviction of Ifor ap Meurig of Senghennydd, or Ifor Bach – 'Ifor the Little, being of short stature, but of great courage', to quote Giraldus Cambrensis. He came to the castle of Cardiff which, Giraldus continues, 'was surrounded with high walls, guarded

Cardiff Castle

by a hundred-and-twenty men-at-arms, a numerous body of archers, a strong watch. The city also contained many stipendiary soldiers; yet, in defiance of all these precautions of security, Ivor, in the dead of night, secretly scaled the walls, and seized the count and countess, with their only son, carried them off into the woods, and did not release them until he had recovered everything that had been unjustly taken from him and received a compensation of additional property.' Few other Welsh leaders are known to have gained similar recompense as a result of such a tenacious gesture of defiance against the invader.

In 1216 the lordship and castle came into the possession of the de Clare family, and by the second half of the century, Cardiff had undergone major improvements in order to combat the relentless assaults mounted by Llywelyn ap Gruffudd, supported by other Welsh chieftains, in his attempt to wrest South Wales from English dominance. The man responsible for such refortification was Gilbert de Clare, 'Gilbert the Red', whose grandfather, another Gilbert, and the first of the family to occupy Cardiff, had been involved in the struggle between King John and the barons. Among the defences that he built were the Black Tower to the left of the present entrance gate, which now accommodates the museum of the Welch Regiment, and a wall to link it to the refortified Norman keep, thereby creating two wards. This wall was demolished in the eighteenth century when the castle was in the process of being turned into a country house by the 1st marquess of Bute, but its foundations were revealed in the nineteenth century and the low wall following the line of the original construction belongs to this century. Such was Gilbert de Clare's territorial ambition that he was responsible for the greatest non-royal castle in the whole of the United Kingdom: Caerphilly, today less than half an hour's journey from Cardiff. Halfway between them he built Castell Coch.

Cardiff Castle passed to the Despenser family in the early fourteenth century, and they were to hold it until the death of Richard Despenser in 1414 when it passed to his sister Isabel's husband, Richard Beauchamp. It was to be a short tenure, and on his death in 1422, Isabel, who was still only twenty-three years of age, married another Richard Beauchamp, earl of Warwick, who played a prestigious rôle in the upbringing of the boy Henry VI, for he was instructed to 'teach him nurture, literature, language and other manner of cunning'. Such responsibilities did not prevent him from making elaborate plans for the development of Cardiff Castle. The period of stability which followed the failure of the Glyndŵr uprising of the first decade of the fifteenth century greatly reduced the concern for defence, resulting in major improvements in domestic comforts.

Beauchamp built a residential range on the west side of the inner ward, and for the first time, the family could descend from the keep. Even so, there was still a suspicion of the possibility of attack, as the construction of the polygonal tower suggests. This has subsequently been known both as the Octagon Tower and as the Beauchamp Tower.

With the death of Richard Beauchamp's son, Henry, the male line of the Warwick Beauchamps became extinct, and the castle came into the possession of Richard's sister, who had married Richard Neville, created earl of Warwick in 1450. Through his wife's enormous inheritance in Wales and the West Midlands, he became one of the greatest landowners in the country, and wielded immeasurably more power than his wife's brother had done. He is best known as Warwick the King-Maker.

No further alterations and improvements were made to the castle until well into the second half of the sixteenth century. These were the work of Henry Herbert, the heir of William Herbert, who had been granted the lordship of Cardiff by Edward VI in 1550. It was during this time that the square tower – the Herbert Tower – was built, together with extensions northwards to the west range. These were the last significant changes to the castle until the eighteenth century when it became, through marriage, the property of one of the most prominent families in the realm: the Butes.

Because of Cardiff's involvement in the Civil War, the castle had become greatly neglected, and John Mount-Stuart, later the 4th earl and 1st marquess of Bute, and son of the Prime Minister, commissioned the most renowned architect of the day, Robert Adam, a fellow Scot, to improve the residential range and to convert the seat of so many illustrious names into a grand and elegant country house. Adam's plans involved converting the existing accommodation into one third of a vast three-winged house, in the shape of a half-hexagon. They were never executed, and it was Lancelot 'Capability' Brown, a successful architect as well as a landscape gardener, together with his son-in-law, Henry Holland, the architect of the Royal Pavilion at Brighton, who were entrusted with the new building scheme. The north-west tower, the Bute Tower, stems from this period, matching the Herbert Tower on the south-west, and giving the Beauchamp Tower a central position. By the 1800s, the west range had an almost symmetrical elevation facing the inner ward. It had become 'a neat Gothic residence'.

The 1st marquess's son had died in an accident, and it was his grandson who succeeded him in 1814. He employed Sir Robert Smirke, the architect of the British Museum, to make alterations to the castle, but his time was mainly taken up by affairs of estate. In 1818, the Bute family's Edinburgh surveyor wrote of Cardiff that he had never seen 'an estate in a more neglected condition. The neglect of centuries cannot be corrected in three or four years . . . The Marquess will not, during his life, be able to repair the consequence of the neglect of his predecessors.' He did not know the firm resolve of the 2nd marquess. A plan was put into operation. Cardiff would be turned into a major port, providing an outlet for the mineral wealth of the Glamorgan hinterland, which he owned, through the judicious marriage of his grandfather. As a result, ground rents would rise, port duties would flow, and the mineral royalties would never cease. The strategy was spectacularly successful. The Bute monopoly transformed the torpid town of Cardiff into the coal metropolis of the world in a matter of decades.

The 2nd marquess was in his mid-fifties when his son was born. He brought the boy on one of his duty visits to Cardiff, to show him to the Glamorgan gentry, and died in his dressing room, 'to awake in eternity'. He was fifty-four years of age, and his six-month-old son was reputedly the richest heir in the country. If his father had made a fortune through the making of Cardiff, the 3rd marquess would spend that fortune transforming Cardiff Castle and giving it a skyline worthy of Camelot.

He developed from an early age into a scholarly aesthete, with a passionate liking for the architecture of the Middle Ages. This was heightened during his undergraduate days at Oxford, and by extensive travel to the greatest cities of Europe and the Middle East. It was the meeting of two like-minded people, with a passion for the medieval world, that turned theory into practice, and transformed an idea and an ideal into a reality. The young marquess of Bute met the older William Burges: between them they presented Cardiff with a castle which gave extravagant substance to a High Victorian dream.

The first manifestation of such a lofty ideal could not be more appropriate: the building of the clock tower on the south-west corner. Its impact on the town, with its ornate decoration is immediate and unmistakable. It dates from 1869 and was designed as accommodation for a bachelor, which Lord Bute indeed was at the beginning of the project. Where the typical grand Victorian country house would have had a separate wing for such a gentleman, it was more appropriate that a castle of Cardiff's lineage should provide that accommodation in a tower and its function would account for its detachment from the main body of the building.

Burges heightened the Herbert and Bute Towers, and the central Beauchamp Tower was given its particular mark of distinction: the very elegant and intricate *flèche*, which

Cardiff Castle, chimney breast of banqueting hall

embodies in an almost playful way, the essence of medieval architecture. This sequence of towers, representing Bute and Burges's ambitiously original scheme, is seen at its most express-ive from the park to the west of the castle.

The exterior of the castle in no way prepares the visitor for the interiors; their range of iconographical intricacy, historical and mythological allusiveness displays the long history of the castle from Roman times, through the Normans and their inheritors, and their eventual Welsh successors, leading to its final possession by the Butes.

Bute said that he was more concerned with 'atmosphere' than with domestic comfort. When Axel Haig's picture of the Smoking Room depicting Bute and Burges, dressed in medieval garb, and imbibing from chalices, was exhibited at the Royal Academy in 1870, the young marquess wrote to his fiancée: 'Please don't imagine, my dear, that the house is all done up as if we are living in the reign of Henry III.' That was a mild understatement.

It is only during the last twenty years that the interiors of Cardiff Castle have been appreciated by the public at large as the artistic aspirations and expressions of a particular period in the development of artistic taste. Previously, they were regarded as either the field-of-study of specialists, or as a figure-of-fun for a public who had not been sufficiently well informed to appreciate the depth and diversity of that wonderful fusion of human, botanical, literary and mythological interests which makes room after room such an intellectual challenge, as well as such a visual delight.

The clock tower contains both winter and summer smoking rooms, with the bachelor's bedroom placed on the floor between them. Off it is a Roman marble bath, decorated with suitably aquatic creatures, ranging from an octopus to a newt. The Summer Smoking Room, which occupies two floors, is reached by passing the door that leads to the clock mechanism. The arduous ascent of 101 steps is rewarded by the glories of the room, with its all-embracing chandelier, depicting Apollo, god of the sun.

The Herbert Tower contains Lord Bute's study, and also the remarkably ornate Arab Room, with its cedar wood-lined walls and coffered ceiling, said to be Lord Bute's favourite room. The Beauchamp Tower houses the Chaucer Room, with stained-glass windows illustrating scenes from *The Canterbury Tales*. The very ornate castellated fireplace in the banqueting hall bears the words *Robertus Consul Com Glo*, Robert Consul and earl of Gloucester. The last two abbreviated words bear a striking resemblance to *Cwm Glo*, 'the valley of coal'. It might well have been one of Bute and Burges's thousands of punnish indulgences throughout the castle. In this case it was not biblical, mythological, historical or literary: it was fact. The wealth that created the glories of the 3rd marquess's showpiece at Cardiff – and at Castell Coch – was based not on illustrious genealogy, but on black diamonds – coal.

Carew, Caeriw (Pembrokeshire)
On A477, 3.5m (5.6km) NE of Pembroke, turn N onto A4075,
Open: Easter–October, Admission charge, Pembrokeshire Coast
National Park

Carew is one of the most strikingly handsome of all the castles in South-West Wales. This is partly due to its situation on the

Carew Castle

tidal creek of the river Carew, but mostly due to the structure of the castle itself, for it combines the elements of powerful defensive systems and the most luxurious displays of palatial comfort, brought about by changes in more settled times.

The founder is reputed to be Rhys ap Tewdwr, Prince of Deheubarth who according to tradition gave it as a dowry to his daughter Nest, acclaimed for her beauty, when she married Gerald Windsor, Constable of Pembroke Castle from 1093–1116. In 1212, Carew was referred to as *domus de Carrio*, probably by then the property of Gerald's grandson who adopted its name. The Old Tower is the only remnant of the stone castle which was built to replace the original earth and timber stronghold, and it was a descendant, Sir Nicholas de Carew who was responsible for much of the basic structure we see today, a quadrilateral enclosure, with powerful round towers, a first-floor hall built over a vaulted basement, and a semi-octagonal tower which accommodated the chapel. Forty

Carew Castle

years of building between 1280–1320 produced a domain where equal attention seems to have been given to stately show and defence. The castle remained the property of the family until 1480 when Sir Edmund Carew sold it to Rhys ap Thomas, an ardent Lancastrian who was to support Henry Tudor, the earl of Richmond, in his claim to the Crown. Rhys accompanied him from the moment he landed at Dale, not far from Carew, after fourteen years of exile in France, throughout his march across Wales and over the border to defeat Richard III at the Battle of Bosworth in 1485. He was rewarded for his loyalty by the young Henry VII, as he had now become, with a knighthood.

Sir Rhys built a gatehouse between the outer and inner wards, and the existing buildings were made far less defensive by the introduction of more ornate fenestration and by the addition of fine façades. He added an oriel window on the north end of the fourteenth-century great hall and a three-storey porch on the south end. The porch bore the arms of Henry VII, his son Arthur, Prince of Wales, and Arthur's wife, Catherine of Aragon, a gesture of gratitude as well as allegiance to the king, for in 1505 Rhys had been made a Knight of the Garter, an honour which he celebrated lavishly at Carew with a great tournament, to which all the leading Welsh noble families were invited.

There was a change of family fortune, however, when in 1531 his grandson, Sir Rhys ap Gruffydd, was beheaded for treason. Carew became Crown property and remained so until 1558 when it was granted to Sir John Perrot, reputedly the natural son of Henry VIII. This next phase in the evolution of Carew from fortress to stately home is the result of Perrot's building flair, which he also exercised at Laugharne Castle.

His addition consists of two rows of mullion-and-transom windows and two large oriel windows, an array of splendour which is enhanced by its reflection in the water of the estuary. It all turned out to be a vain display of success and glory, because in spite of a distinguished political and diplomatic career, Perrot was arrested for high treason, and condemned to death. He died in the Tower in 1592 – of natural causes.

Carmarthen, Caerfyrddin (Carmarthenshire)
In town centre, View from outside only, Local Authority

Crossing the bridge over the river Tywi one is confronted with the uncompromising bland front of the County Hall standing sentinel over the whole area. Such a site deserves an Amboise or a similar Loire-type château. In the early nineteenth century, however, there would have been at least the ruins of a castle on this elevated spot, commanding the river crossing. Most of these ruins are still there but by today they have been masked by urban development, and the twin-towered gatehouse in the middle of the town's shopping area gives very little indication of the fortress's original size and dominating situation.

This was not the first Norman stronghold in the area, the previous one being probably sited further down stream. Its name *Rhyd y Gors* ('the ford over the fen') indicates the importance of the river crossings to the Normans, who had, during their advance into South and West Wales, built their castles at the mouths of rivers. They also very often followed routes established by the Romans and, sometimes, as at Cardiff, built their castles within the Roman fort. Both Norman castles at Carmarthen, however, were built some distance away from the Roman *Maridunum*, the remains of which were still visible in the late twelfth century, according to Giraldus Cambrensis in his *Itinerary*.

In 1275 there was a tantalising reference to 'certain good "dungio" made of five little towers'. Mention was also made of a great tower, hall, kitchen, chapel and gatehouse. This was the work of William Marshall, earl of Pembroke, in order to refortify the castle after its capture and destruction by Llywelyn ap Iorwerth in 1215. Further additions and improvements were made to the castle in the fourteenth century, including the gatehouse and the south-west tower which we see today. Despite these defensive measures, Carmarthen suffered badly during the Owain Glyndŵr rebellion, when the Welsh force included formidable French support. As a result, the castle required considerable rebuilding after 1405.

By 1456, Edmund Tudor (father of Henry, later Henry VII), was given possession of the castle, as the king's representative.

Centuries of strife had proved that Carmarthen was a pivotal factor in controlling routes to the north (Cardigan), the south (Swansea), the east (Brecon) and the west (Pembroke). As a consequence it had become a powerful administrative centre. The Yorkist William Herbert took the castle in 1456 and Edmund Tudor was taken prisoner. He died soon afterwards, on 3rd November and was buried in the Grey Friars. At the dissolution in 1536, his remains were removed to the choir of St David's cathedral.

Like the castles of Flint and Haverfordwest, Carmarthen became a county prison in 1789, and extensions to it in 1869 took up the space previously represented by the outer ward.

In spite of the sparse remains of the castle, Carmarthen town still manages to convey a great deal of its long and significant history.

Carreg Cennen (Carmarthenshire)

From Llandeilo, take A476 S to Ffairfach (0.5m/0.8km). Take left at crossroads, then right. Follow signs to Trapp and castle (3m/ 4.8km). Open: standard hours, Admission charge, Cadw

The distant view of Carreg Cennen from the road between Crosshands and Llandeilo embodies the spirit and atmosphere of medieval warfare. It stands lofty and proud, a man-made fortress securing its hold on the natural stronghold of a limestone rock. The Reverend Eli Jenkins in Dylan Thomas's *Under Milk Wood* refers to it as 'Carreg Cennen, King of Time', and it does seem as if it has always been there, overseeing age after age of man coming to grips with his land and his enemies.

The discovery of first- and second-century coins nearby suggests that the Romans had appreciated the formidable and forbidding character of this rocky elevation, and yet, it has inspired no myths nor is it associated with the legendary exploits of any national heroes, unlike, for example, Tintagel, the precipitous coastal site in Cornwall, associated with Arthur, and no references to its existence appear until the twelfth century.

Like Dinefwr and Dryslwyn, also in Carmarthenshire, it was a native Welsh castle. Unlike them, it is untouched by the sign of neighbouring habitation or vegetation, and stands in uncompromising and awesome aloofness.

During the twelfth and thirteenth centuries, following the death in 1197 of the Lord Rhys of Dinefwr, the stability which he had achieved in Deheubarth was severely undermined by inter-dynastic wrangles which involved these three castles, though not the structures whose remnants we see today.

During Edward I's first Welsh campaign of 1277, Carreg Cennen was taken, and its seizure was challenged first by Llywelyn ap Gruffudd, shortly before his downfall in 1282, and five years later by Rhys ap Maredudd who attacked the English-occupied Dryslwyn on the same day.

Carreg Cennen, at the time of Rhys ap Maredudd's attempt at retrieval, was in the possession of John Giffard, lord of Brimpsfield in Gloucestershire, who had also been granted Llandovery Castle by Edward I as a gesture of appreciation for his support during the king's campaign against Llywelyn. The masonry castle of Carreg Cennen dates from Giffard's tenure, and between 1283–1321, he and his son were responsible for the complex and compelling remains which confront us today: complex because the defences had to conform to the terrain rather than to prescribed notions of military strategy, and compelling because of the nature of the site.

Carreg Cennen was vulnerable on its north and east sides, around which the outer ward was built, thereby offering protection to the inner ward which on its west and south sides was defended by vertiginous drops.

Entering through the gatehouse of the outer ward, the assailant had several obstacles to overcome: a left-hand turn to reach the barbican which was protected by at least one further gate, before negotiating another sharp left-hand turn leading almost immediately to the formidable twin-towered gatehouse which challenged, rather than welcomed, entry into the inner ward.

The domestic range was situated to the east of the gatehouse, and beyond it is the entry into a passage-way in the cliff which leads to a natural cave, its mouth partly walled in order to provide compartments for nesting pigeons. Access to the cave from the castle itself safeguarded one of the fortress's vulnerable points.

In 1321 Giffard's occupancy of Carreg Cennen ended in ignominy because of his part in a rebellion against Edward II. By the middle of the fourteenth century it had come into the possession of the Lancaster family who also owned Kidwelly. A co-heiress of this family married John of Gaunt, and through their son, Henry Bolingbroke, the future Henry IV, both castles became the property of the Crown.

The castle, under its constable John Skydmore, yielded to Owain Glyndŵr, after a lengthy siege. It underwent a further period of activity during the Wars of the Roses, when in 1455, Sir Gruffydd ap Nicholas of Dinefwr, a Lancastrian supporter, gave orders for its refortification. After the Lancastrian defeat at Mortimer's Cross in 1461, Gruffydd's sons, Thomas and Owain, sought refuge at Carreg Cennen until the following year, when Sir Richard Herbert of Raglan and Sir Roger Vaughan of Tretower took the castle for the Yorkists. By August 1462 orders were given for its demolition, which was carried out by 500 men 'with bars, picks and cross-bars of iron and other instruments necessary for the same purpose'. The operation cost £28 5s 6d, and it achieved its aim, which was 'to avoid inconvenience of this kind happening there in future'.

In recognition of his services to the Tudor cause, Henry VII granted the castle to Sir Rhys ap Thomas, and it passed by marriage to the Vaughans of Golden Grove, and through that family to John Campbell, the ancestor of the Earls of Cawdor. In 1932, the 5th earl placed Carreg Cennen in the guardianship of the then His Majesty's Office of Works.

Many artists have attempted to depict Carreg Cennen's defiant profile above the lush pastureland of the surrounding peaceful countryside. Few, if any, have succeeded. 'King of Time' was a far more succinct and successful description of its uniqueness.

Castell y Bere

Castell y Bere (Gwynedd)
7m (11km) inland from Towyn, Open access, Admission free, Cadw

In the galleries devoted to the medieval period in the National Museum of Wales, Cardiff, fragments of carved columns from Castell y Bere give some suggestion of the exceptional standard of ornamented masonry that must have been characteristic of this castle. This should not be surprising, for it was the castle of a Welsh prince, Llywelyn ap Iorwerth. Like two of his other castles, Cricieth and Dolbadarn, it was later adapted to suit the needs of Edward I, but what remains of Castell y Bere dates from Llywelyn's building of 1221. This, according to *Brut*, was the result of his discontent with his son, Gruffudd, from whom he took away the *cantref* of Meirionnydd and the commote of Ardudwy, and 'began to build a castle there for himself'.

The remoteness of its location in the Dysynni Valley is near the formidable rock outcrop of Craig yr Aderyn (Bird Rock), the only inland nesting site in Wales of cormorants. The area brings to mind the awesome characteristics of Argos, with its mighty palace of Mycenae dominating the surrounding Greek plain. Yet no gruesome myths or legends are attached to this fertile valley which was brought into prominence in the nineteenth century by the increasing tourist awareness of the impressive Cader Idris range which is a natural sentinel over the region.

Castell y Bere was no Welsh attempt to offset the English onslaught; it was rather a challenge to any compatriot bold enough to defy Llywelyn's territorial supremacy. The plan of the castle was determined by the contours of the narrow rock on which it was built, utilising every possible naturally defensive vantage point. Its situation accounted for the irregular shape of the curtain-walled ward, strengthened by towers, two of which were D-ended, a style of military architecture which was favoured by the Welsh, and of which there is a good example at Ewloe. Further fortified by deeply-cut ditches and drawbridges, this citadel, probably the most isolated of all the castles in Wales, was essential for defending the mountainous route between Dyfi and the Mawddach estuaries.

After Llywelyn ap Gruffudd's death in 1282, the enormous weight of the Welsh resistance movement fell upon the shoulders of his brother, Dafydd, who used Castell y Bere as his base for the final stand in 1283 against the Edwardian conquest of Wales.

The combination of remoteness, the sparse – though eloquent – remains of a Welsh fortress, with its minimal improvements introduced by the English, the very little written evidence of the site's military importance, all contribute to make Castell y Bere the most enigmatically engaging of the castles of Wales.

Castell Coch (Cardiff)

Tongwynlais 5m (8km) N of Cardiff. Take A470 Merthyr road. Signposted in Tongwynlais. Open: standard hours, Admission charge, Cadw

By any standard Castell Coch (the Red Castle, because of the colour of the stone) is an intriguing anomaly: a stronghold with Norman origins, refortified in the thirteenth century and perfectly habitable at the end of the nineteenth, with living and sleeping quarters that were highly decorated, a portcullis in sound working order, and a drawbridge that still takes the weight of heavily uniformed soldiers on white chargers. Castell Coch, however, is in no way similar to other castles in Wales, like Chirk, or Powis, which overcame attacks over the centuries and survive up to the present day as comfortable country houses whose interiors are prized by the National Trust. The four centuries which divided the masonry fortress of the de Clares, earls of Glamorgan, at Castell Coch and its nineteenth-century appearance represented a span of neglect and decay, and the castle was described by John Leland in the late 1530s as being 'all in ruin no big thing but high', and as late as the 1870s, it was described as a 'picturesque ruin [standing] boldly on a craggy declivity facing the Taff, high enough to command a view of the Channel beyond Cardiff'.

'The channel', or otherwise Cardiff Bay, and the road from Penarth conversely command a view not of a 'picturesque ruin' but of a Rhenish *schloss*, its conical roofs prominent against a heavily wooded backcloth. The magical transformation of the thirteenth-century ruin into a functionable 'fortress', offering the somewhat unconventional amenities of a small country house, is the result of the wizardry that William Burges (1827–81) exerted over his patron, the 3rd marquess of Bute (1847–1900). The first had a courageous spirit of discovery, research and interpretation which was equalled by his imagination and his scholarship; the other had keen erudition, a restlessly inquisitive nature and insatiable acquisitiveness. He was also extremely rich. His dreams, and those of Burges, could become a reality – or an exotic and fantastic version of reality. Castell Coch takes precedence over their other collaborative recreation, Cardiff Castle, only by the dramatic nature of its site and by the much smaller scale of the building which has retained its original contours. As such it not only epitomises every child's idea of a fortress, but powerfully evokes the spirit of the medieval defensive attitude towards life. The earlier mention of white chargers on the drawbridge refers to episodes in more than one film or television play depicting chivalric romance and knightly challenge.

The castle is ovoid in shape, with two round towers flanking a hall on the south side, and a third tower on the north-east side which is not matched by one on the north-west. This basic plan forms the available accommodation space capable of being restored. It had its obvious limitations, resulting in only four rooms of any status: the banqueting hall above the servants' hall, leading to a drawing-room in the keep tower, which had above it Lady Bute's bedroom, with its double-domed ceiling. Lord Bute's bedroom is located above the windlass room, where the mechanism which controlled and operated the drawbridge was placed.

The rooms are extremely varied in their appeal. The servants' hall which now offers a fully comprehensive exhibition of the history of the castle and its nineteenth-century restoration should be visited both before and after a tour of the rooms themselves. Above the servants' hall is the banqueting hall, whose main feature is the hooded lofty chimney breast on which is carved Lucius, King of Britain in about 200AD and founder of the diocese of Llandaf. Centrally placed on the mantel are the arms of the Butes, made up of the two major families in their lineage, and in their surname since the eighteenth century, Crichton and Stuart. The predominantly religious theme of the decoration was carried out after Burges's death, and its chaste restraint in no way prepares the retina for the onslaught of colour, form and design of the domed drawing-room. The polygonal shape of the room, the gallery, with the divided-quatrefoil balustrading, the rib-vaulting, the frieze, the inset panels, the fireplace surmounted by the three Fates, are all overwhelmingly powerful in themselves. To this one has to add not only the colour, but the detail of Burges's figures, representing Aesop's fables, and the magic and mysteries of the natural world in general.

Above the drawing-room is Lady Bute's bedroom, occupying the two top floors of the keep. Its double-dome fits into the conical roof. Centrally placed under the dome is a Victorian Moorish-style bed. In fact, the entire room has a distinctly Moorish or Oriental look, a taste cultivated by many country house owners after the appearance in 1842 of Owen Jones's book on the decorations of the Alhambra in Granada. The

Castell Coch, washstand

theme of the bedroom is 'Sleeping Beauty', and the panels of
the dome are painted with monkeys and pomegranates,
entwined with thorns and brambles. Lord Bute's bedroom is
reached by a spiral staircase which also gives access on the way
to the gallery of the drawing-room, offering an excellent vantage point from which to appreciate the intricacy of Burges's
decorative schemes. The marquess's bedroom, like the banqueting hall, is relatively unadorned, and suggests an almost spartan
disregard for comfort. Leading from it is a wooden bretache,
or hourd, a projecting wooden gallery, offering added defence
to the entrance to the castle.

As if struck by the similarity of his own high-perched castle
to those of the Rhine or the Loire, Bute started his own vineyard, an event which did not go unnoticed by one of the comic
satirical papers of 1875.

The Marquess of Bute has, it appears, a BUTE-iful vineyard
at Castell Coch, near Cardiff, where it is to be hoped such
wine will be produced that in future HOCK will be superseded by Coch, and the unpronounceable vintages of the
Rhine will yield to the unpronounceable vintages of the Taff.
Cocheimer is as yet a wine *in potentia*, but the vines are

planted, and the gardener, Mr. Pettigrew, anticipates no petty growth.

The success of the vineyard was short-lived, but the collaboration between Bute and Burges on the castle itself is as intoxicating an experience as even the finest vintages can produce.

Chepstow, Casgwent (Monmouthshire)
N of town centre, Open: standard hours, Admission charge, Cadw

Chepstow could be called the first castle in Wales, for geographical as well as historical reasons, for not only does it lie just inside the border, on the south bank of the river Wye, but it was the first Norman foothold in South-East Wales, secured by William FitzOsbern, earl of Hereford, as early as 1167. On the narrowest point of the ridge above the river he built a large rectangular hall-keep, remarkable not only for its prominent position, but because it was from the outset a stone structure and, as such, one of the earliest in England and Wales. Its site, commanding the river crossing which linked the route from England into Wales, and its closeness to the river Severn were of enormous military importance.

William FitzOsbern decided to build on the narrowest point of a promontory between the river Wye and a ravine, and only to the west and to the east was there any space for a ward or bailey. It was the rigid limitation of the site which gave it its defensive nature, and resulted in the elongated outline of the castle.

FitzOsbern's building was a first-floor hall, entered through a round-headed decorated doorway which was reached by external steps. This inherently defensible arrangement was later to become characteristic of the successor to the rectangular keep, the round tower, examples of which can be seen at Bronllys and Tretower (Powys), at Skenfrith (Monmouthshire) and at Pembroke (Pembrokeshire).

Stylistically the early Chepstow was abreast with the stone hall-keeps that were appearing in France. In Langeais, on the Loire, for example, such a building or *domicilium* dates back

Chepstow Castle

to 1000. The hall and other domestic quarters were lit on the side of the Wye, from which there would have been few, if any, chances of attack. The service rooms below were barely lit at all. The appearance of this buttressed building must have been grimly unyielding.

In 1075 FitzOsbern's son, Roger de Breteuil, lost the earldom as a result of a plot against King William and the castle became Crown property until 1115 when Henry I granted it, together with the lordship of Striguil – the Welsh name for the area – to Walter FitzRichard, a member of the illustrious de Clare family whose name was to have such a resounding influence on South Wales. In 1131 he founded Tintern abbey, the first monastery of the Cistercian order to be established in Wales.

When Walter died childless in 1138, his lands were re-granted to his nephew, Gilbert, whose son Richard 'Strongbow' was the conqueror of Leinster. It was through the marriage of Richard's daughter Isabella, 'the damsel of Striguil', and William Marshall, 'the flower of chivalry', that Chepstow came into the hands of an outstanding soldier, with a passionate interest in military architecture.

It was the acquisition of Pembroke as well as Chepstow through his wife that enabled him, and later his sons, to transform both castles into the most innovative defensive systems in the whole of South Wales. His principal contribution to the development of Chepstow was to strengthen the eastern and most assailable approach to the castle. A drum tower was built to defend the south-east corner of FitzOsbern's stronghold. The original entrance into the outer bailey was blocked, and a D-shaped tower was built slightly to the north, where it protected the new entrance, placed far nearer to the cliff edge. Though the gateway itself could have seemed neither threatening nor challenging, the appearance of the round and rounded towers introduced a new concept of defence.

When William Marshall died in 1219, he was succeeded by his son, also William, and in turn by four other sons, none of whom produced an heir. Their contribution to Chepstow was considerable, and resulted in the addition of a bailey, with a curtain wall intersected by a D-shaped tower on the south-east corner, on the east side. This was entered through a twin-towered gatehouse. A barbican was built on the west side, with a drum tower protecting its south-west corner. The upper bailey was given a rectangular tower at its south-west corner. The hall underwent significant improvement by the insertion of far more generous and decorative windows, and a gallery was added along the whole of the north side of the building which was now almost literally on the cliff top. The extra storey that was added over a third of the western side must have given the hall the appearance of a very large church. By the death of Anselm, the last of the Marshall brothers, in 1245, Chepstow had been transformed from a basic defensive unit into a fortress which displayed not only a sophisticated awareness of military architecture, but a growing appreciation of the more residential aspects of castle life. This latter consideration played an extremely important part in the next development of Chepstow, when it came into the hands of Roger Bigod III, the grandson of Maud, the eldest of the Marshall sisters. He was earl of Norfolk and Marshal of England.

A gatehouse was added to the barbican, and the tower on the south-east corner of the lower bailey was enlarged in order to provide accommodation, including a chapel, for Bigod's private use. It became a self-contained, and completely separate defensive unit. The third storey of the hall was now extended eastwards to cover the entire length of the building. The most spectacular addition was the construction of an extensive domestic range against the north wall of the lower bailey. This contained not one hall but two, each with its own pantry and buttery. Between the vast kitchen and the gatehouse was a three-storey block containing chambers.

Bigod's building programme was both ingenious and extensive and although he provided the castle with the most luxurious and spacious accommodation, he did not forget the principal purpose of such a building. The might of the castle which he had inherited, and which he improved with such vigour, is obvious even in its fragmented state, and his awareness of the importance of defence also lay outside and beyond the boundaries of the castle itself. He fortified the town with a wall which started at the west tower of the barbican and extended south-eastwards towards the banks of the river Wye. Parts of it still survive, including the Town Gate. Bigod's mind was also on more spiritual matters and his great generosity towards Tintern abbey continued the tradition established by Walter FitzRichard. Later generations considered him as the abbey's founder. Like many builders he became heavily in debt. He bartered with King Edward over the future of his estates, and it was agreed that they should become Crown property after his day, on the understanding that he would be supported by an annuity. He lived only four years after that agreement, and with his death in 1306, nearly 250 years of military-architectural innovations and advancement came to an end.

In the sixteenth century Chepstow was in the control of the Somerset family of Raglan, a property which had come to them through marriage with the Herberts. Not only were new and larger windows inserted, and fireplaces renewed, improved and installed, but whole buildings were modified and adapted to a more secure existence. Unlike Raglan itself, Chepstow was not the Somerset seat, and therefore did not flaunt wealth and position by displays of ornate masonry.

It was a Somerset, Henry, earl of Worcester, who declared

for the king during the Civil War, and held Chepstow for the Royalists until it surrendered in October 1645. Three years later, having been regained in the king's name, it was attacked by Cromwell's men after which, like many other castles, it became a prison – with a difference: its inmates were political prisoners, and included Jeremy Taylor, Chaplain to Charles I, and after the Restoration Henry Martyn, one of the men who signed Charles I's death warrant, who was held for twenty years in the tower on the left of the main entrance which bears his name to this day. Considering that the tower once accommodated Bigod's private apartments, and that it was vastly improved in Tudor times, Martyn's was no ordinary incarceration.

Chepstow Castle spans the whole range of defensive building in Wales from the very first years of the Norman Conquest to the last land warfare in this country. As such it is a reflection of man's innate nature, his accomplishments and his weaknesses. It is, above all, a magnificent ruin.

In 1950, having had no useful purpose for at least two centuries, apart from being a wonderful subject for artists, it was put in the guardianship of the Ministry of Works, the predecessor of Cadw.

Chirk, Castell Y Waun (Wrexham)
Near village, Open: standard hours, Admission charge, National Trust

It was after the defeat of Llywelyn ap Gruffudd, that Roger Mortimer, a firm supporter of Edward I in his campaign against the Welsh, was granted the lands of Llywelyn Fychan at Chirkland by the king. This member of a powerful Marcher family began work on the castle in 1295, or soon afterwards, but certainly close enough to the time of the construction of Beaumaris Castle in Anglesey for both buildings to have had a very similar lay-out of the inner ward. This constituted a generous rectangle protected by massive angle drum towers, one centrally placed on two of the four sides. The original plan for Chirk was either never executed or, if it had been, was drasti-

Chirk Castle

cally changed for some unspecified reason at a much later date, leaving the stronghold half the size it was designed to have been. The claims for the striking resemblance between these two castles are substantiated by the fact that Edward visited the site at Chirk soon after establishing his castle at Beaumaris and that the site in Clwyd offered the same opportunity for a major concentric development.

Just as the king's fortresses had ringed the North Wales coast from Flint, via Rhuddlan, Conwy, Caernarfon, Harlech and Beaumaris, so he devised a similar inland defensive system, with the building of Denbigh, in the *cantref* of Rhos and Rhufoniog, by Henry de Lacy, earl of Lincoln; of Ruthin, in the *cantref* of Dyffryn Clwyd, by Reginald de Grey; and Holt, in Bromfield and Yale (the commote of Yale and Welsh Maelor), by John de Warenne, earl of Surrey.

Speculation about the original height of the magnificent drum towers of the castle is aroused by their stunted appearance, because they rise no higher than the curtain walls. The outer ward was obliterated by landscaping projects in the sixteenth century, if not before, but the vestiges of formality seen in Badeslade's depiction of the forecourt in the early eighteenth century (clearly displayed as part of the castle exhibition section, adjacent to the National Trust shop) support that they were part of that original defensive area.

Had Chirk been completed, it would have exhibited the symmetry of Beaumaris. Had Beaumaris been completed, and occupied, like Chirk, for 700 years, it would have represented the perfect development and evolution of castle to country house. Such perfection has rarely been achieved in the history of any castle.

The entry into the inner ward is by means of a passage-way in the north curtain wall, and the range of cross-fire provided by the drum towers on either side of it was as effective as any attack from the most awesome of the gatehouses. Although the entrance has retained its portcullis grooves, and is generally unwelcoming, it has none of the forbidding and challenging aspects of its contemporary, though ruined, equivalent at Denbigh. This dark passage, with the National Trust ticket booth assigned to an even darker corner, opens into the inner ward, now so welcoming in its expansiveness, and glowing with its south-facing climbing foliage. The contrast between the stern and grey exterior and this most civilised of Oxbridge quadrangles is one of the delights of Chirk.

As a result of taking a leading part in the attack in 1321 against the Despensers, father and son (Edward II's favourite), Mortimer was forced to surrender to the king, and was imprisoned in the Tower of London where he remained until his death four years later in 1326, an ignoble end for someone who had wielded such power in Wales and the Marches. It has often been suggested that it was this dramatic change in fortune that accounted for the curtailment of Chirk's building programme, and with it the incompletion of the southern half of the inner ward which would have been entered, presumably, through a great gatehouse, either on the scale of one of the two at Beaumaris, or of the complexity of that at the other seigneurial castle in North Wales, Denbigh.

After the Mortimers, Chirk passed to a succession of baronial families, until Edward IV presented it to Sir William Stanley, the supporter of Henry Tudor at the Battle of Bosworth. Stanley undertook several improvements, some of which were noted by John Leland during his visit in the 1530s when he recorded that 'there is on a smaul hille a mighty large and stronge castel with dyvers towers, a late welle repayred by Syr Wylliam Standeley, the Yerle of Derby's brother.' In 1495 Stanley was executed for his involvement in the plot surrounding Perkin Warbeck, who claimed to be Richard, duke of York, Edward IV's second son, whose death in the Tower in 1483 could not be proved legally.

Chirk was subsequently in the hands of the Crown until 1563, during which time it was given by Henry VIII first to Henry Fitzroy, duke of Richmond, on whose early death at the age of only seventeen, it was given to Sir Thomas Seymour, Lord High Admiral of England, who married Catherine Parr, the king's widow. It was during this period – in 1529 – that the 'new lodgyngs' of the south range were built by the Crown.

In 1563, the lordship of Chirk, along with Castell Dinas Brân and Denbigh, was given by Queen Elizabeth to her favourite, Robert Dudley, whom she created earl of Leicester. Her gift to him of Kenilworth dates from the same time, and it is no doubt because of the lavish sums which he expended on that, the most accessible of his acquisitions, that few improvements were made at Chirk. His absorption with the building of a church at Denbigh, supposedly intended to supersede St Asaph as the cathedral church in North-East Wales, might well have been another reason why Chirk was given only minor consideration.

There is always the possibility that any work undertaken by him might have been obliterated during the Civil Wars.

In 1595, Chirk was sold to Sir Thomas Myddelton, a man of great entrepreneurial skills, matched by those of his brother, Sir Hugh, who built a water conduit from Ware in Hertfordshire to London by which the capital city was provided with its first water supply. A mere fragment of eight feet, representing the thirty-eight-mile wooden pipeline of the New River Company, laid between 1609–13, is exhibited in the castle.

The elevation of Sir Thomas himself to Lord Mayor of London in 1613 displayed his wide-ranging financial acumen and adventuring spirit. He was involved in establishing the East India Company, and supported the enterprises of Sir Francis Drake and Sir Walter Raleigh. It was this spirit of speculation that spurred him to buy Chirk Castle. His father, Richard Myddelton, was governor of Denbigh Castle, and he himself was probably born there. His mind was not only on material gain and in 1630, together with another highly successful and wealthy London Welshman, Rowland Heilyn, he published a cheap edition of the Welsh Bible. It cost a crown, and became known as Y *Beibl Bach Coron* (The Little Crown Bible) – twenty-five pence in today's money.

Like so many members of the Tudor ascendancy, the Myddeltons claimed descent from a distant and illustrious tribal past. In this case the ancestor was Ririd Flaidd, a name which signified his innate gifts of leadership, since the two elements are 'ruler' and 'wolf'. It was not uncommon for Welsh personal names to suggest the attributes of animals, as in Arthur, a possessor of bear-like qualities, or Bleddyn, who displays those of a wolf.

The £5,000 which Sir Thomas Myddelton is reputed to have paid for Chirk was a fraction of the expense he incurred by the conversion of the formidable stronghold into a grand residence. He concentrated his efforts on the north range, and this accommodation was modified to comply with the domestic requirements and aesthetic tastes of each subsequent generation.

Chirk, under his Parliamentarian son, the second Sir Thomas, was taken by the king in 1643. Although Sir Thomas was successful in capturing Powis Castle, the Herbert Royalist strong-

Chirk Castle

hold, he regained his own property only through bribery. Damage to the castle during the Civil War cost £30,000 to repair. The eastern side of the castle was rebuilt after 1660, following its former defensive structure, though possessing none of its original strength. The improvements included a long gallery, very much an anachronism, but one of the great attractions of Chirk. All this was the responsibility of Sir Thomas Myddelton IV, and the 2nd baronet, as his father had been created a baronet by Charles II. He was succeeded in 1684 by his brother, Sir Richard Myddelton who, in 1712, commissioned the magnificent iron gates from the Davies brothers, the local blacksmiths, whose remarkable expertise was sought by the greatest landowners of North-East Wales and Cheshire, including Sir George Wynne of Leeswood, and Sir Thomas Grosvenor of Eaton Hall. Richard's son, Robert, was responsible for placing them as a ceremonial entry to the north front, where they were flanked by two gigantic lead figures of Mars and Hercules, as recorded in the previously mentioned engraving of 1735 by Badeslade. They were moved to their present position in 1888, and the significance of the wolves is immediately obvious when one remembers the name of the founder of the Myddelton family, Ririd Flaidd.

The castle underwent major changes in the second half of the eighteenth century by the Chester architect, Joseph Turner, who was responsible for the handsome Adamesque staircase placed with enormous assurance in one of the drum towers of the north range. In the 1820s, Thomas Harrison gothicised the east wing, part of which is open to the public, and some twenty years later, A.W. Pugin was responsible for redecorating the Turner classical interiors. It was an irksome challenge, as testified by his anguished words: 'Such a job as Chirk is enough to drive any man mad. All little things are as difficult to get properly done as the greatest. It is worse than the House of Lords.'

Although most people who visit Chirk go there for the 'country house experience', the evidence of medieval fortification and the hardships of life under threat is seen not only in the portcullis entrance, but by the presence of the dungeon, entered from the formidable Adams Tower, and by the stone staircase leading to the watch tower.

Another major attraction of Chirk is the garden, with its regimented yew trees, perhaps in keeping with the battlements of the building itself; its mixture of formality, woodland, shrubbery, and its spectacular views.

Cilgerran (Pembrokeshire)
From Cardigan, take A478 Tenby road S for 2m (3.2km). At crossroads, turn 1m (1.6km) E to Cilgerran. Open: standard hours, Admission charge, National Trust/Cadw

Cilgerran is one of the few castles in Wales whose site cannot be fully appreciated by the public. That privilege belongs to the coracle men on the river Teifi which the fortress commanded with unchallenged assurance. It was the view enjoyed by eighteenth- and nineteenth-century 'tourists' as they came up-stream from Cardigan (Aberteifi), and the depictions of Richard Wil-

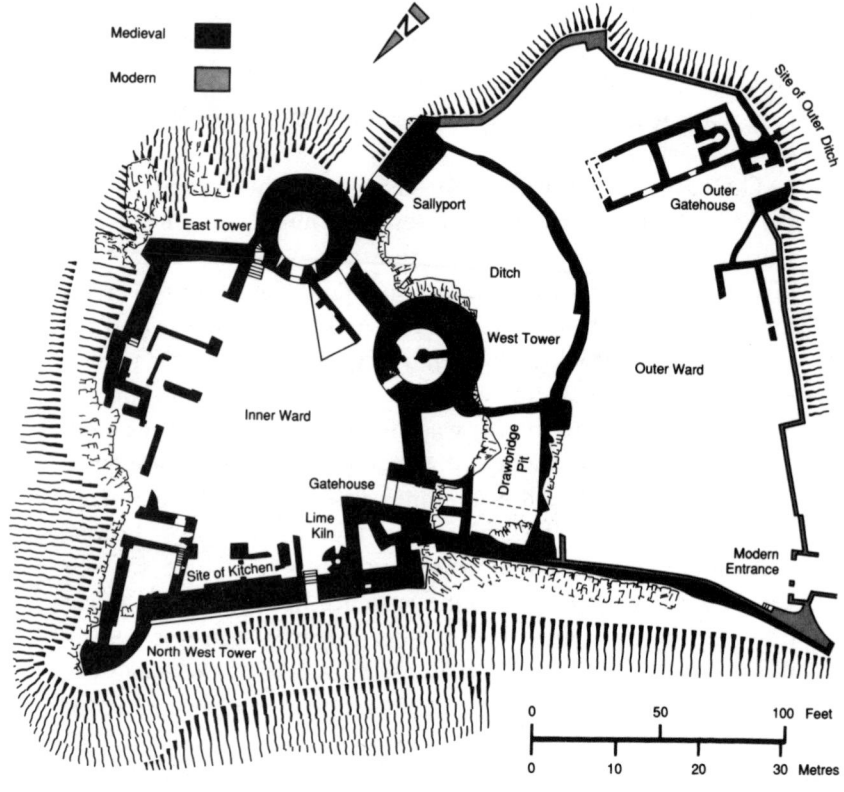

son, Peter de Wint and J.M.W. Turner are memorable evocations of the spectacular grandeur of the castle on the rock.

The earliest stronghold on or near this site was built on the command of Henry I, in order to strengthen his hold on the Norman occupation of South-West Wales, and the lordship of Cilgerran was granted to Gerald of Windsor who already held Pembroke for the king. During a Welsh attack on the castle in 1109, Gerald of Windsor's wife, Nest, the daughter of Rhys ap Tewdwr, the ruler of Deheubarth, was abducted by Owain ap Cadwgan, later to become Prince of Powys; he died seven years afterwards in an ambush set up by Gerald.

Cilgerran is not mentioned by name until 1164, when the Lord Rhys captured the stronghold. In 1204, William Marshall, earl of Pembroke, regained the castle, though not for long. In a major campaign organised by Llywelyn ap Iorwerth (Llywelyn the Great), several West Wales castles were taken, including Carmarthen, Cardigan and Cilgerran itself. Llywelyn lost his hold on all three in 1223, and William Marshall II set about building a masonry castle at Cilgerran which followed the general lay-out of the previous earthwork defences.

If his father's dominant feature at Pembroke had been the great round keep, William II's distinctive contribution to Cilgerran was the building of the two strong towers astride the curtain wall, thereby allowing more space in the inner ward for other accommodation. Since their primary aim was defence, the outer and more assailable sections of the walls were considerably thicker than those facing the inner ward. Both towers consisted of four storeys and the upper floors were lit with windows but again, only when they faced the relative security of the inner ward. A further precaution was taken by cutting a ditch in the rock of the outer ward.

The outer gatehouse, of which only low footings survive, was placed in such a way that anybody coming through it would have seen the two round towers beyond the ditch as unyielding and indomitable. The visitor cannot but be impressed by their power even today.

The three-storey inner gatehouse is on the left of the west tower and would have been reached only by skirting the ditch. It would have had a drawbridge as an extra obstacle. The modern entrance to the castle is placed in line with the inner gatehouse, but on the perimeter of the outer ward.

The north-east and north-west constructions belong to a later period and by the close of the thirteenth century the castle had come to the end of its useful life. It was only the threat of a French invasion in the 1370s that brought about its revival, when Edward III ordered its refurbishment, along with the castles of Pembroke and Tenby.

In 1405, during the uprising of Owain Glyndŵr, the castle was severely damaged. Soon afterwards it became Crown property. Just before the Second World War, having previously had several private owners, it was presented to the National Trust, who handed it over to the Ministry of Works in 1943. It is now in the guardianship of Cadw.

Coity Castle

Coity (Bridgend)

1.5m (2.5km) NE of Bridgend, Open: standard hours, Admission charge, Cadw (key available from 94 Heol West Plas, opposite west end of castle)

Like Newcastle, a mile or so away, the beginnings of Coity were an earthen ringwork established by Payn de Turberville, Y Cythraul (the Demon), who acquired the lordship of Coity from Richard FitzHamon, who was at the forefront of the conquest of Glamorgan. It was completely surrounded by a deep-sided ditch.

In the 1180s a curtain wall was built to follow the original earthwork, and a rectangular keep was added. This reinforcement might have been necessitated by a Welsh revolt which followed the death of Earl William (1147–83) who had succeeded as lord of Glamorgan. It was probably the same reason that motivated Payn de Turberville II to replace the nearby Newcastle's earthwork in stone. Coity's masonry, however, is nothing like as distinguished.

No additions seem to have taken place in the next century, and the major building works were undertaken in the fourteenth century, resulting in the middle gatehouse, the improvement of the keep, which included an annexe to the north. The domestic and ancillary buildings which arose on the south side included a first-floor hall, and a tower designed specifically – as at Manorbier (Dyfed) – for garderobes. The expansion of the outer ward was another fourteenth-century improvement.

The rule of the powerful Turbervilles who had been the mainstay of Coity for three centuries came to an end when the male line failed, and the property passed to Sir Lawrence Berkerolles, who had married a sister of the last Turberville, who was besieged at Coity by Owain Glyndŵr's men. His predicament resulted in a plea to the king for a relieving force, but neither the first under Prince Henry, nor the second, under the king himself, succeeded. The effectiveness of Owain Glyndŵr's attack is evident in the north walls of both outer and inner wards.

On Berkerolles' death without an heir, the property went to William Gamage, the heir of another sister of the last Turberville. It was through the marriage of the sole heiress, Barbara, to Robert, Sir Philip Sydney's brother, that Coity, like Newcastle, became the property of that family, who owned it until the eighteenth century. By 1811 it was in the possession of Thomas Wyndham of Dunraven Castle, and by 1833, Coity was described as 'extensive and magnificent even in its ruins'.

Coity, in its extensiveness, is second only to Caerphilly, as far as Glamorgan castles are concerned, yet it arouses less interest and curiosity than many smaller strongholds. Its stern medieval fortifications are surrounded by indifferent housing development which does little to convey the feeling of the past and its continuity through the centuries.

Conwy (Conwy)
Near town centre, Open: standard hours, Admission charge, Cadw,
A WORLD HERITAGE SITE

'A more beautiful castle never arose' was the opinion of the Welsh traveller and naturalist, Thomas Pennant (1726–98) in the second volume of his *Tour in Wales*, published in 1781. The lesser known Pembrokeshire 'tourist', Richard Fenton (1747–1821) who undertook a visit to the castle and town in 1810, offered practical advice on how to take full advantage of its quality.

> Conway, to be duly appreciated as a picturesque object, and to be properly admired, should be seen in all sides and at all hours, for there never was a scene that took so many changes, shifting its features at every look and every variation of light and shade; and I would recommend it to every traveller, not to be satisfied with two or three Views of it, making no doubt that the last will still be the most pleasing.

He could well have been writing up his notes as a travelling painter, as well as a 'diarist'.

More than a century later, making a bold stand for the superiority of Conwy, Sir Goronwy Edwards in 1946, asserted that 'Taken as a whole, Conway is incomparably the most magnificent of Edward I's Welsh fortresses.'

Such claims are by no means exaggerated. Although many visitors will often be undecided as to their preference between Conwy and Caernarfon, partly because both are alike in basic ground plan, they will readily concede that what makes Conwy unique is its relationship to the fortified town walls, which still stand in a remarkably good state of preservation, making it the best preserved of all Edward's boroughs.

The most advantageous way to appreciate the extent of their survival, and the compactness of the medieval settlement which they defended, is to approach Conwy from the east, along the A55 express road, from which the traveller can see the apex of the towered and battlemented triangle, looking so improbable

Conwy Castle by Julius Caesar Ibbetson

that it might be an idealised pictorial representation of a chivalric romance.

The reasons for its foundation, however, were not aesthetic. Edward's choice of site was characteristically judicious, based on hard practicalities, the foremost being defence and marine access. In this respect, his plans were conspicuously served by a major river, the Conwy, and its tributary, the Gyffin. On its rising ground, the fortified town was an extension and an integral part of the king's design for his third great stronghold in his attempt to throttle the spirit of Welsh independence.

Nevertheless, the site was new and untried in strict military terms, though, ironically, it had up to then been used for far more peaceful purposes, for here stood once a Cistercian abbey, founded by Llywelyn ap Iorwerth as part of the *llys* of the Welsh princes, but transferred to a new site at Maenan, further inland along the Conwy Valley. Though still forming a very prominent position – in fact, the original lay-out of the borough was planned around it – the existing church of St Mary and All Saints owes most of its structure to major restoration work undertaken in the fourteenth century. Of the utmost significance as far as Edward was concerned was the fact that the abbey was the burial place of Llywelyn ap Iorwerth. The king's order was an act of the utmost defiance against the reality of Wales and the existence of her leaders.

The Conwy Valley was essential to Edward's plans for further advancement westwards, in order to debilitate the formidable resistance movement in Snowdonia. His success in overwhelming Dolwyddelan in 1283 resulted in his hold over the entire corridor to the sea. The rocky spur between two rivers seemed to be an ideally situated place from which to establish possession and to consolidate dominion. Conwy Castle was the result of such planning. However frantic and frenzied the building programme activated by the king's decision, the results were so accomplished that even now, over 700 years later, the level of military subtlety and the extent of domestic sophistication is astounding.

Within four years, Edward, in conjunction with his incomparable builder, Master James of St George, introduced a new concept of hard defence, side by side with regal comfort. In terms of military strategy, Conwy Castle on its narrow but awesome rock, was a great advance forward for the English cause, for it now controlled the western bank of the estuary, thereby ensuring a greater grip on the people of Gwynedd. Degannwy, on the opposite bank, the site of a former *llys* and a Norman castle, but refortified by Edward I's father, Henry III, was now redundant, and the king's attention was concentrated on his new fighting machine at Conwy.

The most distinctive feature of the castle is the outline of its eight battlemented drum towers, four of which are surmounted by turrets. This is no mere attempt at added defence, nor only a decorative device; the arrangement has a symbolic significance, for the turrets indicate the royal apartments in the castle's almost square inner ward whose entrance from the outer ward was protected by a drawbridge and a small gatehouse. The accommodation included the King's Hall, the King's Presence Chamber, the royal bed-chambers and the chapel royal in the north-east tower, always referred to as the Chapel Tower. Like its counterpart at Beaumaris, this is the best preserved of the castle apartments, with five arcading and slender lancet windows. Although traditionally known as Queen Eleanor's Chapel, during neither of her visits to Conwy had the chapel been completed, and when Edward next came to spend Christmas here in 1294, he had been a widower for four years. This inner ward, with its handsome apartments which had cost £320, with a further cost of £100 for fine woodwork supplied by Master Richard of Chester and Master Henry of Oxford, had its own separate entrance by way of the east barbican. This was a larger version of its western counterpart, with its own garden and lawn for the queen's enjoyment, its turf shipped from further upstream. One of the queen's squires, Roger le Fykeys was paid 3d for attending to its first watering. The eastern boundary walls rose sharply from the river, to which the access was through a water gate at the side of Chapel Tower.

Master James's plans were intended to make the inner ward completely self-sufficient, capable of its own defence, as well as offering means of escape in emergency. He thus created two separate strongholds which were given a most satisfying unity of design by the regular placing of the towers. Seen from the quayside, the castle appears to be a symmetrical composition, and it is only after entering the outer ward that the visitor realises by the curve on the south side how the rocky ridge was utilised to its full defensive capacity. This is accentuated by the almost jointed form of the great hall, the focal point of the social and communal life of the castle, whose permanent garrison of thirty fencible soldiers, fifteen of whom were bowmen, came under the direct authority of the constable who lived in the outer ward with his family. He was responsible not only for the protection and discipline of the castle, but for the prisoners incarcerated in the tower on the apex of the great hall, and the general supervision of the town.

The residents of the outer ward included an armourer, a smith, a carpenter and a mason and, as in the case of major royal castles, Conwy had a permanent chaplain. Good and friendly relations would have been of the utmost importance

Conwy Castle

because of the lay-out of the building itself, for on entering through the west barbican, every component part of the estab-lishment is within sight and sound. Unlike most castles, Conwy seems to invite the visitor in one direction: forward, and in this respect it is not unlike a great medieval cathedral, where the plan is designed to facilitate the ritual of parade and procession.

This was a stronghold without antecedents or history and its name has found itself in neither myth nor romance. It served one purpose: to show the Welsh at the beginning of Edward's second campaign that now since Llywelyn ap Gruffudd and his brother, Dafydd, were dead, the king's word was beyond dis-pute and his actions not to be challenged. By 1287, his great undertaking at Conwy, comprising castle and a girdle of battle-mented town walls and towers, was complete. The king's bold, limewashed statement of supremacy had cost £15,000.

Edward's next move was westwards to Caernarfon; nothing lay in his way. He had, however, underestimated the resurgent spirit of the people of Gwynedd, who found in Madog ap Llywelyn, a kinsman of Llywelyn ap Gruffudd, a fearless leader and champion. In 1294, they rebelled against the English mis-rule, and in January 1295, Edward was besieged in his magnifi-cent fortress at Conwy.

The king's pride of place and possession was vulnerable not only to attack by the Welsh, but by a less visible enemy: rot. As early as 1321 a survey reported alarmingly that 'in the Hall of Conwy Castle several of the roof trusses have failed, and in the other buildings and towers many of the trusses and much of the rest of the timber have perished for want of covering of lead.'

This was the beginning of the fortress's structural decline. Three hundred years later, the survey of 1627 was, understand-ably, even more devastating, for by now the entire fabric was in danger, 'the leads being decayed and broken above and almost all the floores fallen downe'. Repairs of a sufficiently substantial nature were undertaken in order to make Conwy an effective Royalist station during the Civil War. These were financed by a native of the town, John Williams (1582–1650) who was descended on his father's side from the family of Penrhyn, Bangor, and on his mother's from the Wynns of

Gwydir. Referred to invariably as Archbishop Williams, having been Archbishop of York in 1641, he wrote in 1645 about his refortification of Edward's great castle: 'from the bare walls, I have repaired, victualed and supplied it with ammunition at mine own charge.' A serious dispute with the king's commander, Sir John Owen, resulted in Archbishop Williams switching his allegiance to the opposing side and in 1645, Conwy fell to the Parliamentarians.

In the late eighteenth and nineteenth centuries the castle was the inspiration of a wide range of artists, to whom the ruinous state of the fabric, the invasive greenery, and the battlements against the skyline had a powerful romantic appeal. The description by Sir Richard Colt Hoare of one of his favourite castles seems to sum up the attitude of both artist and traveller:

> For a short interval the road becomes uninteresting – when Conwy's proud towers burst suddenly on the sight. I envy the traveller (if such there be) who not knowing such a castle existed should be thus unexpectedly and pleasingly surprised . . . The castle itself is a most noble structure and of the most picturesque form and in a much less dilapidated state than most baronial and royal castles with which this country abounds . . . In short the whole is so beautiful in all its parts and so judiciously situated that I could almost suppose the artist, not the engineer, had directed its construction.

This, like Fenton's description already quoted, belonged to the time before Telford's suspension bridge (1822) to carry the road, and Stephenson's tubular railway bridge (1846–48) had been built. The addition of the second road bridge earlier this century made the suspension bridge redundant, though it makes a striking picture, giving the impression of an ornate entrance into the east barbican.

Thanks to the intervention of the marquess of Anglesey and the Secretary of State for Wales at the time, Nicholas Edwards, now Lord Crickhowell, plans for yet another road bridge were thwarted in favour of a tunnel. Built in the 1980s it has relieved the traffic jams which damaged Conwy in every way. As a result it is now far easier to appreciate the unique character of this compact medieval walled town with its twenty-one towers.

In addition to the parish church, the town has two buildings of outstanding historic and architectural interest: Aberconwy House, a late medieval merchant house, now administered by the National Trust and open to the public, and Plas Mawr, the finest surviving Elizabethan town house in Wales, with few rivals in the rest of the British Isles.

Craig-y-Nos (Powys)
Head of Swansea Valley. Opera House open occasionally. House clearly visible from the adjacent Brecon Beacons Country Park. Private ownership

Bryn Melin, the house that T.H. Wyatt designed in the 1840s for a local landowner, Rhys Davies Powell, was a sturdy structure incorporating a number of architectural ideas but failing to result in a coherent entity. Perhaps it was the inclusion of a tourelle and the suggestion of battlements in the entrance porch that gave the purchaser of Bryn Melin from the original owner the idea of calling the house the 'castle' of Craig-y-Nos (Rock of the Night), the prominence that gives the area an arrestingly romantic appeal. The person who fell under such a spell was Adelina Patti, the world famous operatic soprano who acquired the property in 1885. She added to the north and south of the Wyatt building, thereby quadrupling the size of the house. On the north appeared a castellated block with turrets and mock machicolations which justified calling the new creation a castle. Beyond that is the clock tower and a private theatre, seating 150 people, where the 'Queen of Song', as Patti was called sang Marguerite, among other roles, to the Faust of her husband, Ernesto Nicolini. After her death in 1919 the diva's creation went into sad decline.

It became a tuberculosis hospital, and after that a home for geriatric patients. Following a short, well intentioned but misguided attempt at regaining something of the house's former dignity by converting it into a restaurant, Craig-y-Nos was bought by a dedicated couple who had both been brought up locally but had spent most of their professional life abroad.

The theatre is used for a short season every summer by Neath Operatic Society.

Cricieth (Gwynedd)
On the edge of the town, Open: standard hours, Admission charge, Cadw

The first glimpse of the castle as one approaches Cricieth from Portmadog is unforgettable, standing boldly as it does on its green and rocky promontory. Its renowned siting is rivalled and probably eclipsed by that of Harlech on the opposite side of Tremadoc Bay which is so generously arched that it almost takes on the guise of a vast lake. The two fortresses seem to be in constant watch over one another, weather permitting, for in this part of Wales, the moody light plays the most theatrical tricks on both land and seascapes. The native Welsh stronghold at Cricieth predates the English one at Harlech by at least half a century, but the spectacularly placed sea-girt fortress that conveys such compelling power, even in its ruins, is nevertheless heavily dependent on Harlech for its later defensive sophistication. This in no way diminishes the powerful position and prestige of the castle which Llywelyn ap Iorwerth built at Cricieth in the 1230s, when he transferred the court here from Dolbenmaen to the north, which had been the *maerdref*, the administrative centre, of the commote of Eifionydd, and which was originally a Norman motte-and-bailey.

Like all castle builders, Llywelyn chose the form and size of his stronghold to take the best possible defensive advantage of site and surroundings; this accounts for the irregular outline of the curtain walls. In this respect, the difference between his ability and that of Edward I's master-builder, Master James of St George, was one of degree rather than kind. After his overthrow of the Welsh in 1282, Edward was in a position to upgrade Llywelyn's fortress to the standard that would not shame those castles over which he had had complete design and building control from their beginnings. Nevertheless the £353 which the king spent on the modernisation of Cricieth between 1285–92 is a paltry sum compared with the £8,000 that

Cricieth Castle

he lavished on his new creation, Harlech, in the same period.

Llywelyn's castle at Cricieth is traditionally reputed to be patterned on the formidable stronghold of Beeston, known to everybody who has travelled on the railway between Crewe and Chester, where its defiant height breaks the lush monotony of the Cheshire Plain. Beeston was built in the 1220s by Ranulf, the 6th earl of Chester, and was greatly influenced by the principles of military architecture which he had assimilated during his experiences in the Crusades. An ironically successful alliance between Ranulf and Llywelyn had brought peace to Cheshire so that the Welsh prince was in a position to acquaint himself with the most recent defensive system brought into these islands. This was the gatehouse. It soon grew into more than a mere entrance, and incorporated two flanking D-ended towers which were gradually extended inwards to the castle ward, thereby forming a passage-way. This, in turn, could be provided with a sequence of hostile devices, each one progressively more challenging. Such an extension brought about a considerable increase in the range of accommodation and function, so that this development, together with the intricate system of defence, overtook the keep in importance, and eventually superseded it.

Another probable pattern which Llywelyn followed was the lofty stronghold of his arch-enemy, Hubert de Burgh, at Montgomery, which he attacked on two occasions while this new Anglo-Norman castle was being built. Whatever the source of its military inspiration, the gatehouse is the most prominent and substantial feature of what remains of Llywelyn's fortress.

Reference was first made to the castle in 1239, when an entry in the *Brut* refers to the imprisonment of Gruffudd, Llywelyn's illegitimate son. According to Welsh law, he had as much right to succeed to his father's possessions as the king's legitimate offspring, Dafydd, and it was the son of the illegitimate Gruffudd who was to continue the building history of Cricieth. He, too, was called Llywelyn: the second – and last – of that personal name which is synonymous with the idea and ideal of Welsh nationhood.

He asserted his claim on Cricieth with the addition of an outer ward, thereby enlarging the castle to such an extent that it crowned the hillside. The considerable extensions included a south-western tower, which probably contained residential accommodation, since it was decorated with carved stone and was larger than the other tower addition on the northern apex. As a result the triangular shape of Llywelyn ap Gruffudd's outer ward was greatly accentuated. Considering its prominent position, this north tower was capable of defending two sides of the outer curtain, and reference to it as the Engine Tower suggests that its function was to stage heavy artillery, such as a mangon or mangonel, or a trebuchet that would endanger the life of any intruder. This defensive strengthening was probably the work of Edward, who raised the height of the gate-house. This, the most prominent and abiding feature of Cricieth's visual identity was raised yet again during the reign of Edward I's son, Edward II.

Edward I's refortification programme also included the encas-ing of the south-eastern tower, often referred to as the Leyburn Tower after Sir William Leyburn who was made constable of the castle in 1284, the same year that the king established a free English borough of Cricieth. Here Leyburn had in his charge a garrison of between thirty and forty men. Similar numbers were stationed at Harlech and at Aberystwyth, further south along Cardigan Bay, both of which were also pre-eminently coastal fortifications, a significant military feature during the last nation-wide Welsh rebellion against Edward I, between 1294–95, led by Madog ap Llywelyn. He claimed the title of 'Prince of Wales', although his status was that of a member of a cadet branch of the dynasty of Gwynedd. Sustained by food supplies from Ireland, Cricieth, like Harlech and Aberystwyth, with-stood months of siege, whereas Caernarfon and Denbigh were captured.

In 1359, Edward the Black Prince, eldest son of Edward III, appointed as constable of the castle Sir Hywel ap Gruffudd, who had served him in the Hundred Years War, and who had distinguished himself both at the Battle of Crécy (1346) where he was probably knighted, and at the Battle of Poitiers (1356), where his military prowess was described by the court poet, Iolo Goch (1320–c. 1398) so exuberantly, that it comes as no surprise that the Welsh warrior was nicknamed Syr Hywel y Fwyall (Sir Hywel of the Axe), and became a legend in his own lifetime.

> Shaving with mighty blow on blow
> The head and beard of many a foe,
> And shedding lightly, yea, foot high
> The blood of any his strength would try.

The poet applied the same enthusiasm in describing the castle over which the fearless knight was constable until his death in 1381.

In 1404, the castle was destroyed during the Glyndŵr uprising, and the varying heights of its ruins have changed little since then. In architectural terms, Cricieth has posed problems and quandaries of period, material and style for generations of historians. What is beyond dispute is the impact of its setting, and the views from its remains. The mountains of Snowdonia are still the genuine fortresses, and the waves of Cardigan Bay the most effective defences. In the 1990s Cricieth is still a modest and peaceful seaside town, mercifully unexploited to become a 'resort'. It is now probably best remembered as the place where the Liberal Prime Minister, David Lloyd George made his home for the last years of his life.

There is a comprehensive interpretation display.

Crickhowell, Crughywel (Powys)

Signposted from A40 in the town, Open access, Admission free, Local Authority

Like Abergavenny Castle, Crickhowell Castle (also once known as Ailsby's Castle, after a warder of the Tower of London, who was warder here in the late thirteenth century) enjoys a peaceful setting with provision for pleasant walks and recreational activities, to which the remains of the fortification form a picturesque backcloth. Crickhowell takes its name from Crug Hywel (the cairn or tump of Hywel), an Iron Age hillfort situated about three miles from the town, and was an important site on the Roman route between Abergavenny (*Gobannium*) and Brecon, and therefore one that could be followed by the Normans in their westward advance.

The original eleventh-century motte-and-bailey was thrown up by the Turbervilles in order to command a vantage point on the river Usk. As in so many instances, the later masonry developments observed the outline of the original defences, and this stone castle would have had at its core a motte surmounted by a shell keep, so that it would have resembled the similar structure at Tretower and, to a lesser degree, the one at Cardiff, which was faceted rather than round. The person responsible for these improvements was Sir Grimbald Pauncefote, to whom

Crickhowell had come through his marriage to the Turberville heiress. Hardly any visible remains exist of this prominent defence. In fact, only a section of a round tower and a rectangular tower have survived.

Crickhowell was given a murage licence in 1281, but nothing remains of the town walls, though the lay-out of this small and delightful market town observes distinct boundaries and limits.

Sir John Pauncefote, Sir Grimbald's great-grandson, was given orders by Henry IV to make the castle defensible against Owain Glyndŵr's forces, but to no avail, for they left it 'in ruins'. It was granted to Sir William Herbert of Raglan, later to become the first earl of Pembroke in the late fifteenth century, and through him it eventually passed to the earls of Worcester and finally the dukes of Beaufort.

Cyfarthfa (Merthyr Tydfil)

1m (1.6km) from Merthyr Tydfil town centre off A470, Open: standard hours, Admission charge, Local Authority

Cyfarthfa Castle is a castle only in so far that the man who built it, William Crawshay, one of the iron masters of South Wales, chose to call it such. Its towers and battlements are for display only and were the means by which a man of recent wealth could proclaim his prestige. Although it was an indulgence characteristic of his class and his period, it was, as far as his father was concerned, an act of sheer folly. 'Ambition', he admonished, 'has directed you to build a great and expensive house, but I advise you to do no such thing. Is it wise at any time to build on so large a scale? No man can say what it will cost to finish, to furnish, to maintain.'

The 'castle', designed by Robert Lugar, reputedly cost £30,000, and was completed between 1824–25, but its existence as a private residence lasted for less than a hundred years. In 1909 it was acquired by Merthyr Tydfil Borough Council, and became the local grammar school soon afterwards, while also serving as a museum. After the departure of the school to other premises in the 1980s the entire building became a museum and

Cyfarthfa Castle

art gallery. The castle grounds are a much appreciated public amenity.

Degannwy (Gwynedd)
Above the town, Open access, Admission free, Local Authority

Little remains of the stronghold of Degannwy, although success- ive rulers and usurpers built and rebuilt fortifications here up until the thirteenth century. Even with such slight evidence, it is easy to discern the enormous strategic importance of the site, for its two steep mounds, about a quarter of a mile (0.5km) east of the Conwy estuary, would have been a daunting challenge to the hardiest. The discovery of coins points to the occupation of the site in Roman times, but it was in the sixth century that Degannwy had a particularly important native significance, when it was the *llys* of Maelgwn Gwynedd, one of the five kings of Britain, and described by the sixth-century monk and chronicler, Gildas, as 'the dragon of the island', a reference to his aggressive attributes rather than to his protective qualities. In most respects he was totally unlike one of his descendants, Cadfan, whose virtues are commemorated in the parish church of Llangadwaladr, near Llangefni, on the isle of Anglesey, with a stone bearing the words: *Catamanus Rex Sapientissimus Opinatissimus Omnium Regum* – 'the wisest and most circumspect of all kings'.

Nothing remains of this early Welsh settlement, as it was, according to the *Annales Cambriae*, destroyed by the Saxons; nor is there any evidence of its successor which was completed in 1080 by Robert of Rhuddlan, a cousin of Hugh of Avranches, the 2nd earl of Chester, in his westward advance from his foothold at Rhuddlan. Any ambition that he had to gain territory the other side of the Conwy estuary, and thereby making him the virtual lord of Gwynedd, was obliterated by the sudden appearance of three Welsh ships which had landed near the Great Orme, led, according to tradition, by Gruffudd ap Cynan (1055–1137). Women and children were taken aboard as captives, the land was pillaged, and the cattle stolen. Robert, in his wrath and before he could muster his own men, reputedly descended from the heights of his stronghold with only his armour-bearer in a futile attempt to put an end to the onslaught. He was killed, and his head nailed to the mast of the leading ship as a sign of the Welshmen's victory.

The next major figure to be associated with Degannwy was Llywelyn ap Iorwerth 'the Great' (1173–1240) to whom it came by inheritance in 1200. Within ten years or so, the castle was destroyed by the Welsh, in the face of an English advance, rebuilt by the earl of Chester, and recaptured by Llywelyn in 1213. A handsome corbel of a crowned head found on the site, and now one of the prized medieval exhibits at the National Museum of Wales in Cardiff, might well be a depiction of Llywelyn. In 1241, as in 1210, the castle was again destroyed, and for the same reason: to resist attack by the English Crown, not on this occasion by King John, but by his son, Henry III. Although he had ordered the refortifying of the castle of 'Gannok', progress was severely impeded by Welsh intervention, and it was only when the king himself arrived at

Degannwy, where he stayed from the August until the October of 1245, that serious work was started. In 1248, free burgages were made available and within the next few years the burgesses had been provided not only with markets and fairs, but with permission by a royal charter stating that 'the burgesses may enclose the [said] town with a dike and wall.'

Whatever its development, both town and castle were destroyed by Llywelyn ap Gruffudd in 1263 when he achieved the total control over Degannwy that had eluded him on his attempt of 1257.

The ensuing decade and more had brought Llywelyn consistent prominence and intermittent dominance; to the new king, Edward I, he was more than a territorial challenge, he was an intellectually invigorating rival; a man whose ancestry gloried in position rather than in possession, in Llywelyn's case, Snowdonia. Gwynedd, *Pura Wallia*, was that embodiment of a positive Welsh identity which, for reasons of terrain, and therefore of temperament, could not be cajoled into postures of compromise and positions of submission, like the inhabitants of the accessible fertile plains of Powys.

Edward immediately assessed the strategic value of Degannwy, and found it wanting. For all its height, it had its pitfalls. The opposite side of the river offered greater strengths and more immediate threats. It was at sea-level, and commanded equal control over the estuary, but it was also on the territory occupied by the relentlessly and aggressively possessive enemy: the proud Welsh of Gwynedd. He found the place on which to build his mighty engine of war which would be capable of crushing any rebelliousness into abject submission. It was an elongated plateau on an elevated rocky ridge. Every natural attribute of the site pronounced defensive strength; any built additions proclaimed invulnerability. It was to be the castle of Conwy.

In spite of its scarcity of ruins, Degannwy, because of its position, is one of the most striking examples in Wales of the development of defensive sites from at least the Roman period, up until the thirteenth century. Its associations with the early rulers of Gwynedd, its involvement in constant internecine intrigues, its resilience in the face of successive invasions, have all added their fascination to the weather-torn, man-ravaged site above that crucially important river Conwy, which was such a decisive factor in the manipulative power of the native princes of Gwynedd and Norman and English invaders.

One side of the estuary possesses the bold statement of Conwy Castle and its magnificent town walls, the other side possesses a fortress whose long defensive genealogy is now remembered only in the name of Degannwy Castle Hotel, near which one turns into York Road, which ultimately, through arduous pathways, leads the visitor to one of those landscapes which encapsulate the principles of primeval and subsequent attempts at supremacy.

Denbigh, Dinbych (Denbighshire)
Dominating the town, Open: standard hours, Admission free, Cadw

Denbigh is an anglicisation of the Welsh Dinbych, 'a small fort' (cf. Dinbych-y-Pysgod, the Welsh for Tenby, in Pembrokeshire), a name which clearly indicates the existence of such a building, but belonging to an unrecorded period. Although its precise location is not known, it presumably occupied a central site on this spectacular eminence dominating the Vale of Clwyd. It might well have been, later, the position of a *llys* in the time of Llywelyn ap Iorwerth (d. 1240) who for the last twenty years of his life was the most powerful prince of native Wales (*Pura Wallia*).

Nor does anything remain of the stronghold which Dafydd, the younger brother of Llywelyn ap Gruffudd, built for himself here in 1277 and which fell into English hands in 1282. Edward I's victory resulted in the redistribution of that land between Gwynedd and Powys called Y Berfedd-wlad (in English the Middle Country), or the four Cantrefs, because it was divided into the *cantrefi* of Tegeingl (or Englefield), Rhos, Rhufoniog, and Dyffryn Clwyd. The king kept Tegeingl with its two castles of Flint and Rhuddlan for himself, and Dyffryn Clwyd he gave to Reginald de Grey. Rhos and Rhufoniog, together with the commote of Dinmael, were to form a new lordship, taking its

Denbigh Castle

name from its administrative centre and castle, Denbigh. The grantee was Henry de Lacy, earl of Lincoln (1251–1311), the chief military commander of Edward I's armies in Wales.

He applied here the building principles to be found in other strongholds where town and castle were to function as a unified system of defence, namely the practice of first erecting an outer wall which would form a protective shell sufficiently strong to withstand attack while the castle itself was being built. During the initial stages of the operation, Edward stayed for ten days at Denbigh with de Lacy, and it is possible that the king's master mason, James of St George might also have been there. The presence of both would certainly have indicated the significance of the new castle, not only in terms of military strategy but in seigneurial prestige. Once satisfied that the programme had been sufficiently planned, the king left the responsibility of the fortification on de Lacy's shoulders.

Within two years of his occupation, the defences were well enough advanced to give Edward the confidence to send the earl '40 bucks and does . . . to stock his park at Denbigh'. Such assurance of the castle's durability was ill-founded. In 1294, the uprising of Madog ap Llywelyn, a relation of Llywelyn ap Gruffudd, created havoc here as it did at a number of English castles. As at Caernarfon, Denbigh's town defences proved inadequate, and the castle itself was no great challenge to the spirited assailants. Edward had under-estimated the spirit of revolt among the native Welsh population.

The uprising was quelled within a year, but this display of grievance was a powerful sign to the king that he had to consider more aggressive means of asserting his authority and sustaining his territorial supremacy more forcefully. The fact that several of the castles in his carefully planned defence system had been overrun by the Welsh resulted in a fresh strategy: he would demolish, he would re-construct, and he would build. Castell y Bere, a castle of the Welsh princes, but in English hands since 1283, fell into the first category, Caernarfon and Caergwrle (or Hope Castle), along with Denbigh, rose again from ignominy, and Beaumaris, the first and only Edwardian castle on the isle of Anglesey, made its first appearance.

Henry de Lacy died without a male heir in 1311, both his sons having met awful fates: the elder, Edmund, according to tradition, had fallen into Denbigh Castle well. John Leland noted 'Sum say that the Erle of Lincoln's sunne felle into the castelle welle and ther dyed: wherupon he never passid to finisch the castelle.' The younger, John, had fallen from the battlements of the family's other castle at Pontefract, while running after a ball. Denbigh therefore became the property of his daughter Alice whose husband, Thomas, earl of Lancaster, supervised the continuation of the building scheme. His tenure lasted only eleven years, for in 1322, at Pontefract, the other castle acquired through marriage, he was beheaded for treason. Similar fates awaited the next two occupants: Hugh le Despenser, the favourite of Edward II, at Bristol in 1326, and Roger Mortimer, at Tyburn in 1330. He was the first of four Mortimers who were to hold Denbigh which by 1400 was under as serious a threat as it had been just over a hundred years previously.

The assailant on this occasion was Owain Glyndŵr, and for the next two and a half years the castle was held for the king, Henry IV, by Henry Percy 'Hotspur', with, reputedly, a garrison of 150 men. Although he changed sides, Percy was in no position to be of any great assistance to the Welsh cause as he was killed at the Battle of Shrewsbury soon after his defection.

As the Mortimers were keen supporters of the Yorkists, Denbigh Castle was to be one of the most powerful centres of their cause in North Wales, and the failure of Jasper Tudor, earl of Pembroke, the half-brother of Henry VI, to take the castle, resulted in his burning the town instead. It was this extreme measure and its consequences that led the inhabitants to establish a new town further away from the defensive walls which had become increasingly vulnerable with each rebel attack since 1294.

In 1563, Robert Dudley, a favourite of Queen Elizabeth, was given the titles of Baron Denbigh and earl of Leicester. With the first title went the castle and lordship of Denbigh, although he spent little time in North Wales, as he devoted his social and artistic energies to the refurbishment of Kenilworth Castle. His one major contribution to the region was his plan for a new church, possibly to replace the neighbouring St Asaph, as cathedral. It was left in an unfinished state because, according to Thomas Pennant, writing in 1786–89, 'of the public hatred he [Dudley] had incurred on account of his tyranny'.

During the Civil War, Denbigh Castle was held for the king by William Salisbury of Rûg, near Corwen, and Charles I found refuge here for three nights after the defeat at Rowton Heath, near Chester. When, a year later, Salisbury was 'invited' by Major-General Mytton to surrender, he declined on the grounds that 'being loyall to my King . . . for the keeping of this place, His Majesty's own house, which (without regard to my own life, lands and prosperity) with God's assistance, I will endeavour to make good for him to my last gasp. Soe I rest your poor kinsman and old play fellow.' He did not surrender until he had the written consent of the king himself. The castle was then handed over on the 26th October 1646. 'If I must quit this place, I confesse I had rather you had the honour of it than any other person in England of your party.' Salisbury, 'Old Blue Stockings' as he was often called, had financed the necessary fortification of Denbigh Castle in 1643.

With the Restoration in 1660 came the decline of the castle, its masonry being consistently robbed by the neighbourhood, a great deal of it put to effective use in the building or aggrandising of the houses of the local gentry and tradesmen. This pillaging was held in check in the mid-nineteenth century by the formation of a 'Castle Committee' by a group of local people who were concerned about the state of disrepair. Work was undertaken to 'secure' the ruins and make them not only less dangerous but a less attractive quarry. In 1920 both castle and town walls were transferred to the Commissioner of Works who, having then become the Department of the Environment, are now called Cadw.

The crowning glory of Denbigh Castle is the Great Gatehouse, whose design showed as acute an awareness of aesthetics as of tactical defence. Its spatial arrangement answered the most relentless demands of medieval combat; centuries later, in peaceful times, such a distribution of rooms in a country house would have elicited appreciative delight. Looked at through the eyes of a military historian or through those of an architectural connoisseur, such a structure must surely be considered amazing in its inventiveness. The Great Gatehouse consisted of three octagonal towers, which surrounded a vaulted octagonal hall, a plan which was repeated exactly on the floor above.

Its lay-out was enough to cause the greatest confusion to an attacker, if indeed he reached this point, for he would already have had to contend with a barbican, only to find himself faced with the problems of a drawbridge, before confronting two portcullises, a door and then murder-holes. In the complexity of its arrangement, it is often compared with the King's Gate at Caernarfon, a further indication that Master James had been consulted very closely at Denbigh. It was, according to.John Leland, 'a mervelus strong and great peace of work, but the *fastigia* of it were never finischid. If they had beene, it might have beene countid among the most memorable peaces of workys yn England. It hath diverse wardes and dyverse portcolicis. On the front of the gate is set the image of Hen. Lacy Erle of Lincoln in his stately long robes.'

Although the Great Gatehouse is the most prominent feature of Denbigh Castle, there are ample remains which testify to the importance of this lordship castle occupying such expansive space that it dominates the hillside, its walls forming a coronet if not a crown, since Denbigh never was a royal castle. Unlike

Caernarfon, Conwy and Beaumaris, and to a lesser extent, Harlech, there are few 'rooms' that one can enter or passage-ways that one can explore, or wall walks on which one can parade in rain, wind or sunlight. The compensation is the incomparable view of the rich Vale of Clwyd, one of the lushest and most historic regions of this part of Wales. Although the town walls are not complete, sections are open to the public, and the remains of Burgess Gate and, to a lesser extent, Exchequer Gate point to the defensive importance of Henry de Lacy's Denbigh.

Dinas Brân (Denbighshire)
Marked footpath from Llangollen, Open access, Admission free, Local Authority

These much painted and photographed ruins are the stuff of which calendars are made, and have almost become an emblem of the International Music Eisteddfod held every July in Llangollen. They are seen to picturesque advantage from the A483 between the Llangollen/Whichurch exit and the Halton roundabout, a stretch which offers an unrivalled view of the Dee Valley.

The lords of Powys Fadog – the northern part of Powys, as opposed to the southern area, Powys Wenwynwyn, both regions named after territorial chieftains – in building the castle in the 1260s, further defended the Iron Age hillfort with ditches cut into the surrounding rock surfaces. The castle's assertiveness was emphasised by curtain walls, a rectangular keep, a characteristically Welsh apsidal or D-ended tower, and a twin-towered gatehouse.

Rather than submit to English forces when, in 1277, Edward I embarked on his first Welsh campaign, building castles at Aberystwyth, Builth, Flint, Rhuddlan and Ruthin, the native garrison of Dinas Brân ('fortress of the crow') burnt the castle. After the downfall of Llywelyn ap Gruffud, Llywelyn the Last, in 1282, the stronghold became the property of the Crown and was granted to John de Warenne, earl of Surrey, who abandoned it in favour of another royal gift, with lands not only on the very banks of the Dee, but on the English border and within civilised distance of Chester.

Daunting though the climb is, for those young or agile enough to confront the challenge, the rewards are enormous, not only for the views from such a vantage point, but for the substantial remains which show considerable decorative details, indicating that life here must have been as civilised as it was military. What, from a distance, appears to be a wild and romantic outline, belonging to the world of myth and legend, in reality is a castle which was built with all the means and expertise which the Welsh had at their disposal.

Dinefwr (Carmarthenshire)
Llandeilo. Through the park of Newton House (NT), Open: standard hours, Admission charge, Cadw

The August 1996 setting of the Royal National Eisteddfod of Wales, the great annual festival of competitions in all branches of the spoken, performing, visual and literary arts, could not have been more appropriate, for the backcloth to this vast field with its centrally placed pavilion, surrounded by smaller temporary structures was the spectacularly placed castle of Rhys ap Gruffudd, the Lord Rhys, a great patron of the arts, and the founder of the first eisteddfod at Cardigan, another of his domains, in 1176.

Dinefwr had been the capital of the ancient Kingdom of Deheubarth from the time of Hywel ap Cadell, who ruled from about 910AD until his death in about 950AD; later in his life, his authority also extended over Gwynedd in North Wales and Powys in Mid-Wales. His fame rests on the fact that he was the law-giver of medieval Wales, and that he became known after his death as Hywel Dda ('the Good').

With the Norman Conquest, one of Hywel's descendants, Rhys ap Tewdwr (d. 1093) the last independent King of Deheubarth, virtually became a vassal to the English Crown, on payment of annual dues of £40 to King William. The Norman-Welsh liaison was further strengthened when his daughter Nest, famous for her beauty, married the Norman,

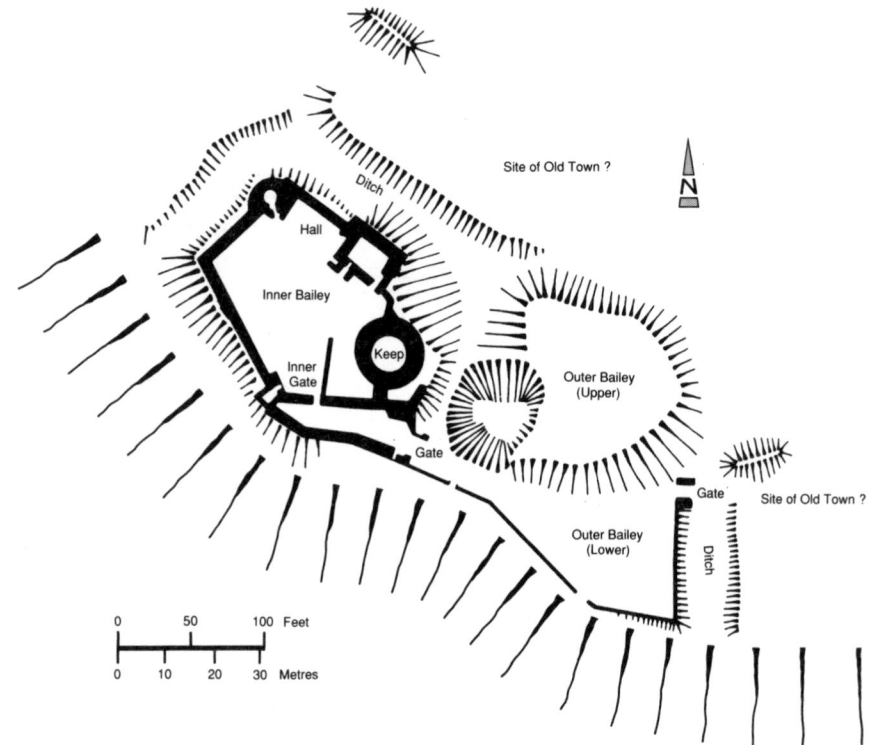

Gerald of Windsor. Nest was to become the grandmother of Giraldus Cambrensis, Gerald of Wales, whose account of his journey through Wales in 1188 is such a rich mine of fascinating information.

Rhys ap Tewdwr's grandson, the previously mentioned Rhys ap Gruffudd, came into possession of Dinefwr in the 1160s and the initial refortification of the castle might belong to this period. During most of his long tenure he played a dominant rôle in the political affairs of the whole of Wales, and was made justiciar of South Wales by Henry II. He was generous in his patronage of monastic foundations, and both Ystrad Fflur (Strata Florida) and Tal-y-llychau (Talley) were the outcome of his beneficence. He relinquished the regal status which his ancestors had held and adopted the title the Lord Rhys, a compromise that made his relationship with the Normans far

Dinefwr Castle

easier, without in any way undermining his feeling of national pride and his independence of spirit, which could often be aggressively asserted in the dynastic animosities between the Welsh princes.

With his death in 1197, Dinefwr was gained by his third son, Rhys Gryg after challenging the rightful heir, Gruffudd, who died in 1201, leaving two sons. This situation was to result eventually in the attack made on Dinefwr by one of the avenging sons of Gruffudd, Rhys Ieuanc, who in 1213 'made for the castle' and, according to the account in the *Chronicle of the Welsh Princes*,

> on the following day he placed engines and contrivances to lay siege to the castle, and made ladders against the walls for his men to climb over the walls. And thus he gained possession of the whole of the castle except for one tower. And in that the garrison undertook to fight and put up a defence with missiles and other engines; and outside there were archers and crossbow-men and sappers and knights besieging them. And thus they were forced before afternoon to surrender the castle.

Within five years it was to be the scene of another upheaval, this time with far more drastic results. After the sealing of the Peace of Worcester, whereby Llywelyn ap Iorwerth swore to the young King Henry III that the Welsh princes should be brought to the king's peace, the Princes of Deheubarth rebelled, and none more than Rhys Gryg whose refusal to agree to pay homage to the king led him to take extreme measures. By the time Llywelyn had brought his men to South Wales to force them to comply, Rhys Gryg had dismantled the seat of his ancestors. It was an act of proud defiance. Llywelyn wrote to the king of the destruction of a stronghold 'once famous, now ruined, to which once pertained as the capital of Deheubarth, the dignities of the whole of the province'. Within a few days, Rhys Gryg yielded to Llywelyn, and became not only one of his supporters, but a feudal vassal of Henry III.

The rebuilding of Dinefwr might well date from the period between 1220 and Rhys Gryg's death in 1234. The round keep represented the trend of such castle defences in the early part of the thirteenth century, and there is a similar structure at Dryslwyn, further down the river Tywi. The best known of such cylindrical towers are those at Bronllys in Powys and Skenfrith in Gwent, both Norman castles. The evidence at Dinefwr suggests that the keep had a first-floor entry, with access to basement level through a trap door. This conformed to the usual arrangement of the period. It stood at the eastern side of the inner bailey, which was roughly a pentagon, whose masonry curtain walls probably followed the lines of the original defences. The entrance to the castle is from the east, into an upper and lower outer bailey, bare of any remains of buildings. A gate on the south side leads into a narrow passage; at its north side a further gate gives entry to the inner bailey. On the north was a hall, a later addition. The exact site of the original town of Dinefwr is not known, but in 1298 Edward I established a new settlement to the north called, appropriately, the Newtown of Dinefwr, Y Drenewydd.

After his success in gaining the crown from Richard III at the Battle of Bosworth in 1485, Henry VII presented Dinefwr as a reward to one of his staunchest supporters, Sir Rhys ap Thomas. Any improvements that he made to the building were clearly not of the high standard of his embellishments and additions at Carew and, to a lesser degree, Weobley. A descendant was the builder of the Tudor mansion which had been altered and modified in subsequent years until it was to be given capped turrets at each corner, a *porte-cochère* over the main entrance, and a heavy Venetian Gothic garden front in 1857. This has been recently acquired by the National Trust and was opened to the public in the spring of 1996. It has now reverted to its original name of Newton House, having been known for generations as Dynevor Castle. Among the pictures on display are some fascinating depictions of the medieval fortress, which had such an active past, and which is now reached by passing through the serenity of a 'Capability' Brown park.

Dolbadarn (Gwynedd)
.5m (.8km) SE of Llanberis, Open access, Admission free, Cadw

Dolbadarn is one of two stone castles built by the Princes of Gwynedd within the rugged contours of Snowdonia, that once-awesome fastness which in the late eighteenth and early nineteenth centuries became such a challenge to tourists and painters. The contrast between Richard Wilson's version of Dolbadarn and that of J.M.W. Turner shows the range of response that such a setting could elicit (see pp. 25–6). The builder of Dolbadarn had no such compositional or aesthetic considerations in his mind. His preoccupation was to establish and secure the best means of defence to protect the inland route from Caernarfon to the upper valley of the Conwy. This entailed the constant surveillance of any movement through the formidable Llanberis Pass.

It was Llywelyn ap Iorwerth who was responsible for the building of Dolbadarn, whose round tower is a dominant feature above Llyn Peris, adjacent to Llyn Padarn. This structure itself shows an acute awareness of the trends of contemporary Anglo-Norman military architecture and, as such, bears a very recognisable likeness to Bronllys and Tretower in Powys, and to Skenfrith in Gwent. In all three, access to the building was at first-floor level, and the ground or basement level was entered only internally by trap door, though none of them matched in scale and impact, their precursor and inspiration, the enormous cylindrical keep of Pembroke Castle.

Like all of them, Dolbadarn consisted of three storeys, a sophisticated innovation for a native Welsh castle. Unlike its English-built counterparts, the communication between one storey and the next was not by means of intra-mural stairs following the contours of the walls of the keep, but by an ingenious newel arrangement, where the direction of the steps is reversed in mid-flight, thereby disorienting the invader. The castle was further strengthened by a portcullis, again an indication of Llywelyn ap Iorwerth's full awareness of the prevailing defensive devices of his enemy.

This notable tower of the 1230s has survived in a considerably more substantial state than its component parts. The outline of the curtain wall which enclosed the entire fortress has often been likened to a boomerang, and within it, the footings of the accommodation essential to a military base indicate their function.

History has assigned Dolbadarn importance as a prison rather than as a castle of strategic and crucial significance. Llywelyn ap Iorwerth's offspring, Dafydd, his son and successor by his wife Joan, the daughter of King John, lived for only six years after Llywelyn's death. The continuity of the line of the Princes of Gwynedd was now seriously threatened. Llywelyn's grandson by his illegitimate son, Gruffudd, changed the course of Welsh history. Llywelyn the Last displayed those strengths of leadership that should guarantee the independence of Gwynedd and of Wales. The Treaty of Montgomery of 1267 recognised him as Prince of Wales. Such acknowledgement of power was not to go unchallenged. The contender was someone who claimed equal right to the inheritance: his brother, Owain, whose stance resulted in an imprisonment at Dolbadarn which lasted for over twenty years. His fate aroused the sympathy of contemporary bards, one of whom refers to him as 'A man in the tower, a prolonged guest.' The remains of the built evidence suggests that Owain Goch had his own small sleeping apartment, with an adjacent latrine.

Dolbadarn was later used as a prison in the early fifteenth

century when Owain Glyndŵr held his arch-enemy, and the instigator of the entire uprising, Earl Grey of Ruthin, within its walls, though some of the stronghold's effectiveness had been debilitated in the early 1280s when Edward I removed much of the castle's timber for his grand designs at Caernarfon.

What the majority of the artistic depictions of Dolbadarn did not record was the enormity of the slate quarry of Dinorwic, in the mid-nineteenth century one of the most important in Europe. It towers arrogantly above both Llyn Padarn and Llyn Peris, the greens, blues and purples of its faces and facets constantly changing with the unpredictable light of Snowdonia. Although now a spent force, it has the majesty and mystery of a smaller version of an Inca citadel, and its picturesque appeal is enormous. The slate was railed from here to the small sea outlet of Port Dinorwic, on the main road between Bangor and Caernarfon, a corridor settlement known also by the far more pleasing sounding Y Felinheli (the Sea-water Mill) whose harbour has now become a marine development. In 1941, Sir Michael Duff, a descendant of the quarry's owner, Thomas Assheton Smith, placed the castle in the guardianship of what was then the Ministry of Works, now known as Cadw.

Dolforwyn (Powys)
1m (1.6km) W of Abermule, Open access, Admission free, Cadw

The building of Llywelyn ap Gruffudd's castle at Dolforwyn in 1273, the only one built entirely by Llywelyn as a new foundation, was an assertive indication of his increasing control over the area of Cedewain which had been granted to him by Henry III in 1267, when the king, through the Treaty of Montgomery, recognised Llywelyn as Prince of Wales.

Llywelyn's ambitious building scheme aroused Edward I, who was away on crusade, to instruct his officials to write to Llywelyn, expressing his extreme displeasure, which amounted to an 'Inhibition . . . of his creating a castle at Aberunal [Abermule] . . . or a borough or a town there, or a market . . . as the King learns that he proposes to erect anew the said castle . . . and a borough or town and market.'

Dolforwyn Castle

In no way were Llywelyn's plans to be thwarted. His reply was a crisp refusal to submit to the royal command: 'you know well that the rights of our principality are entirely separate from the rights of your kingdom . . . though we hold our principality under your royal power . . . We pray you not to listen to those who try to inflame your mind against us.'

The building of the castle and the attached town which had begun in 1273 proceeded during the following year and, at Easter 1274, Llywelyn ap Gruffudd visited Dolforwyn, where Gruffudd ap Gwenwynwyn was summoned to him, not only to be upbraided for his treacherous actions, but to be deprived of Arwystli and thirteen townships of Cyfeiliog. Llywelyn's final act of revenge was to take Gruffudd's eldest son, Owain, under his authority in Gwynedd.

Dolforwyn, which had consumed more than £174 of

Llywelyn's income, was in 1277 surrounded by the earl of Lincoln and Roger Mortimer. It surrendered after a fortnight, because of lack of water, and became a Mortimer border stronghold. By the end of the fourteenth century it was derelict.

Llywelyn's short-lived attempt to establish himself at Dolforwyn led to the strengthening of the castle and town of Montgomery in 1279. Roger Mortimer, having been granted Cedewain, was given the right by Edward I to hold a weekly market and an annual fair within the manor. This was to develop as Newtown.

Dolforwyn is one of the least known of the castles of the native princes, and it is only since excavations during the 1980s that its basic plan of a rectangular curtain wall, fortified at the west by a rectangular keep and at the east by a round tower, has come to light.

The site of Llywelyn's town is still a matter of conjecture. The castle remains to occupy a splendid position above the river Severn.

Dolwyddelan (Gwynedd)
1m from Dolwyddelan off A470, Open: standard hours, Admission charge, Cadw

Because of the mountainous nature of Snowdonia and the proximity of the two important passes which Dolwyddelan and Dolbadarn safeguarded, these two castles of Llywelyn ap Iorwerth stand closer to one another than any of the other fortresses that he built. For this reason and for the fact that they both contain the same initial syllable (meaning 'meadow'), the two strongholds are almost invariably linked in the national consciousness.

In other ways they share very little in common. The difference in their layout is not the result of subtle military ploys and strategies but that of the more basic consideration of taking full advantage of a naturally defensive site. The curtain wall of Dolwyddelan, therefore, obeys the contours of the rocky knoll on which it is built, resulting in a roughly hexagonal plan, whereas similar principles of defence at Dolbadarn produced the boomerang shape.

The most prominent difference between Llywelyn's two castles lies in the nature of the keeps. Dolbadarn's is cylindrical, suggesting that Llywelyn had assimilated the salient features of French military architecture. His rectangular counterpart at Dolwyddelan was equally indicative of his grasp of current trends in defensive design, but when built, sometime between 1210–40, consisted of two storeys, unlike Dolbadarn's three. The addition of its third storey dates from the late thirteenth century, and was the work of Edward I, soon after his conquest of Gwynedd. Unlike Dolbadarn, the keep at Dolwyddelan is in a remarkably good state of preservation, not because of any quirky sequence of historical and military circumstances, but because in the mid-nineteenth century, a programme of substantial restoration was undertaken with similar enthusiasm – though obviously on a much smaller scale – to that shown by the 4th marquess of Bute at Caerphilly in Glamorgan. The person responsible for this work was Lord Willoughby de Eresby, to whom the property had come through marriage. The derelict state of the keep prior to his undertaking is picturesquely depicted by some of the indefatigable painters of the late eighteenth and early nineteenth centuries whose works tended to emphasise and indeed exaggerate the ferocity of the terrain. Although this romantic aspect has been deadened by the invasion of forest plantations, the former strategic importance of Dolwyddelan above the Lledr Valley, now stern in its stony silence, is still obvious as the visitor stands in the courtyard, whose curtain walls, even at a fraction of their original height, impart a sense of power, which was Edward's intention when he strengthened them. At the same time he rebuilt the tower on the west, not only to provide greater domestic convenience, but to make a more visible assertion of his sovereignty.

It was not always consistent with military prowess to make so bold a statement of one's presence. The king's accounts for the winter of 1283, for example, suggest that camouflage was of vital importance to the newly installed English garrison, whose numbers were to be protected by white tunics and stockings. The snows of Gwynedd arrive in advance of most other parts of Wales; communications can still suddenly come to a complete halt. The grip of winter was a bitter enemy of the medieval population of Gwynedd, to the English it was an adversary which could generally be overcome by superior strength, allied with subtle strategy. For all the lessons gleaned from contemporary sources of military architecture, Llywelyn's two best known fortresses, Dolbadarn and Dolwyddelan, succumbed to the determination of Edward.

It was not until the late fifteenth century when Maredudd ap Ieuan ap Robert purchased the lease of Dolwyddelan that further improvements were made to the castle. These were governed not only by considerations of domestic convenience, for he had an expanding family, but by those of safety. In this remote and mountainous region, hostility rather than conviviality prevailed.

Maredudd died in 1525, and a brass of him can be seen at the nearby church of St Gwyddelan which he rebuilt and which he would attend for worship from his new house at Penamnen nearby, only having taken the greatest precautions by having the doors of his home 'sure barred and bolted and a watchman to stand guard at Y Garreg Big during divine service being a rock whence he might see both the church and the house and raise the cry if the house were assaulted'.

With the interests of Maredudd's descendants centred on other properties, notably at Gwydir, near Llanrwst, Dolwyddelan was increasingly neglected, and by the mid-eighteenth century had become a ruin.

Dolwyddelan was reputedly the birthplace of Llywelyn ap Gruffudd, though the prince was probably born in an earlier castle situated nearby and abandoned when the Dolwyddelan that stands today, much restored, was built.

Although near the popular tourist attraction of Betws-y-Coed, and the slate town of Blaenau Ffestiniog, with its narrow gauge railway to Porthmadog, the feeling that the visitor still gets at Dolwyddelan is one of refreshing isolation.

Although there is ample parking space, there is a considerable walk to the castle, via a farmyard, where tickets are sold, and where there are toilets and a refreshment kiosk.

Dryslwyn (Carmarthenshire)

2.5m (4km) W of Llandeilo on A40 or B4300. From either road take B4297. Open access, Admission free, Cadw

Ironically for a castle foundation, Dryslwyn must now be one of the best examples in Wales of a pastoral spot where only the steepness of the grass escarpment, with its sparse grey-stone remains, suggests the turbulent days of its origins. What is now a charmingly somnolent hamlet was in the thirteenth century a borough, very much in the prevailing English fashion, with burgages outside the castle defences and extending downwards towards the river Tywi. It could even boast its own annual fair.

There is no reference to Dryslwyn until 1245, and it seems to have been engaged in no hostility between then and 1287 when Rhys ap Maredudd made a brave stand against Edward I and did not surrender without the boldest assertion of independence. In fact such a strong determination on his part resulted in one of the most dramatic sieges during Edward I's Welsh campaigns. An army of 11,000, led by the earl of Cornwall, besieged the castle. The consequences for the English attackers were disastrous, and 150 of them were crushed by their own attempt to undermine the defences.

After it was eventually taken Dryslwyn was refortified at a cost of £338 13s 4d, and it remained in the control of the Crown until the rebellion of Owain Glyndŵr. It is not known what part it played in this national uprising and, since there is little reference to it afterwards, the reasons for its dismantling and disintegration are not recorded.

Dyserth (Denbighshire)

Not accessible, but site is clearly visible

By tradition, this is the first stone castle in North-East Wales. It was built by Henry III in 1241, when he defeated Dafydd, the successor to Llywelyn ap Iorwerth 'the Great', and gained the region of Tegeingl (Englefield). The stronghold, referred to in the *Brut* as *Castell-y-garreg* (the Stone Castle), was built at a height of 60m above sea-level, looking towards the Irish Sea, as well as commanding views over much of the Vale of Clwyd. It was a site which had probably been occupied since Neolithic times. Soon after the castle was built, burgages were available for tenancy 'near the castle', and a further inducement to prospective settlers was the fact that the infant borough was given the liberties of Chester, the most accessible English town.

Such promise was reduced to nothing with the attack in 1263 by Llywelyn ap Gruffudd who destroyed the king's fortress and its satellite settlement. In regaining the territory for the rightful owners, Henry III's son, Edward I, saw that Dyserth had one major virtue – access to tidal waters. It was a consideration which governed the siting of almost all his fortresses during the first and second campaigns. However his attitude to Dyserth was similar to that at Degannwy: forget, start again – elsewhere. He therefore favoured the site of Rhuddlan, whose defensive advantages had been appreciated by the Normans. By making the river Clwyd navigable up to his new stronghold, he was able to ensure those strengths that were naturally at almost all of his other castles.

Henry III's castle probably bore some resemblance to his construction at Montgomery. Extensive quarrying over centuries has deprived Dyserth, sometimes also known as Dincolyn or Caerfaelan, of those defences. Today its site holds considerable interest for archaeologists and view-seekers, and the present settlement of Diserth is removed in every sense from that intended by Henry III.

Ewloe (Flintshire)
On B5125 between Ewloe and Northophall and off A548 at Connah's Quay. Open access, Admission free, Cadw

It is easy to miss Ewloe Castle, because although there is a sign on the B5125, the only available parking space is a lay-by, and the local terrain in no way suggests a suitable place for a defensive building. Having followed the castle sign, the visitor sees a field through which nothing more than a track leads to a wooded area at the end of the sloping lie of the land. Here the ground drops suddenly, and in the hollow, surprisingly, stand the ruins of fortified walls 'built . . . in the corner of the woods', as Llywelyn ap Gruffudd's castle was once described. Even if it was a statement of his repossession from the English of his family's manor of Ewloe, as part of the *cantref* of Tegeingl, or Englefield, in 1257, its position was far from ideal, and however high the original walls might have been, or however strong and deep the rock-cut ditches, they would have offered no serious challenge to a determined assailant.

The other approach is from the built up area of Connah's Quay and Shotton, through Wepre Park, where there are parking facilities and a visitor centre. By following this route, Ewloe takes on a more menacing aspect, due to the impressive tower which defended what was obviously regarded as the principal approach to the castle. This two-storey rectangular fortification, probably the castle keep, was characteristically Welsh in that it had an apsidal or curved end. This was by no means a recent innovation; both Castell y Bere and Cricieth had such defences thirty years earlier, for the practical reason that this almost semi-circular shape provided such an extensive field of fire. The keep was entered at first-floor level, and on the right of the entrance to the main chamber, lit by large windows, a mural stairway, still remarkably intact and lit by a small surviving window, led to a wall-walk, which no longer exists. From the top of the stairs, it is possible to see what the internal arrangements of the basement level were.

A high curtain wall divides this upper ward from the lower one, whose chief features are the well and the lower part of a round west tower which was built against the face of the rocky spur which gives the castle much of its natural defensiveness. Both wards would have had temporary structures to accommodate all the ancillary needs of garrison and family.

With Edward I's increasing dominance of North-East Wales as a result of his first campaign of 1277, Ewloe's defensive role was greatly diminished. It was certainly no match for the sophistication of nearby Flint, with its highly original plan and its immediate access to the Dee estuary.

Ewloe, in its deep woodland setting, conveys the spirit of myth, legend, romance and adventure, whereas the castles of Gilbert de Clare in the south and those of Edward I in the north excite sensations of awe. Few can leave Ewloe without feeling that they have been, in some magical way, transported back to the early days of their own personal fantasy.

Flint (Flintshire)
Inadequately signposted on left of A5119 in the town. Small turning leads over railway bridge to ample car park adjacent to castle. Open access, Admission free, Cadw

The first of Edward I's northern strongholds in his campaign of 1277, Flint commanded the Dee estuary dividing Wales from England, and the coastal plain from the Point of Ayr to Chester, a route now basically followed by the railway. With the Treaty of Montgomery of 1267, Edward's father, Henry III, had bestowed on Llywelyn ap Gruffudd not only the title of Prince of Wales, but the region of Tegeingl, which by nature of its frontier position had passed from Welsh to English hands for centuries. Llywelyn had deliberately chosen to disregard one of the conditions of the title: that he should pay homage to the king, and the Welsh prince's recalcitrance angered Edward to the extent that there seemed to be one solution: to reduce Llywelyn to a state of complete subjection.

Although Flint is much reduced, enough remains of its original structure to understand the stronghold's lay-out: an outer and inner ward, the latter square-shaped, with angle towers, one of which was detached from the others and more aggressive in purpose. This separate round donjon was in principle not unlike a Norman keep, in that it offered final protection to the garrison in times of siege. It was a construction which the king's Savoyard architect, Master James of St George, was not to repeat anywhere else in his Welsh plans. In high tidal waters, such as those of February 1974, the highest for 300 years, the castle can be seen just as the king and architect had envisaged it: a place where the sea itself provided forceful defence.

The Great Tower, as well as having its own moat, had a drawbridge to connect it to the inner ward, and its height and position outside that court gave it undisputed command over

Flint Castle

the area. In its strength – its walls were 23ft thick – in the ingenuity of its plan and in its ample provision of residential accommodation, it might be regarded as a castle within a castle. A gallery, reached by a mural staircase known only to the garrison, gave them not only means of escape from the invading forces who had penetrated this final defence, but an opportunity to shoot down at the enemy, as they found themselves in a confined round space, with no visible means of escape. In its outward appearance, the Great Tower of Flint has been compared to the Tour de Constance at Aigues-Mortes. Yverdon in Savoy, where Master James would have been employed a decade earlier, also bears a striking resemblance to Edward's first castle of his first Welsh campaign.

The building of Flint was a military enterprise on a grand scale, involving 970 diggers, over 300 carpenters, about the same number of woodmen, 200 masons, twelve smiths and ten charcoal burners. The men were recruited from the Midlands and beyond, and were all subjected to what amounted to forced labour. What material the diggers were not able to produce on site was provided by boatloads of stone from the quarries of the Wirral peninsula between the Dee and the Mersey.

The castle of Flint, where there had been no previous habitation, was linked with its satellite urban development to form a defensive unit, an arrangement seen also at Aberystwyth, Caernarfon and, most strikingly, at Conwy. A modified scheme based on the same principle is discernible at Rhuddlan and Beaumaris.

Edward's work force was therefore needed to dig ditches over a far more extensive area, in order to safeguard the *bastide*, or plantation town, which had the advantages as well as the restrictions of an economy controlled by the landowner. The scheme and its distribution of land resulted in a distinctive lay-out, where geometrical division assured fairness of allocation. Flint town was protected only by earthworks, rather than built defences, and its arrangement of access and thoroughfares conformed with the grid system. The cost of the town and castle amounted to £7,000.

John Speed's map of 1610 indicates that the town's original lay-out was still intact and little change was made to it until the incursion of the Chester to Holyhead railway in the 1840s. In the 1960s the medieval plan was completely distorted by the erection of monstrous high-rise flats, totally out of character with the low-lying area of the coastal plain.

Although Edward's castle superseded that of his father in Dyserth, it played no major active rôle in the English-Welsh wars. It was nevertheless instrumental in instigating Edward's second campaign. On Palm Sunday, 1282, Flint was attacked by Llywelyn ap Gruffudd's brother, Dafydd, from his base at Caergwrle, and the town was burnt. This assault, like those on Hawarden and Rhuddlan on the same day, was an act of aggression which led eventually to the formal loss of national independence. Madog ap Llywelyn, a distant kinsman of Llywelyn ap Gruffudd, attempted to redress this state of affairs by his widespread revolt of 1294 which resulted in the town being burnt again, this time by the castle's constable. His act was a drastic measure to deny food and shelter to Madog's supporters who were laying siege to the castle.

In August 1399, Flint Castle was, ironically, the scene of the downfall of an English king, Richard II. On his return from the Irish campaigns, having been under constant threat from his rival, the rebellious Bolingbroke, the king sought refuge here, an incident depicted in Shakespeare's *Richard II*.

Percy:	The castle is royally manned, my lord, Against thy entrance.
Bolingbroke:	Royally! Why, it contains no king?
Percy	Yes, my good lord, It doth contain a king; King Richard lies within the limits of yond lime and stone . . .

Soon afterwards, 'having heard Mass', Richard walked along the castle walls before facing the penultimate ignominy.

Richard:	Down, down I come; like glistering Phaethon . . . In the base court? Where kings grow base . . . Down, court, down king!

He was soon afterwards in London, where he was forced to abdicate, Bolingbroke becoming king in his stead, as Henry IV.

During the Civil War, the castle was initially garrisoned by Royalists but changed hands twice between 1643–45. It was demolished soon afterwards and by 1652 had lost all semblance of a castle.

Buck's view of 1742 not only shows the Dee lapping at the walls of the castle, but in the distance a mass of chimney stacks belching industrial smoke. In fact the area is still heavily industrialised, although in recent years the general environment immediately surrounding the castle has been much improved.

Although nothing remains of the buildings in the inner ward, the sturdy outline of the defences and the formidable might of the Great Tower and the North-East Tower are full of interest.

Fonmon (Vale of Glamorgan)
Near Rhoose, 4m (6.4km) W of Barry, Open: by previous written appointment, Sir Brooke Boothby, Bt

Fonmon Castle is no mere fanciful name for a country house, any more than its castellations are a mere adornment of a building seeking claim to a significant ancestry. In fact, the core of the house belongs to the late twelfth or early thirteenth century, and as such it is the only castle in Glamorgan that has been lived in continuously since then, and has changed hands only once during all that time.

The original rectangular stone keep, with its 6ft thick walls, is clearly discernible to the left of the present entrance, although the Venetian window softens the unyielding military look that it would otherwise still have. The site owes its existence to Oliver St John, one of the twelve knights who, having helped Robert Fitzhamon in the conquest of Glamorgan, was granted the Manor of Fonmon, and it was a secluded spot about a mile (1.6km) from where the river Thaw enters the Bristol Channel that a descendant of Oliver St John chose for his castle. It was naturally defended on the east and north-east sides by a ravine and, in spite of today's vegetation, the strategic placing of the fortress is impressively awesome.

Substantial additions were made to Fonmon in the late thirteenth century and again in the seventeenth. In 1656 it was sold under a decree of the Court of Chancery to pay the debts of Lord Bolingbroke and his son Oliver, descendants of the original family. Four and a half centuries of St John family associations came to an end.

The purchaser was Colonel Philip Jones, Controller of Oliver Cromwell's Household and the leading Parliamentarian in South Wales. He added the block on the north of the house. It was over a hundred years later, however, that the most dramatic change took place, when a descendant, Robert Jones III, transformed the castle into an eighteenth-century country house of considerable refinement. The Venetian window mentioned earlier belongs to this period. Inappropriate though it might appear from the outside, its contribution to the interior is immeasurable, as it graces one of the finest rococo rooms in Wales, the library, a dignified space created in the first-floor hall of the original keep. It is the elegance of so much of the eighteenth-century remodelling, together with the unexpected twists and turns of newel staircases, glimpses of a deep closet here and a guard-room there, that makes Fonmon a place of endless fascination and speculation.

Grosmont (Monmouthshire)

On B4347 10m (16km) NW of Monmouth on Pontrilas to Rockfield road, Open access, Admission free, Cadw (Guidebook from Post Office)

The name, 'Big Mound', itself conveys its elevated position on the west bank of the river Monnow, which is all that separates it from England, thereby making it a rival to Chepstow, which has the river Wye between its fortifications and England. Grosmont, Skenfrith (Ynysgynwraidd) and White Castle were all three built close enough together to form what was effectively a unified defence system, known either as the Three Castles or as the Trilateral.

They owe their origins to William FitzOsbern, earl of Hereford, who had established his conquest of South-East Wales at Chepstow, where he built the first stone castle in Wales. From here and from his later foothold at Monmouth, he was able to extend and exert his power by building smaller strongholds at points which owed their strategic significance, for the most part, to river crossings, since this part of Wales lacks Gwynedd's formidable mountain ranges. If the Norman invasion of South-East Wales was relatively effortless, the recently gained territory had nevertheless to be safeguarded. For the usurpers presence was all, especially if, like Grosmont, it was in a position to challenge major lines of communication, such as that between Herefordshire and the Usk Valley.

The three earth-and-timber strongholds were granted by King

Grosmont Castle

John in 1201 to Hubert de Burgh, the king's chamberlain. Grosmont's original earth defences, like those at White Castle, were put to good use when he set about refortifying the castle in masonry. His initial work, done between 1201–04, was the rectangular block which comprised a first-floor hall and solar, entered by an external timber staircase. The ground floor or basement was accessible only internally, and the fenestration of the two storeys clearly indicates the defensive nature of the lower, and the more residential nature of the one above it. This departed very little from the arrangement which William FitzOsbern had introduced at Chepstow well over a hundred years previously.

In 1204, during the war against France, Hubert held Chinon, on the Vienne, against the king, Philip Augustus, and although he was taken prisoner the following year, his military exploits must have stimulated his interest in current French military architecture, of which Saumur, with its four corner towers, could well have been a major influence. When he regained his possessions in 1219, he was in a position to implement the most recent trends in defensive techniques.

As at Skenfrith, a stone curtain wall was erected at Grosmont, incorporating circular towers which projected boldly at each angle, thereby providing ample range for cross-firing purposes. Unlike Skenfrith, however, it was given a sturdy gatehouse.

Hubert de Burgh, earl of Kent and royal justiciar, nevertheless fell from royal favour in 1232, when he was deprived of his much prized Gwent castles, on which he had expended considerable architectural expertise, as well as enormous sums of money. The Trilateral was granted by Henry III to his younger son, Edmund Crouchback, earl of Lancaster in 1267, and his son Henry of Lancaster so favoured Grosmont as a home that his own son, as his name Henry of Grosmont suggests, was born there. This represents the third phase in the castle's architectural evolution, when the north-west block underwent major changes in order to provide apartments that reflected the royal status of Grosmont's owners. Larger windows were installed, more fireplaces were added, and the number of garderobes increased.

A fascinating remnant of this transition from fortress to grand residence is an elaborate octagonal chimney, unlike any other such survivor in a Welsh castle.

Owain Glyndŵr's attack in 1404 was relieved by a small force led by the Prince of Wales, the future Henry V, who later wrote to his father: 'Your people held the field and conquered all the said rebels and killed of them according to a fair account in the field to the time of their return from the pursuit some say eight hundred, some say a thousand, being questioned on the pain of death.'

The castle declined in importance in subsequent years and was in ruins by the sixteenth century. The majestic church of St Nicholas, dating from about 1100, was completed by Queen Eleanor, wife of Henry III, and gloriously reflects the importance of Grosmont in medieval times.

Gwrych (Denbighshire)
Seen only at a distance from Abergele, Private ownership

The front of this elegant modern mansion extends nearly
five hundred yards, with a noble terrace on either side, four
hundred yards in length . . . It commands an extensive view
of the sea, which on this part of the coast is generally alive
with shipping, upwards of two hundred vessels being often
seen at the same time with sails full spread for different
directions.

So runs a description of this, probably the most idiosyncratic
manifestion of the 'castle' cult in Wales, written soon after it
was built in 1815. Although Charles Augustus Busby (1788–
1838) exhibited his designs for 'Gwrych Castle' at the Royal
Academy in 1814, evidence suggests that he had little part in
the irregular structure which so conspicuously clads the hillside,
and which appears far removed from an 'elegant modern mansion'. In fact, it embodies the principles not of elegance and
modernity so much as those of rugged medievalism. The last
two decades of neglect have reduced this rambling extravaganza
to a state of decay and disarray similar to that reached by the
Norman, Welsh and Edwardian castles in the eighteenth and
nineteenth centuries, which inspired the work of so many
famous artists.

In spite of its sprawling castellated walls built in the local
limestone, with their towers and turrets and sally ports, the
residential nucleus of Gwrych is surprisingly small; the rest is
for effect, and represents gradual addition and development, as
new ideas and whims assailed the owner, Lloyd Bamford Hes-
keth, whose father had acquired the property by his marriage
to Frances, the daughter and heiress of John Lloyd of Gwrych.

In the second half of the nineteenth century, a Bamford Hes-
keth heiress married the earl of Dundonald in whose family the
property remained until it was sold in 1946. Several attempts
over subsequent years at making effective use of this extraordinary concoction of idealism, fantasy and bravado have failed;
not even medieval jousting tournaments succeeded. The place
is now probably beyond repair. From a distance, its array of

Gwrych Castle

battlements set against the wooded hillside above Abergele is
one of the most dramatic settings in Wales.

Harlech (Gwynedd)

20m (32km) N from Dolgellau along A496 via Barmouth, Open:
standard hours, Admission charge, Cadw, A WORLD HERITAGE SITE

In the four twelfth-century Welsh native tales entitled *The Mab-*
inogion, the second of them opens with the description of King
Bendigeidfran sitting on the rock at Harddlech in Ardudwy,
his court, in the company of his brother and his retinue when
they see thirteen ships coming from the direction of Ireland.
On board one of them is Matholwch, King of Ireland, who is
coming to seek the hand of Branwen, Bendigeidfran's sister, in
marriage. Nobody who has read *Branwen Daughter of Llŷr* can
visit the Harddlech – Harlech – a name interpreted as 'high
rock', without thinking of the Irish sea, which in medieval times

Harlech Castle

would have lapped at its feet, and imagining the thirteen sets
of sails coming across Cardigan Bay with the wind behind them.
However arresting the opening of the story may be, there is
no archaeological evidence to suggest that either a defensive
settlement or a *llys* existed here before Edward I started building
his castle in 1283, although it is easy enough to understand
how such an awesomely majestic site might have inspired the
most heroic legends of any literature.

Harlech was one of a trio of castles begun in the same year,
as part of the king's second Welsh campaign, following the
death of Llywelyn ap Gruffudd, Llywelyn 'the Last', near Builth,
the previous year. With the native Prince of Gwynedd at last
out of the way, the king sought to consolidate his triumph
by ráising strongholds which would unequivocally express his
superior strength and obliterate the spirit of Welsh pride and

independence. Of the three, Harlech is undeniably superior to Conwy and Caernarfon by the very nature of its site, for the precipice on which it stands is a fortress in its own right. Even today, the visitor approaching the castle by its most accessible route, with the aid of modern solid timber walkways over the rock-cut ditch and timber steps up to the gatehouse, cannot but be overawed by the powerful volume of the fortress.

Harlech gains its distinction not only from the forceful impact of the military construction itself, but from the views of Snowdonia, an area made up of one natural defence after another, with such irregularity that for all the precision and symmetry of Edward's castle, he might well have felt occasionally that there was a strength in those mountain ranges which was greater than that which even his master mason, James of St George, could match.

It is rare these days that a place can have changed so little that it is possible to agree with the viewpoint of an early nineteenth-century traveller. Richard Fenton's description applies equally now: 'the castle is a most superb building, whether we consider its magnitude, its site, or its masonry and style of architecture . . . Looked at from every way, it is a most beautiful and magnificent pile, and when you couple it with the great features of the Snowdonian tract, and the lovely outline of Lleyn, which must come into every view of it, nothing can surpass it.'

However precipitous the rock on which Edward's fortress was founded, it afforded enough level area for James of St George to apply the principles of concentric planning. The confined space of the narrow outer ward was adequately compensated by the sheer drop on the north and west, and by the rock-cut dry moats on the other two sides. It was an exercise which served him very well when, twelve years later, in 1295, he began work on Beaumaris in Anglesey, on a flat and unhindered site where the unparalleled concentric plan was put into operation.

Harlech was to be the site of another of James of St George's ingenious innovations in his Welsh castle programme; the concentration on the gatehouse not only for defensive power, but for domestic apartments which could offer standards of comfort suitable for people of rank. Neither of the contemporary castles of Caernarfon or Conwy had a similar building; in fact, Conwy had no gatehouse at all, apart from the building which separated the inner from the outer ward. As in the case of the perfecting of the concentric plan, it was Beaumaris which was to refine the concept of the gatehouse as a building which was sufficiently fortified to withstand attack as well as providing accommodation of a high level of sophistication and opulence.

The outer elevation of the gatehouse at Harlech is protected by two solid turrets which are part of the curtain wall, and are very miniature versions of the D-ends of the main gatehouse. Its outward show of defiant aggression with its narrow square-headed apertures on each floor belies the inner elevation, with its three generous traceried windows on each of its first and second floors. At Beaumaris, James of St George was to build two identical gatehouses, their inner-facing elevations identical, and the number of windows on each floor increased from three to five. Unlike those at Beaumaris, which though unfinished, were intended to be luxurious royal apartments for the king and his son Edward of Caernarfon, the three-storeyed gatehouse at Harlech fulfilled more than one function.

The gate-passage itself was defended by a series of daunting deterrents: a sequence of stout wooden doors, the first port-cullis, arrow-loops, a second portcullis and a second door constituted as formidable a challenge as any military architect could devise.

Offices and storerooms were accommodated in the basement, and the guard-rooms were housed on the ground floor. The principal apartments, the residence of the constable, faced the inner ward and, in addition to the relative luxury of being well lit, they were heated by fires from hooded chimney breasts. On the east side of the first floor, over the entry, was a barrel-vaulted chapel, which had nothing like the dignified beauty of its counterpart at Conwy and at Beaumaris, and its strange location meant that it had another function: in its roof were the pulleys controlling the two portcullises which were part of the elaborate system to protect the gate-passage.

External steps led to the first floor of the main accommodation apartments and connected them to the rest of the castle.

Harlech Castle, rear view

A sixteenth-century survey refers to them as 'a stately stayre', and in fact the whole of this inner-facing elevation of the gatehouse has the semblance of the principal facade of a country house in the early stages of its development. The structure has a simple elegance which is remarkable for its date and for the troubled times which brought it into being. It would have been a worthy home for the man who was appointed the castle's constable in 1290 – Master James of St George.

The inner ward was surrounded on the other sides by essential castle accommodation built against the curtain walls, of which only the footings remain. The largest of these rooms was the hall, the hub of castle life, with four large windows facing

Cardigan Bay, and probably three facing the inner ward. A screens passage would have divided the hall from the buttery and the pantry, beyond which was the kitchen. On the opposite, north side, was the dais end which led to the garrison chapel.

Adjoining the kitchen, against the south curtain wall, are the traces of what is referred to as Ystumgwern Hall, the home of Llywelyn ap Gruffudd, Prince of Wales, and removed from a place of that name four miles (6.4km) from Harlech in the early fourteenth century. The dwarfing of its ground area is as effective an indication as any of the difference in scale, let alone in volume and mass, between Edward I's great fortress and the residence of his arch-enemy. The symbolic significance of such a removal was far more potent: there was to be no doubt in people's minds as to who now had the upper hand.

Harlech is also remarkable for its defended Way from the Sea, a stairway of 108 shallow steps cut into the western rock face from the Water Gate which, like Beaumaris, had direct access to the sea, though it is unlikely that it was equipped with a dock.

By the time the castle was completed, the whole enterprise had cost between £8,000 and £9,000, and had involved nearly 950 men, comprising 115 quarriers, 227 masons, 30 smiths, 22 carpenters and 546 labourers. For Sir Otto de Grandison, who had first spotted the enormous military significance of the Harlech site, during his march northwards, fresh from his conquest of Castell y Bere, the completion of the Edwardian enterprise must have been infinitely satisfying.

Only five years later, the spirit of Welsh independence was to rise again, this time under the leadership of Madog ap Llywelyn, a relation of Llywelyn the Last. Although the castle was completely cut off by land, like Cricieth across the bay, its coastal position was as good a guarantee as any of necessary supplies reaching them from Ireland. As a result, both castles held out. As soon as Madog was defeated, precautionary measures were taken at Harlech. The deep rocky ravine which defended the north-west side of the castle was given the added protection of a wall of stone and lime.

The revolt of Madog ap Llywelyn was a minor episode in the military history of Harlech which was to see more action than any of the other Edwardian castles, although it was over a hundred years before another attempt was made to retrieve North Wales from the grip of the English.

The protagonist was Owain Glyndŵr to whose forces Harlech fell after a long siege, in the spring of 1404, three years after his first unsuccessful attack on the castle. Having ultimately gained possession, Owain established not only his family home here, but a base for his political plans and prospects. It was, no doubt in his own mind, and in the eyes and actions of his followers, the Welsh royal court to which all his energies had been directed, and where he was formally acknowledged, by the very act of being crowned, as the Prince of Wales. According to tradition, the ceremony at Harlech was witnessed by representatives of Scotland, Spain and, particularly, of France, on whose forces Owain had relied so heavily during his campaign. It was at Harlech that he called a parliamentary meeting where he presented his policy for establishing not only an independent Welsh church, but two universities.

Such an affirmation of the revival of Welsh independence was negated by the recapture of Harlech after a long siege between 1408–09, by Harry of Monmouth's men, Gilbert Talbot, and his brother John, later the first earl of Shrewsbury, sons of Richard Talbot of the Marcher castle of Goodrich. The outcome of Gilbert's achievement in bringing the siege of Harlech to a successful end was his being given a year later, in 1410, command of 900 men to keep control over the borders between England and Wales. Even so, Harlech's capitulation had not been brought about without considerable cost, requiring the skills of 300 men-at-arms and 600 archers.

Later in the century, Harlech was involved in disputes and skirmishes not between the Welsh and the English but between supporters of the House of Lancaster (Red Rose) and the House of York (White Rose), a major internecine struggle which lasted for thirty years and which was not decisively concluded until Richard III was defeated at Bosworth in 1485 by Henry Tudor, then to be crowned Henry VII, and thereby heralding a new, and Welsh, dynasty – the Tudors.

During the earlier part of the Wars of the Roses, after the capture of Henry VI at Northampton, his wife Margaret of

Anjou fled to Harlech which was held for the Lancastrians by Dafydd ap Ieuan ap Einion, the constable appointed by Jasper Tudor, the king's half-brother. His particular rôle, if not his name, will go down in the history of those wars as the last commander in England and Wales to yield to the Yorkists; in the case of Harlech, to the force led by William Herbert, later to be earl of Pembroke, and his brother Sir Richard Herbert of Coldbrook. This arduous and courageous siege is by tradition the inspiration of '*Rhyfelgyrch Gwŷr Harlech*' ('The Campaign of the Men of Harlech'), the rousing march which has almost the identity of a national anthem.

During the Civil War, Harlech yet again had the distinction of being the last fortress to hold out against the adversary; on this occasion by the tenacity of its Royalist constable, William Owen. Its surrender in March 1647 after nine months' siege was brought about on 'the 16th day, being Tuesday, [when] the Governor, Mr William Owen, delivered the keys of the castle to General Mytton'. The transfer of power signalled the end of the Civil War in Wales.

In 1914 Harlech Castle was placed in the charge of the Office of Works and is today the responsibility of its successor, Cadw.

Outside the castle is a bronze of Bendigeidfran on horseback, depicting his return from Ireland where his sister Branwen is now the tragic wife of Matholwch. Executed in the 1980s by Wales's distinguished sculptor, Ivor Roberts-Jones, it is a powerful glimpse of the enchanted world of *The Mabinogion*.

Unlike Edward's other three great fortresses of the second Welsh campaign, Caernarfon, Conwy and Beaumaris, Harlech never had a planned and defended town, though its present popularity as a tourist venue belies an early seventeenth-century description of the place as 'a very poor towne ... having no traphicke or trade', a state of affairs which persisted in 1808 when Richard Fenton referred to it as 'the most forlorn, beggarly place imaginable'. How things change!

Haverfordwest, Hwlffordd (Pembrokeshire)
In town centre, Exterior only, Open: standard hours, Admission free, Local Authority

Until earlier this century the Western Cleddau was navigable up to the point which has now become the shopping-centre of the town. Its river-sea connection accounts for its former importance and the subsequent need for defence. In the Middle Ages, Haverfordwest was far more important than Cardiff, for example, and although its prestige declined where that of others increased, its former strategic position is still evident, as the castle, standing proudly 80ft above the river, all too clearly indicates.

The fortress, even in ruins, still seems to have the entire area firmly in its control, and few castles in Wales can match it for its dominance. Giraldus Cambrensis, Gerald of Wales, visited it in the company of Archbishop Baldwin in 1188, when it was an earth-and-timber structure which was superseded by the stone castle whose remains we see today.

This was the work of William Marshall, a distinguished soldier whose experience in warfare abroad had given him great insight into the intricacies of defensive buildings and had whetted his appetite for applying those techniques himself. His marriage to the daughter of Richard de Clare (Strongbow) brought him both Chepstow and Pembroke, where he was able to demonstrate his outstanding gifts of originality and his ability to adapt and adopt.

In 1215 Llywelyn ap Iorwerth failed to take Haverfordwest, although Kidwelly, Carmarthen, Llansteffan, Laugharne and Cilgerran had all yielded to his onslaught. In 1220 the second of Llywelyn's attacks failed, although on this occasion he succeeded in burning all the town up to the gate of the castle itself. Almost two hundred years later, Marshall's stronghold resisted even the endeavours of Owain Glyndŵr and his considerable French supporters.

For all its resolute show of impregnability, it was in a distressed state by the sixteenth century, and like so many other castles which had been similarly demeaned, Haverfordwest was refurbished during the Civil War, during which the occupancy of the castle changed continually between the Royalists and Parliamentarians.

The walls and the south-west tower of the hall ranges, together with those of the chapel are impressive, even in their ruined state, and give a tantalising suggestion of the castle's former distinction.

In 1779 a gaol was built in the inner ward, but this was replaced in 1820 by similar provision in the outer ward. Having been afterwards the headquarters of the Pembrokeshire Constabulary, it became in 1963 a county record office, museum and art gallery. The adjacent building, once the prison governor's house, is now the town museum reflecting its rich history.

Hawarden, Penarlâg (Flintshire)
In centre of town, Open: occasionally in summer, Admission charge, Privately owned

The existing remains do not belong to the original strongholds. It is likely that when Hugh Lupus d'Avranches, earl of Chester, and nephew of William the Conqueror established a military base here, he was profiting from the defensive advantages of much earlier fortifications which commanded the slopes down to the river Dee and across the vast Cheshire Plain and beyond.

Mentioned as Crown property during the reign of King John, its frontier position made it particularly vulnerable to Welsh claims for repossession, and in 1265 it was destroyed by Llywelyn ap Gruffudd. It was only one gesture of assertion and defiance among many. In an attempt to assuage the grievances of his considerable adversary, Henry III acknowledged Llywelyn as Prince of Wales by the Treaty of Montgomery of 25th September 1267. It was a new title which carried with it certain conditions and obligations, including paying tribute and doing homage to the English king.

In that same year, with the confidence that his gesture of appeasement would bring an end to hostilities, the king restored the lordship of Hawarden to the de Mohaut (or Montalt) family, who owned the property that had been rendered unten-

Hawarden Castle

able by Llywelyn. The royal gift, however, carried with it one important condition: that no new castle should be built at Hawarden for thirty years. The king's will was clearly not honoured, for by 1282 a defensive structure of sufficient aggressiveness had been raised there to provoke another Welsh assault. The attacker on this occasion was not Llywelyn, but his brother Dafydd, one-time ally of Edward I.

From his castle of Caergwrle, referred to as Hope Castle in English records, he descended on Hawarden on Palm Sunday, capturing the English commander, Roger de Clifford, and killing the garrison. The raid inevitably led to the king's second Welsh campaign, a decision which precipitated the building of Conwy, Caernarfon and Harlech Castles in an attempt to quell the threat to his supremacy.

This sovereignty was further challenged in 1294 by the revolt of Madog ap Llywelyn and his attack on the crucially placed Hawarden. It was soon afterwards that the castle was refortified in stone, the ruins of which are still so impressive.

The principal remaining features are the round tower or keep on its mound of challenging height, and sections of walls, in particular a part-elevation of the great hall, with its two handsome windows. Various foundations and footings suggest that the castle did not observe a regular plan. Only the basement, which contained prisons and a cesspit, remains of a sturdy square tower and the defensive strength of the stronghold also lay in an intricate system of sally ports. Hawarden's crowning glory, however, is the round tower or keep, worthy of the inspiration of Master James of St George.

During the Owain Glyndŵr uprising, the Welsh supporters, many locally based, laid siege to Hawarden, but it was during the Civil War that the castle experienced its greatest hostility since medieval times. In 1643 the garrison of 120 Parliamentarians was besieged, only to surrender within a few weeks, when many of their number were taken to Wrexham where they were 'crewelly used by some Welshmen, who did beat and wound some of them, slew other some and tooke the . . . clothes from other some.' This was after they had been confronted by the Royalist commander with the threat that 'if you put me to the least trouble or loss of blood to force you, expect no quarter for man, woman or child.'

In 1653 the castle, which had been granted to Sir Thomas Stanley in 1453, was sold by Stanley's descendant, the earl of Derby to John Glynne, sergeant-in-law. Through inheritance, the neighbouring property, Broadlane Hall, also became the possession of the Glynne family. In the early 1800s it was extended and castellated and renamed Hawarden Castle in order to be consistent with its medieval backdrop, which became a grand eye-catcher, forming the focal point of pleasure gardens and wooded walks.

Through marriage, the property became the home of the Prime Minister, W.E. Gladstone, whose vast personal library forms the nucleus of St Deiniol's Library, founded by him as a centre for Christian learning, and housed in a handsome building of 1899, standing next to the parish church of the same name.

Hay Castle

Hay, Y Gelli (Powys)
In the town, Outside views only, Private ownership

Like those at Brecon and Builth, Hay (from *La Haie*, 'a hedge' or 'enclosure') town and castle are the result of Bernard de Neufmarché's seizure of Brycheiniog, which had been completed by 1110. Along with members of the de Braose family, he had direct control over the districts that were dependent on these first Norman timber strongholds. Hay, like the others, was rebuilt in stone, and in 1230 had major additions, including refortifying the gateway which survives to this day, with its portcullis groove.

The castle and the lordship of Brycheiniog became the property of the dukes of Buckingham in the fifteenth century. They had also acquired land in Gwent, including the castle of Caldicot, near Chepstow. It was this family which was responsible for the square tower near the gatehouse. Their name is also commemorated in Buckingham Place in Brecon. Three dukes of Buckingham came to a sad end (see Caldicot Castle).

The remains of the castle, together with the ruined seventeenth-century mansion which stands alongside it, form an elevated and attractive feature of this small border market town, whose thirteenth-century walls have for the most part disappeared. Nevertheless, as in so many medieval settlements, the spirit and awareness of a distant age gives Hay a recognisably different quality. Its chief attraction throughout the year is its reputation as a community of bookshops, a phenomenon which no doubt led to the Literary Festival held every spring, in the shade of the castle.

Holt (Denbighshire)

4.5m (7.2km) from Wrexham, via A534 towards Nantwich. Park in village. Open access, Admission free, Local Authority

Tantalisingly too little stands of this Edwardian castle for us to be able to discern its idiosyncratic lay-out – if an early seventeenth-century illustration is any indication. Its pentagonal shape was referred to by one surveyor as 'a five-sided square'. Set quite low in a quarry of red sandstone from which the stone was obtained, its close proximity to the river Dee, dividing Wales and England, and navigable as far as Holt, gave it considerable military clout, a rôle which in less stressful times was to be taken by the bridge which connected the settlement of Holt itself and English Farndon.

Edward I's victory over Llywelyn ap Gruffudd in 1282 and the death of Llywelyn's brother, Dafydd, a year later enabled him to divide much of his newly acquired property among his supporters, including the de Greys, the de Lacys and the de Warennes, who were now on a par with those families long established in the mid- and south Marches, names as resonant as Mortimer and Clare.

It was John de Warenne, earl of Surrey, who was granted the lands of Iâl and Bromfield, with its castle of Dinas Brân, built by Madog Prince of Powys in the 1270s. For reasons of accessibility and convenience, de Warenne chose Holt as his base and work on the castle started soon after 1282 and proceeded into the first decade of the next century. Because of the lion sculpture set above the gateway it was known as Chastellion or *Castrum Leonis.*

A survey of 1315 recorded the existence of 159 burgesses and about 200 other tenants. The original lay-out of the town is still discernible and, although the Black Death and the uprising of Owain Glyndŵr contributed much to its decline, John Leland between 1536–39 was able to write that 'Holt is a praty Walsche toune, governid by a maire, having ons a year a fair, but surely now no celebrate marked. In it a pretty church, and a goodly castel.' By 1620, according to John Norden, 'the goodly castel' was 'now in great decay', an impression not indicated by his drawing made at the same time.

Both the castle and bridge at Holt played a significant part during the Civil War, the latter then having a centrally placed gatehouse, further protected by a drawbridge and gates. Small though the castle might have appeared, it was capable of resisting a nine-month siege against the Parliamentarians, a record slightly surpassed by Harlech, before eventually yielding in 1646.

Given the originality of its plan and the sophistication of its defences, it is possible that the king's architect might have had a hand in its design, but any true appreciation of its quality must rest on archaeological analysis and surmise, since most of the stonework was removed from the site in order to build Eaton Hall between 1675–83 for Sir Thomas Grosvenor. Few castle sites in Wales have been left so bereft.

Kidwelly, Cydweli (Carmarthenshire)

10m (16km) S of Carmarthen, on A484. Castle signposted in town. Open: standard hours, Admission charge, Cadw

Like Laugharne and Llansteffan, Kidwelly is eminently accessible by sea, and its situation on the west bank of the Gwendraeth Fach was chosen with great military care, for it formed part of a girdle of coastal defences. The lay-out of the castle is often compared with a bow, and it is clear that the choice of the original fortress was determined by the steep slope which fell down to the river Gwendraeth and which offered valuable natural protection. Where the castle was more vulnerable to attack, a deep semi-circular ditch was built, thereby resulting in a basic plan which owed more to necessity than to any form of design.

The man responsible for it was Roger, Bishop of Salisbury, who had been granted the lordship of the south-west coastal plain by Henry I. It was he who also founded the Benedictine priory of St Mary, around which the first settlement of Kidwelly developed. All three were established soon after 1106. By 1139 the castle and lordship of Kidwelly had been granted to Maurice de Londres, whose family was responsible for the building of Ogmore Castle in Glamorgan.

Three years previously, Maurice de Londres had been involved in a battle nearby, when Gwenllian, the daughter of Gruffudd ap Cynan (c. 1055–1137) King of Gwynedd, and wife of Gruffudd ap Rhys, lord of Deheubarth, had led a small army and attempted to take the Norman settlement. Maurice defeated and killed her, and the site of the skirmish is called to this day Maes Gwenllian (Gwenllian's Field).

The castle was attacked on several occasions by the Welsh, and in 1159, during a concentrated raid on the south-west by Rhys ap Gruffudd (the Lord Rhys), Kidwelly, along with other castles and their towns, was burnt. In the ensuing years, the control of the castle changed hands between Anglo-Normans and the Welsh with varying lengths of tenure and tenacity, until 1231 when Llywelyn ap Iorwerth 'made Cydweli', along with Neath, 'level to the ground'.

In 1244, Hawise, the de Londres heiress, married Patrick de Chaworth, and it was his son, Payn, who was responsible for the next phase at Kidwelly. His was to be a major contribution, for he was well acquainted with the most recent developments of castle building, as he had recently returned from Edward I's crusade in the Holy Land, where they would have seen those fortifications which inspired the king himself, and which gave him and his master-builder, James of St George, so many of the ideas that went into the first two castles of Edward's first Welsh campaign: Flint and Rhuddlan, both raised in 1277.

Into Roger Salisbury's earthwork defences, Payn de Chaworth built a rectangular masonry structure, with massive towers at each corner, thereby creating an inner ward, which was entered by gateways to the north and south. This was

Kidwelly Castle

the initial stage in the formation of a concentric castle, whose strength and sophistication were to be perfected by its next owner, Henry, earl of Lancaster, to whom Kidwelly had come by marriage to Matilda de Chaworth. Soon after 1298, the transformation began: the castle was to reflect the elevated status of its new owner, resulting in the eastern range which consisted of a hall and a solar and, one of the most immediately identifiable of Kidwelly's features, the chapel tower with its spur buttresses. The semi-circular earlier defences which gave the castle its unique bow-like shape were walled with masonry, and the result was probably a unique castle plan: a semi-concentric castle.

This outer defence was reinforced by three semi-circular mural towers and a gateway on the north and south sides completed the plan. The twin-towered south gatehouse is a building of immense presence, its stature as symbolic as military. It was greatly restored by Henry IV and Henry V, following extensive damage done to Kidwelly during the Owain Glyndŵr uprising, when the castle was besieged by Henry Dwnn, aided by French reinforcements. Although the town fell, the castle itself resisted attack for three weeks.

On the ground floor of the gatehouse was the porter's lodge, on the left-hand side of the entry; on the opposite side was the prison. The floor above contained a chamber, with access to a wall-walk, a hall and a kitchen. The machinery for operating the portcullis, as well as access to the murder-holes, was located here, a rather less convenient arrangement than at Harlech, where such defensive mechanisms were placed in a non-domestic room, the chapel. The gatehouse was a completely self-contained defensive unit.

Sir Rhys ap Thomas, the ardent Tudor supporter who was knighted after the Battle of Bosworth in 1485, gleaned as part of Henry VII's acknowledgement of his allegiance, several honours and properties, including Kidwelly, to which he made substantial additions and improvements to increase the residential comforts and reflect his status. The larger hall built on the western wall of the outer ward is probably his work.

Kidwelly played little part in the Civil War and its state of preservation is outstanding. An appreciation of its unusual lay-out can be further heightened by a walk around the castle boundaries, and better still, from the opposite bank of the Gwendraeth Fach, from which the semi-hexagonal chapel tower makes a splendid impression.

The early fourteenth-century town gate still stands to remind us of the prestige of the early settlement.

Laugharne, Talacharn (Carmarthenshire)
In town centre 4m (6.4km) S of St Clears on A4066, Open:
standard hours, Admission charge, Cadw

The castle is built on a low cliff skirting the mouth of the river Taf (not to be confused with Taff), and commands a magnificent view of the 'heron-priested shore', to quote Dylan Thomas, who immortalised the small town, and found inspiration in the coastal character with its sloping richly-leaved backdrop, and its colourful inhabitants, for Llaregyb, the village that lies 'Under Milk Wood'. His description of the castle in another work is 'the castle, brown as owls' and he, then, would have had a view of this defensive structure denied to most other people, for until recently it was still private property, accessible only through the grounds of the handsome pink-washed Castle House. It was for years the home of Richard Hughes, the author of *High Wind in Jamaica* and *In Hazard*, who had found inspiration in that same expanse of water that had moved Dylan Thomas. To the early invaders it was an eminent place from which to lay their claims to recently conquered domains. It had considerable advantages: it was on an estuary, with easy access to Carmarthen Bay, and could be part of a defensive triumvirate, along with Llansteffan and Kidwelly.

In 1189, according to the *Brut*, 'the Lord Rhys gained possession of the castles of St Clears and Abercorram and Llansteffan'. All three castles were in the same line of defence, and it seems more than likely that Abercorram refers to Laugharne, since the early Norman stronghold was constructed on the side of the Coran, a tributary of the Taf. In 1215, the same three castles were destroyed by Llywelyn ap Iorwerth, with the support of the Welsh princes, between their destruction of Carmarthen and their siege of Cardigan. Laugharne, along with Llansteffan again, suffered a similar fate in 1257.

The first stronghold at Talacharn or Laugharne was nothing more than an enclosure surrounded by an earth bank, probably protected by a timber palisade. This basic plan hardly varied from one Norman foundation to another. It was elementary, but it made a powerful statement: possession. Such a mark of assurance could lead to substantial consolidation as the surrounding territory was brought under the control of the usurper.

At the time of the attack of 1257, Laugharne was in the possession of the de Brian family, and their descendants were to hold it until the late fourteenth century. It was a succession of Guy de Brians who were responsible for the transition of the earth-and-timber fortress, first by replacing the original stronghold with masonry, and then by introducing new standards of defence, and eventually higher standards of accommodation and comfort.

After the death of Guy de Brian VII in 1390, the castle underwent a period of semi-obscurity, and it was not until the threat of attack by Owain Glyndŵr's forces that it regained something of its former defensive efficiency, when Henry IV gave instructions that Laugharne should be refortified.

The next significant change is the result of substantial rebuilding and aggrandisement of the castle by Sir John Perrot, whose improvements at Carew are still eloquent testimony to his considerable architectural flair. Perrot's ambition overleaped itself and he was sentenced to death for high treason in 1592, though he died first of natural causes. With his end came another period in the decline of Laugharne, culminating in its final ignominy with its destruction after the Civil War.

In the 1970s Laugharne Castle came into the guardianship of Cadw. Twenty years of research work and sensitive conservation followed. This Norman fortress, with its subsequent additions and improvements, though considerably reduced by circumstances of all sorts, is now open to the public. A rose-garden, a gazebo with spectacular views, as well as exhibiting features of Richard Hughes's work, together with the very impressive defensive and domestic remains of the castle, give an eloquent indication of the history of Talacharn.

Llansteffan (Carmarthenshire)
8m (12.8km) SW of Carmarthen. On A40 W of Carmarthen, take B4312. Open access, Admission free, Cadw

Llansteffan takes precedence over both Laugharne and Kidwelly for its view, although all three were built on strategic positions commanding three estuaries flowing into Carmarthen Bay. Llansteffan is different in another respect also, as there was an Iron Age fort on the site, which might well have formed the basis for the Norman defences of the early twelfth century and which would have conformed to the motte-and-bailey plan, built by the Marmion family, from whom it descended to the de Camvilles.

In 1146, Cadell ap Gruffudd and his brothers Maredudd and

Llansteffan Castle

Rhys 'overcame the castle of Llansteffan in a severe struggle, after many of their enemies had been slain and others wounded'. The Rhys referred to was only thirteen at the time, and was to become the renowned 'Lord Rhys' whose rule over Deheubarth was to challenge the invasions of the Anglo-Normans with varying degrees of success until his death in 1197. It was Maredudd, the middle brother who distinguished himself at that incident, by hurling the scaling-ladders of the enemy into the ditch. Lost to the de Camville family in 1158, Llansteffan was regained by Lord Rhys. It was when the castle was repossessed by the de Camvilles in 1192 that they embarked on the defensive scheme which gave it those architectural characteristics which can be appreciated even in their debilitated state today. Five members of the family in turn controlled the castle up to the middle of the fourteenth century.

The most impressive architecturally-defensive feature at Llansteffan is the twin-towered Great Gatehouse, and its mechanisms are immediately discernible in the murder-holes and the grooves for the portcullis. It bears a striking resemblance to the East Gate of Caerphilly Castle and to the formidable gatehouse at Harlech. It was conceived as a self-contained unit, impressively challenging to any assailant, and yet offering a modicum of comfort for the family. In fact, it was adapted as a domestic residence in the Tudor period, by the walling up of its centralised access at both ends.

Even in its ruins, Llansteffan stands proud and majestic above the unspoilt village at its feet. As in so many castle sites in Wales, there is a dramatic contrast between the concentration of early landmarks of enmity and hostility and the subsequent somnolent domestic development nearby. Few places in Wales convey this dichotomy in such a striking way.

Llawhaden, Llanhuadain (Pembrokeshire)
7m (11.2km) E of Haverfordwest on A40, 3m NW of Narberth.
Open: standard hours, Admission charge, Cadw

Llawhaden is as peaceful a village as one can find, and the presence of such a splendid castle, which somehow seems to be regarded as just another, but much bigger, building at the end of a row of cottages, comes as rather a surprise. It was in fact more of a fortified residence than a fortress, although the reasons for its Norman origins were specifically defensive: to protect the rich estates of the bishops of St David's from the marauding and retaliating Welsh.

As with all such constructions of the period, it was a ringwork of earth-and-timber, and that is what Giraldus Cambrensis would have seen during his visit to Llawhaden in 1175 when, according to his own account, he was entertained by his uncle, Bishop David FitzGerald. The Lord Rhys gained possession of the fortress in 1192 and the following year it was destroyed.

When the castle was regained by the bishops of St David's in the early thirteenth century, its original lay-out was followed, this time with a stone circular wall which incorporated two

Llawhaden Castle

flanking towers, one circular and the other semi-circular, both of which survive.

Although considerable improvements were made in the late thirteenth and early fourteenth centuries by Bishops Thomas Bek and David Martyn, the major extensions were made in the late fourteenth century, the period of the building of the very imposing gatehouse. By this time the accommodation offered suites of apartments for visiting prelates and other dignitaries.

In the sixteenth century Llawhaden was abandoned, and the bishops of St David's moved to Abergwili, on the outskirts of Carmarthen, and still their official residence.

Nearby are the remains of a hospital founded by Bishop Bek in 1287. It administered to the sick and infirm under the authority of a prior until the sixteenth century.

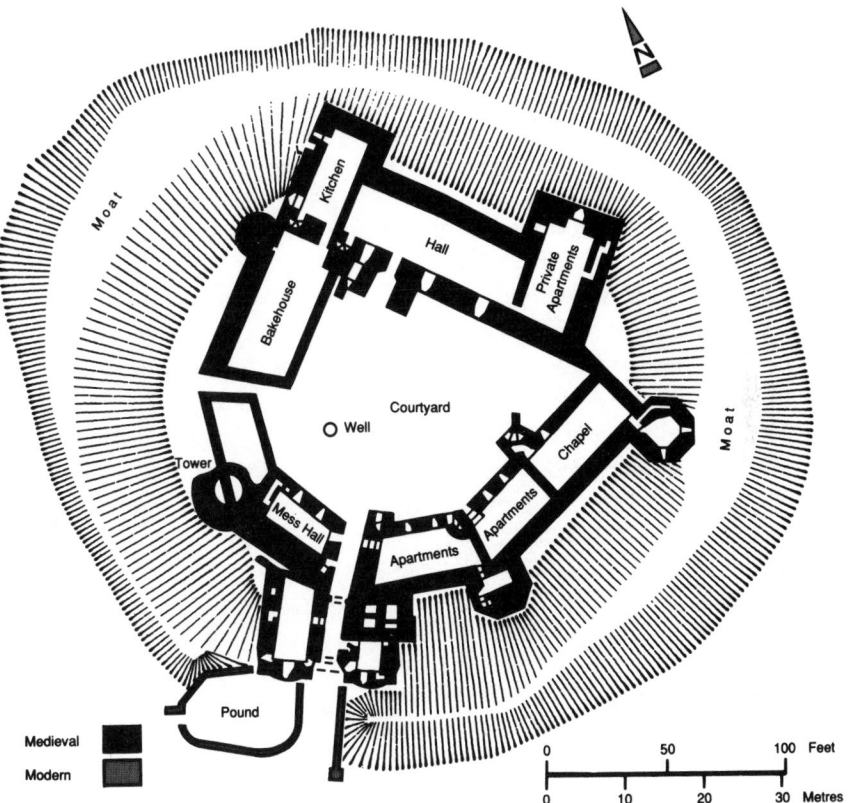

The plan of Llawhaden Castle

Loughor, Casllwchwr (Swansea)
On A484 Gorseinon to Llanelli. W side of Loughor, just before the bridge. Open access, Admission free, Local Authority

The origins of the castle, as its Welsh name, Casllwchwr suggests, go back to Roman times, and its placing on the narrowest point of the estuary of afon Llwchwr indicates that it guarded an important fordable crossing, which facilitated communications between the Roman fort at Cardiff, westwards through Neath (*Nidum*) and onwards to Carmarthen (*Maridunum*). The fact that there was a ferry here up until the nineteenth century and that both railway and road bridges cross at this point are further marks of its strategic significance. The Roman fort of Leucarum was the reason. The Normans took advantage of this Roman site, as they had done at Cardiff, and it was Henry Beaumont, or Henry de Newburgh, to use his other name, earl of Warwick, who had been granted the lordship of Gower (Gŵyr), and established a stronghold of earth and timber which was placed in the care of Newburgh's steward, Henry de Villers, who established the stronghold at Loughor soon after 1106.

Successive building gradually overlaid the Roman foundation. In 1151, Maredudd and Rhys, the sons of Gruffudd ap Rhys, laid siege to the castle of 'Aberllwchwr', as it was called in the *Brut*, and not only burnt it, but 'ravaged the land'. A further attack was made in 1215 when Rhys Ieuanc, or Rhys ap Gruffudd, made a concentrated onslaught on Oystermouth and Swansea as well. The lordship of Gower was in the firm grip of the de Braose family, and the ruins of a tower are the only remains of the medieval castle, which by then showed some indication of domestic comfort.

The importance of the site was recognised early in this century, but it was only after the Second World War, when a broader view was taken of the country's built heritage – whatever the state of disrepair – that Loughor Castle was taken into state guardianship. At that time the district was still heavily industrialised, for this was very much in the heartland of the tin-plate industry, so that the ruins of this once important castle were given scant attention, except from archaeologists and historians. Excavations undertaken between 1969–73 have aroused considerable interest, when the existence of the original Roman fort was revealed, thereby creating a far sharper awareness of the significance of the site, however faint the vestiges.

Manorbier (Pembrokeshire)
5m (8km) SW of Tensy, Open: sumer only, Admission free, Private ownership

The ubiquitous and omniscient Giraldus Cambrensis, or Gerald of Wales, or Gerallt Gymro, to whose wittily perceptive observations we owe so much of our knowledge of life in Wales in the late twelfth century, was justifiably proud of his birthplace,

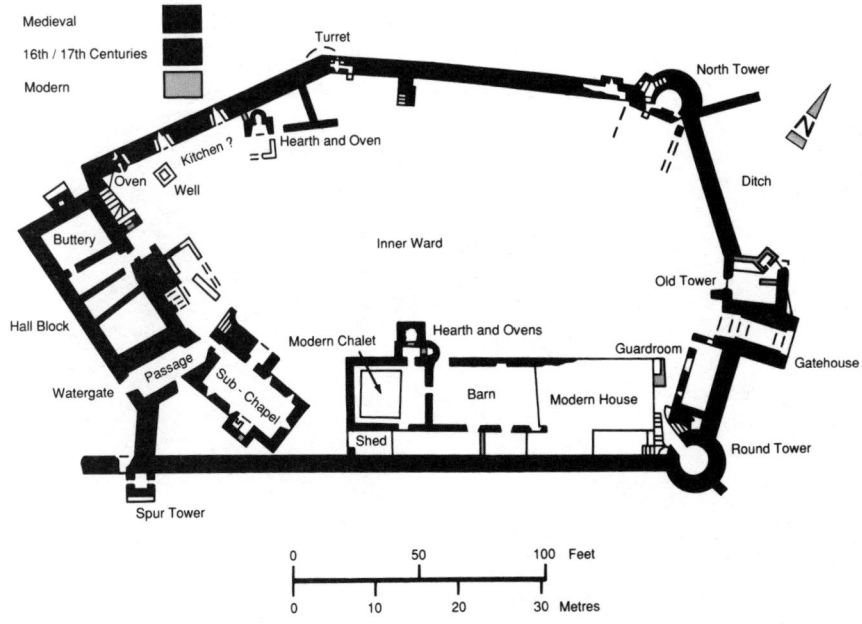

Manorbier, which he described as being 'excellently well defended by turrets and bulwarks, and is situated on the summit of a hill ... having on the north and south sides a fine fish pond ... a beautiful orchard ... enclosed on one part by a vineyard, and on the other by a wood ... the country is well supplied with corn, sea fish and imported wines ... It is evident that Maenor Pirr is the pleasantest spot in Wales.'

Visitors cannot but be taken by the pleasant and peaceful nature of 'the mansion of Pyrrus', and the lawns and flower beds, now such an attractive feature of the inner ward, give no indication of the original nature of the building or of the necessity for its construction.

The Norman Conquest of South-West Wales, as in other parts of the country, was achieved and later consolidated by strongholds which could control and subjugate wide areas surrounding such fortifications. One of the most aggressive was Pembroke Castle, under the control at the end of the eleventh century of Gerald of Windsor, whose wife was the daughter of

Manorbier Castle

Rhys ap Tewdwr, Prince of Deheubarth. She was Nest, often referred to as the 'Helen of Wales' because of her beauty. This, one of the most illustrious of Norman Welsh alliances was repeated in the next generation when their daughter Angharad married a William de Barri whose father held the lordship of Manorbier. Their son, Giraldus, described himself as 'sprung from the Princes of Wales and from the Barons of the Marches'. This must have been a difficult situation for his brothers, all of whom were fighting men, and as a priest, this dual allegiance would have caused no less concern to him. In his *Description of Wales* (1190) his stance is often ambivalent, suggesting on the one hand the most effective means for the Normans to overcome the Welsh, and on the other, advising the Welsh of the most successful way to resist such subjections. All in all, Gerald's emotional ties were far more strongly bound with Wales and the Welsh.

The de Barri family, which took its name from Barry in

South Glamorgan, was in possession of Manorbier until the mid-fourteenth century when it passed to Sir John Cornwall. In 1403 Henry IV, under constant threat of Owain Glyndŵr's uprising, gave orders for it to be fully refortified, but such preparations were never put to the test, and the history of the castle continued to be one of relative peace. Henry VII, who was born at nearby Pembroke Castle to Margaret Beaufort in 1457, granted Manorbier to his mother for life in the late fifteenth century. In the second part of the seventeenth century it was acquired by the Philipps family of Picton Castle, and it is a descendant who now lives in that part of Manorbier which was improved and modernised by J.R. Cobb, an avid castle enthusiast who applied his energy, money and expertise to substantial restoration work at Caldicot in Gwent and at Pembroke in Dyfed.

The inner ward is polygonal, but the chapel, built adjacent to the hall, thereby cutting off an angle, makes it into a hexagonal shape. Manorbier's charm lies in the fact that it is possible to see how buildings were modified and added to according to growing domestic needs, rather than to urgent military and defensive necessity. The inaccessibility of the castle also suggests that its occupants were not aware of the prevailing fashions of fortified buildings in more centrally placed – and therefore more assailable – regions.

Monmouth (Monmouthshire)
In the town, Open: standard hours, Admission free, Cadw

William FitzOsbern's castle at Monmouth, unlike his first foothold in Wales at Chepstow, was not built in stone. FitzOsbern's wooden stronghold of about 1070 brought in its wake soon afterwards the foundation of a borough, though given its situation so close to two rivers, the Monnow and Wye, the Romans would have previously had a fort nearby, possibly the one referred to as Blestium. The borough was entered from the west through the Monnow or Western Gate, the only remaining example of a fortified bridge in Britain dating from 1272. Judging by its menacing machicolations, one can assume that the successor to FitzOsbern's timber stronghold would not have been less aggressive.

The Great Tower of the twelfth century is the oldest surviving part of the stone castle at Monmouth. It was a hall-keep, and as such a direct relation to the structure at Chepstow which owed much to current trends in Normandy, and possibly borrowing ideas from William the Conqueror's own home in Falaise. The ground floor or basement level provided elementary defence, since it provided no access, and was barely lit, except for arrow slits. This principle of first-floor entry was to continue not only through the period of the rectangular keep in such castles as Usk, but in the far more sophisticated and militarily advanced cylindrical keep-tower, of which the one at Pembroke was the most formidable. An additional hall was built at right angles to the Great Tower by Edmund Crouchback, son of Henry III, on becoming earl of Lancaster.

Monmouth Castle was the birthplace in September 1387 of the boy known as Harry of Monmouth who was to succeed as Henry V, King of England and Lord of Ireland on 20th March 1413, aged twenty-five. He has represented throughout the ages a romantic aspect of British monarchy, mostly due to Shakespeare's depiction of him in *Henry IV* and *Henry V*. A lesser, but unforgettable rôle was played in that historical tableau by Fluellen, whose references to Monmouth are amusing and stringently patriotic, when, for example, he talks about the birthplaces of great men, and compares it to the Macedonia of Alexander the Great: 'There is a river in Macedon; and there is also moreover a river at Monmouth; it is called Wye at Monmouth ... but it is out of my brains what is the name of the other river ... but ... there is salmons in both.' At Agincourt, the Welsh 'did good service, wearing leeks in their Monmouth caps'.

Having changed hands three times during the Civil War, the castle was razed in 1647, and on the place where the tower had stood a handsome town house was built in 1673 by the marquis of Worcester, later to be the first duke of Beaufort. Great Castle House, as it is called, was the birthplace on the 2nd April 1684 of the future 2nd duke, 'for his mother the Marchioness of Worcester was ordered by his Grandfather Henry, later Duke of Beaufort, to lie in of him her first Child, in a house lately built within the Castle of Monmouth, near that Spot of Ground and Space of Air where our great Hero King Henry V was born.'

The first duke, having inherited the great estate of Badminton near Chipping Sodbury from his great-uncle, Viscount Somerset, enlarged the house in the grandest fashion, and the family forsook their properties in Wales in favour of Gloucestershire.

In 1875 this handsome house became the headquarters of the Royal Monmouthshire Royal Engineers (Militia) Supplementary Reserve. By the end of the nineteenth century the medieval castle had been put into state guardianship, and it is now the responsibility of Cadw. Sparse as the remains are, the site is far better maintained than it was in the 1770s when William Gilpin visited it and discovered that 'the palace of a king; and the birth-place of a mighty prince: is now converted into a yard for fatting ducks.'

Montgomery, Trefaldwyn (Powys)
Above the town, Open access, Admission free, Cadw

Montgomery owes its name to the builder, Roger of Montgomery, earl of Shrewsbury, whose birthplace was Sainte Foi de Montgommerie in Calvados. It was a motte-and-bailey stronghold started in 1071 which had achieved a sufficient state of completion to be recorded in the Domesday survey of 1088. Its carefully chosen site commanded a strategic crossing over the river Severn.

In the first years of the twelfth century the castle became the focal point of a new Marcher lordship governed by the de Boulers family, one of whom, Baldwin, gave the Welsh name to the settlement, Trefaldwyn. Llywelyn ap Iorwerth's attempt to claim the territory for himself was severely challenged by powerful English forces, led by the young Henry III. It was during the campaign in 1223, according to the chronicler Matthew Paris, that the sixteen-year-old king was shown 'a suitable spot for the erection of an impregnable castle'. This was about a mile (1.6km) away, and what gave the site its 'suitability' was not only the steepness, but the narrowness of the ridge. It must have borne a striking resemblance to Chepstow; in both cases, the structural development of the fortress was dictated by the nature of the terrain. Roger's castle was abandoned and became known as Hen Domen (Old Mound).

The man responsible for the new fortification was Hubert de Burgh who built the irregularly shaped inner ward which was entered by the Great Gatehouse tower, closing 'the entire southern end of the ward like the jaws of a magnet'. This was a particularly powerful structure, and clearly the work of someone who had had extensive military experience. In fact de Burgh had been accustomed to siege warfare in France, and was later able to apply many of the defensive building techniques he had witnessed abroad to British castle architecture. In this respect, he was very similar to William Marshall. The gatehouse was made up of four storeys, the ground floor consisting of a long centrally placed entrance passage, and the floors above occupying the width of the building. Because of its closeness to the curtain wall, as well as its challenging presence, attack from either side would have been almost impossible.

In 1231, Llywelyn ap Iorwerth 'burned the town of Baldwin's Castle' which had received its charter as a borough in 1227. The castle itself was still in the process of being enlarged and fortified when Henry III granted it to his son, the future Edward I, in 1254. The building of Dolforwyn Castle by Llywelyn ap Gruffudd less than five miles (8km) away, must have precipitated considerable development at Montgomery, to counteract the Welsh threat. This resulted in the building of a stone wall in which, according to Leland in the 1530s 'yet remayne broken towrets, of the whiche the whit toure is now the most notable'.

In the fourteenth century Montgomery became the property of the Mortimer family, associated with the great border fortress of Chirk. It was the second generation of Mortimers who were responsible for the last major additions to Montgomery. They reflected the increasing stability of the times, since the emphasis was placed on residential comfort and domestic efficiency, rather than on consideration of defence.

The most notable occupant of Montgomery Castle in later centuries was Rowland Lee, Bishop of Lichfield, who was made

President of the Council of Wales and the Marches in 1534, as Thomas Cromwell's principal agent in Wales. Leland described it at that time as 'late reedified'. Lord Herbert of Cherbury, whose family owned the castle, as indeed they continue to do, built a house in the middle ward on 1622. For all its grandeur – 'an elegant and noble pile, beautiful without and richly furnished within' – it was to be short-lived; it became a victim of indiscriminate destruction in 1649.

Montgomery, like Dolforwyn, occupies a majestic site. Unlike Llywelyn's, Baldwin's settlement has not only survived but is one of the most peaceful and beguiling small towns in Wales, with a striking town hall end-stopping a dignified Broad Street of Georgian red brick houses. St Nicholas church is rich in interest, with a canopied tomb of Richard Herbert and his wife. Their eight children, including Lord Herbert of Cherbury and George Herbert, the Metaphysical poet, appear behind them, paired in arcades. The town and castle of Montgomery provide a dramatic contrast.

Neath, Castell Nedd (Neath–Port Talbot)
Near town centre, External views only of scanty remains, Local Authority

The place takes its name from Nidum, an auxiliary fort built by the Romans in about 75 AD to guard the crossing of the river Nedd. The Normans, as they did in several other cases, raised their own castle nearby in 1130, the same year that its builder, Richard de Granville, founded the abbey of Neath.

In the second half of the twelfth century a second castle was built, this time on the opposite side of the river. Its builder, Robert, earl of Gloucester, showing a similar piety, founded the abbey at Margam. The reason for the existence of two Norman castles of the same period, one on the west bank, the other on the east bank of the Nedd has never been fully explained, but by 1207 de Granville's had been dismantled.

Robert, earl of Gloucester's stronghold was an earthwork defence, but an attack in 1231 when Llywelyn ap Iorwerth 'reduced Caerleon to ashes . . . and made the castles of Neath and Cydweli level with the ground' necessitated its rebuilding in stone, with curtain walls, incorporating two stone towers and a simple gatehouse on the site of the present one, which represents a further rebuilding in the fourteenth century, following an assault on the castle when it was in the hands of the infamous Hugh le Despenser. Only the fronts of the twin-towered gatehouse survive, but a great deal of cleaning and clearing by the Local Authority has made these few, but striking, remains an interesting focal point in an otherwise uninteresting urban scene.

Newcastle (Bridgend)
Near Bridgend town centre on A4063, Open access, Admission free

The view from the tower of St Illtyd's church is the best way to appreciate fully the compactness of Newcastle and its clifftop position. However, even on ground level, there is a great deal to admire in this little-known stronghold within walking distance of the centre of the medieval market town of Bridgend. The town developed on the ford of the river Ogmore (afon Ogwr) which this early Norman castle, established by Robert FitzHamon about 1100, was intended to guard. Although it is called Newcastle, there is some doubt about the existence of any older defence.

The curtain wall, when it does not hug the clifftop, is faceted, forming an almost circular courtyard castle, with two towers built into its south and west sides. The quality of the ashlar masonry and particularly the ornate Romanesque gateway, more characteristic of ecclesiastical decorative detail, are two of the outstanding features of Newcastle, which is outstanding also in the fact that it is a Norman castle that underwent no subsequent major structural changes. In 1217, it became property of the Turberville family, lords of Coity who, regarding Coity as their main residence, forsook the remarkable castle on the hilltop.

Newcastle Emlyn, Castell Newydd Emlyn (Carmarthenshire)
Just outside the town, 11m (17.6km) SE of Cardigan, Open access, Admission free, Local Authority

Although the remains of Newcastle Emlyn are scanty, it is obvious that it gained its defensiveness not from any elevated prominence, but from its low-lying position in a loop of the river Teifi, which makes an almost complete natural moat.

When, in 1240, Maredudd ap Rhys was granted half of the *cantref* of Emlyn by Henry III, he built a castle which was known as 'new' castle Emlyn. There is some disagreement as to which the 'old castle' might be, since both Cilgerran and the motte at Cenarth are contenders, though the former is the more likely. On the other hand, the name might be a plain statement of fact, rather than a comparison between two similar constructions.

Maredudd ap Rhys's stronghold is distinguished by the fact that it is a Welsh native castle built in stone, and is probably the first defensive building of that type in South and South-West Wales. Maredudd's son, Rhys, afterwards held the castle, and withstood several attacks from the English until, on his death at their hands, it was taken by the Crown, in whose possession it remained until 1349. It is to this period that the foundation of the town of Newcastle Emlyn is attributed. Although it was sufficiently threatening to be taken by Owain Glyndŵr in 1403, the castle had lost all semblance of military effectiveness by 1428.

In 1500 the castle came into the hands of Rhys ap Thomas, one of Henry Tudor's keenest supporters in his bid to gain the Crown from Richard III. Rhys, 'good father Ris', as Henry VII was to refer to him in later years, did at Newcastle Emlyn what he did at Carew; he transformed it into a residence which would reflect a new spirit of stability and optimism, thereby turning his back on those earlier considerations of defence, by looking outwards through wider windows at safer unthreatened territories. This castle's fate, as that of so many others throughout England and Wales, was the result not of the century-bridging feuds and skirmishes between Normans, Anglo-Normans, English and Welsh, but the concentrated hostility of the Civil War, where techniques of warfare were more sophisticated and devastating. It was as a result of such internecine enmity that the castle was 'plundered and ever since neglected', except by local people who enjoy the peaceful surroundings, without worrying too much about its turbulent past.

Newport, Casnewydd (Newport)
In the town centre, View from the road, Cadw

Newport, or what little remains of it, is probably the most visible of all the castles in Wales, since it stands between the railway bridge and the road bridge, with the gloomy waters of the river Usk and its mud banks at the feet of the gatehouse, the most substantial part of the fortress to have survived.

Its predecessor, a motte-and-bailey castle, built by Gilbert de Clare, stood on the top of Stow Hill, near the cathedral. The remains of that, too, were to be the victims of railway expansion, when they were buried as part of the excavation work necessary for creating the tunnel for Brunel's Great Western Railway in the 1840s. When de Clare died in the Battle of Bannockburn in 1314, the castle passed to his sister and her husband, Hugh d'Audele. At that time the castle was part of the lordship of Glamorgan, but when Newport was made the headquarters of the lordship of Wentloog, d'Audele decided to build a new castle which would be worthy of its independent status, though the precise dates of its construction are not known.

It suffered a severe attack during the Owain Glyndŵr uprising, and though the refortification might have been to make good the damage, in the main the fifteenth-century rebuilding was a show of pride and prestige by Humphrey Stafford, whose great-grandfather had acquired Newport through marriage. His inheritance brought him vast acres in South Wales, and his work at Newport must have started soon after his coming of age in 1424. Twenty years later he was created the 1st duke of Buckingham, by which time he had developed the castle into a residence worthy of his rank. After the death of the 3rd duke, who was beheaded during the reign of Henry VIII in 1521, the castle went into a period of disuse from which it never re-

covered, and its state of dereliction is poignantly depicted by
J.M.W. Turner. Unlike so many other castles in Wales which
knew medieval battle and bloodshed, but which are now surrounded by pastoral peace and bucolic tranquillity, Newport,
which experienced no such military action, since its function
was principally administrative, is now engulfed by the ceaseless
turbulence of urban transport.

Ogmore, Ogwr (Vale of Glamorgan)

*B4524 Ewenny to Ogmore-by-Sea road. Castle signposted 1m
(1.6km) W of Ewenny. Open: standard hours, Admission free,
Cadw*

To enjoy Ogmore fully, one should approach it from the west
bank of the tidal afon Ewenni – after visiting Candleston Castle,
perhaps – so that by negotiating the stepping-stones of the
river, one can fully appreciate William de Londres' strategy in
constructing his fortress here in the early twelfth century when,
as one of Robert FitzHamon's supporters, he was forging his
way westwards in the Norman attempt to overcome the Welsh.
Like most defensive systems of the period, when time was short
and territorial control was vital, it was an earth-and-timber
structure, probably of two wards, the inner surrounded by a
ditch, so that when there was high tide, there was safety from
attack. Like all such 'emergency' strongholds, Ogmore was soon
given a more solid structure, in the form of an early twelfth-
century rectangular keep built on the left of the entrance to the
inner ward. It represented the first phase of the stone castle,
and was a first-floor entry building, with access to the ground
floor by means of a trap door from the first floor which served
as the hall, and therefore the main living accommodation of
the castle. The social prestige as well as the domestic importance
of the room is indicated by the remains of two semi-circular-
headed windows and a hooded fireplace. This was the work of
William de Londres' son, Maurice, whose tombstone can be
seen at Ewenny priory, which he founded as a Benedictine
community for a prior and twelve monks in about 1141.
Belonging to later in the twelfth century is the so-named

Ogmore Castle

cellar, standing opposite the keep on the side of the inner ward, and not linked up with any other building. This may be the basement of an important part of the castle's defensive plan, but its function has yet to be discovered.

The third phase of Ogmore belongs to the early thirteenth century, and is represented by the faceted curtain wall, which bears a resemblance to that at nearby Coity and Newcastle, and at the keep in Cardiff Castle. The gateway, which is of the same period, is adjacent to the keep. This is a surprisingly simple and unmenacing entrance, showing no indications of a portcullis, or other similarly challenging and protective devices. The hall was built into the north and east facets of the curtain wall, leaving its other two sides to face the ward.

By the late thirteenth century Ogmore passed by marriage to the de Chaworth family, but their time and energies were absorbed by the demands of the castle at Kidwelly which had come into their possession by the same marriage, since the de Londres family had control of that castle as well. Ogmore, as a result, lost its status as a principal residence and became an auxiliary, if not an ancillary, consideration, functioning as an administrative centre and overseeing its considerable feudal responsibilities. The manorial buildings, including the court-house which survived until the mid-seventeenth century, were placed in the outer ward.

A visit to Ogmore is an experience which gives the visitor a feeling of great tranquillity. Parking on the bank of the river, crossing the stepping-stones, hearing children's voices echoing among the walls, the prospect of a farm-house tea nearby, are all part of the pleasures of castle-going, and at such variance with the reason for their construction – and destruction.

Oxwich (Swansea)
Beyond village of Nicholaston on A4118, take minor road S at gates to Penrice Castle (not open). Castle signposted in Oxwich. Open access, Admission free, Cadw

Like Weobley (Swansea), Beaupré (South Glamorgan) and Tretower Court (Powys) Oxwich is more of a courtyard house than an out-and-out defensive building. As such it is an assertive statement of pride of possession, enhanced by its wonderfully commanding views over Oxwich Bay. The 'castle' which stands today is the second structure on the site, though nothing remains of its predecessor. Oxwich was the property of Sir Rhys (or Rice) Mansel whose family name embodies a great deal of the history of Glamorgan; he himself displayed considerable administrative, diplomatic and military skills. He was attuned to current trends in domestic architecture and decorative devices and the gatehouse, bearing his coat-of-arms, and the range to the right of the entrance represent his building programme between 1520–38. He also applied himself with gusto to structural improvements at Beaupré, in which he had a life interest through marriage, and to domesticising Margam abbey which he bought after the Dissolution of the Monasteries. It was Margam which he eventually chose as his country seat, and Oxwich became the property of Sir Rhys's son, Sir Edward, who was responsible for the very lofty east range which even in its ruined state exudes the spirit of the Renaissance and the aspirations of its builder. Two of its principal features were a two-storey hall, and a long gallery on the floor above it.

Only the footings remain of the porch which accommodated

the stairway leading to the first-floor entry into the imposing statement of wordly ambition, sharpened, no doubt, by his marriage to Jane Somerset, the daughter of Henry, 2nd earl of Worcester who was busily embellishing his castle at Raglan.

Within fifty years of its completion, Oxwich was leased, and the building went into a gradual decline, while the earlier and more manageable south wing, the work of Sir Rhys, became a farmhouse.

The self-importance of the Mansel family is splendidly exemplified by the group of sixteenth- and seventeenth-century tombs in the south aisle of the abbey church of St Mary, adjacent to Margam 'Castle', in West Glamorgan.

Oystermouth (Swansea)

In village of Oystermouth, W of Swansea, Open: standard hours, Admission charge, Local Authority

Few castles in Wales can rival Oystermouth for its extensive marine views, and for the remarkable state of its preservation, since almost the entire castle stands to its original height. The first name to be associated with it was William de Londres, the builder of Ogmore Castle, whose son, Maurice, was the founder of the church at Oystermouth. The man responsible for the reinforcing of the castle was Henry de Beaumont (or Henry de Newburgh, to give him his other name), earl of Warwick, who had been granted Gower by Henry I soon after 1106. In 1116 Gruffudd ap Rhys 'sent his comrades to make an attack and a raid upon a castle that was situated near Swansea. And that belonged to an earl called Henry Beaumont. And after burning the outer castle and after the keepers had saved the tower and some of his men had been killed, he turned back again.' In the other onslaught on the castle, this time in 1215, it is mentioned by name in the *Chronicle of the Welsh Princes*. On this occasion the attacker was Rhys Ieuanc who 'made for the castle of Oystermouth, and he encamped around it that night. And on the following morning he took the castle, and he burned it to the ground.' By the thirteenth century, the de Braoses had become lords of Gower and, as such, held the castles of Swansea and Oystermouth, both of which they rebuilt in stone, though they were eventually to adopt Oystermouth as their principal domain.

The destruction of the towers which flanked the castle entrance might have been the result of post-Civil War dismantling, but even so, this main gateway has retained much of its challenging power. The walls to the east are uncompromisingly grim, and it is only at the furthest north point that this unyielding aspect relents and, on the third level, presents the castle's greatest prize, the fine tracery of the east window of the chapel. This belongs to a fourteenth-century addition to the castle, held at that time by the de Mowbray family. It is the largest of the four windows that light the chapel on the highest storey which, although it blends in with the earlier construction, represents a completely different attitude towards residential arrangement and the need for comfort and convenience. Both phases of the castle have their interest, and represent two levels of degree rather than of kind.

Given the remarkable situation of Oystermouth, one can understand why the de Braoses preferred it to the estuary-bound Swansea. In the nineteenth century Swansea Bay, which Oystermouth commands in an imperious way, was compared to the Bay of Naples. Whether one knows that part of the Italian coastline or not in no way detracts from one's appreciation of Oystermouth – for its visual pleasure, rather than for a liking for shellfish. Although oyster beds were known in this area in Roman times, and flourished here up until the nineteenth century, the name of the place has nothing to do with the sea at all, but with a precise description of the setting: *Ystum* (bend) + *llwyn* (grove) + *arth* (hill), giving Ystumllwynarth. Knowing the Englishman's complete inability to cope with other languages, this eventually became Stumarth, which through a process of 'rationalising', became Oystermouth – and delightfully appropriate.

Like so many castles in Wales, this is the setting of *son-et-lumière* entertainments. Few offer a better backcloth.

Pembroke (Pembrokeshire)
In town centre, Open: standard hours, Admission charge, Local trust

John Leland in the 1530s wrote that 'Penbroke standith upon an arme at Milford, the wich about a mile beyond the towne creketh in that so that it almost peninsulatith the toune that standith on a veri maine rokki ground.' His description could not be bettered. At one end of the town lies the West Gate and the castle, and the East Gate lies the length of the town away. The river provided a natural defence on the north side, and a steep escarpment protected the south. The thoroughfare running along the spine was called Main Street, with burgage plots on either side. It is clear why the Elizabethan historian of Pembrokeshire, George Owen, wrote that Pembroke was a town 'without any cross streets'.

It was Roger of Montgomery, earl of Shrewsbury who was responsible for the Norman infiltration of South-West Wales and in 1093, his son Arnulf was granted Pembroke where his 'slender fortress of stakes and turf' was built. This was put in the custody of Gerald of Windsor who 'deposited all his riches, his wife and family and fortified it with a ditch and wall and a gate with a lock on it'.

In 1096, so tradition has it, Cadwgan ap Bleddyn besieged Pembroke and Gerald, in order to deceive the Welsh forces into believing that the stronghold had stocks of food, ordered that the last remaining four hogs should be cut up and thrown from the castle walls in a show of prodigality, although the garrison, in fact, was at starvation point. The ruse was successful, and Cadwgan and his men, convinced that Gerald could hold out indefinitely, abandoned their plan of attack.

In 1138 the earldom of Pembroke was created by King Stephen and conferred on Gilbert de Clare who started to refortify the castle without delay. The building scheme was carried on by his son Richard Strongbow who, as someone who played a significant part in the conquest of Ireland, used Pembroke as his base during the Irish campaigns. With the marriage of his daughter to William Marshall in 1189, the castle passed into the hands of a remarkable family whose fervour for castle build-

Pembroke Castle

ing was to transform the shape, size and outline of more than
one Norman stronghold in South Wales. William's earlier military career abroad had given him ample opportunity to examine
current defensive trends in many of the places he visited, and
he was able to adapt them and probably improve on them when
the need came for him to start on his own building programme.

His major contribution to Pembroke was the monumental
circular keep which dominates not only the castle but the entire

Pembroke Castle by John 'Warwick' Smith

town and the surrounding countryside. What Marshall did was to turn his back on the usual rectangular keep and supplant it with a cylindrical version. His structure was 72ft in height and contained four floors, each consisting of two rooms. A spiral stair connected each floor and led to the battlements. There are indications of the supports for the hoard or hoarding, a wooden gallery protected in front with boarding, which was thrown out from the surface of the wall so that, in times of attack, the platform became a further defence. An external staircase reached the first floor where the original door was sited. The entire structure was roofed with a dome, and the building in its totality represents an extraordinary achievement in military design for such an early date, 1200, since it is one of the few examples of an innovation which was superseded by the principle of the strong curtain wall and projecting angle towers. It occupied a vast area of the inner ward which also included William Marshall's hall and private apartments.

After the Marshalls, Pembroke was occupied by William de Valence who was responsible for the outer defences with their six towers and the handsome gatehouse. In 1456, Jasper Tudor, as earl of Pembroke, entertained his sister-in-law, Margaret Beaufort, while her husband Edmund, earl of Richmond, was fighting for the Lancastrian cause in the neighbouring county, where he died a prisoner at Carmarthen Castle, leaving a fifteen-year-old widow. Three months later, in January 1457, she gave birth to Henry Tudor, the future Henry VII, in the tower which has borne his name since the sixteenth century.

The boy was brought up by his uncle until the age of fourteen. By now the hostility between the Yorkists and Lancastrians was at its height, and the young Henry's slight claim to the throne, through Margaret Beaufort, put him in great danger. He fled to Brittany where he stayed for another fourteen years before returning to Wales in 1485 and, with keen supporters, started on his campaign against Richard III which ended victoriously on Bosworth Field.

Although Pembroke was the chief stronghold of the Parliamentary forces in West Wales from 1642−47, in 1648, its governor declared for the king. The ensuing siege, directed by Cromwell himself, lasted forty-eight days and resulted in substantial damage. The castle was partly restored by J.R. Cobb in the 1880s.

Penhow (Monmouthshire)

7m (11.2km) from the Old Severn Bridge. Midway between Newport and Chepstow on the A48. Open: standard hours, Admission charge, Stephen Weeks

Penhow more than any castle in Wales exemplifies contemporary adventure, boldness, courage, determination, energy . . . one could find a quality for each letter of the alphabet which would in some way describe the enormous efforts that have gone into the presentation of this medieval stronghold, since it was bought in 1973 by a twenty-four-year-old film-maker. He was in no way deterred by the formidable task of restoring this minor border castle to a state of repair that would adequately impart its regional and period importance. He did far more than that: through extraordinary interpretative as well as entrepreneurial skills, he succeeded in bringing the medieval world into the immediate understanding and appreciation of a wide range of people, and particularly schoolchildren, for whom there are comprehensive educational tours.

This part of South Wales was earliest to come under Norman rule and with the building of William FitzOsbern, earl of Hereford's massive statement of power at Chepstow, a number of other castles appeared in order to widen the area of possession – the substantial stronghold at Caldicot, a few miles away was one of these – and to form look-out posts, such as the much smaller Penhow. This would at that time have been in the form of a tower, probably not unlike the later peel towers that were raised in such profusion on the English and Scottish border. Its basic defensiveness would have been greatly increased by its prominent situation on a knoll, which would explain its name, half-Welsh and half English, meaning the top of the hill.

The first Norman occupant came from a village on the Loire, called St Maur, which became included in his surname, as was the case with so many of his compatriots. Sir Roger de St Maur might well have been the first of that name at Penhow; it is certain that he was there in 1129 when he witnessed the charter that founded the priory of Monmouth. Judicious marriages led to the integration of subsequent generations of the St Maurs with some of the most powerful and influential families. The name was eventually modified to Seymour, immortalised by Jane Seymour, one of Henry VIII's wives, whose brother Edward became the 1st duke of Somerset. The male line of the Seymours had come to an end by the end of the fourteenth century and the heiress married a John Bowles, whose descendants lived at Penhow for several generations. In the late seventeenth century, the castle, by now a dwelling house, was further improved, but by the beginning of the eighteenth century it had ceased to be a country seat, and became a tenanted farmhouse until 1966 when it was purchased by a man whose efforts to restore Penhow were thwarted by ill health, and he was forced to sell the property. It was bought by Stephen Weeks.

Only someone of his flair and tireless energy could have achieved what the last quarter of a century represents at the castle. The three main phases of the place's history and evolution from early fortification to country house are excitingly demonstrated by furniture, artefacts, decoration and lighting, from the drawbridge to the great hall and the keep room, and through to the grand comfort of the seventeenth-century improvements. It is a journey that gives not only fascinating glimpses of military ruses and tactics, and later concerns in domestic convenience and display, but also an insight into the imaginative and visual gifts of the man who managed to bring an early Norman tower with its accretions and additions to dramatic life.

Pennard (Swansea)
B4436 to Pennard, then minor road to Southgate, Open access, Admission free, Pennard Golf Club

Pennard Castle occupies one of the most beautiful sites in Wales, with extensive views over Three Cliffs Bay and Penmaen Burrows. It was established by Henry de Beaumont, the 1st earl of Warwick, when he was granted the lordship of Gower by Henry I in 1106. His stronghold took the form of a ringwork with a surrounding bank, further protected by a ditch. Excavations in the 1960s brought to light evidence of a twelfth-century domestic range, including a hall, with a central hearth. The basic outline of the ringwork was followed by a refortification of Pennard in masonry either late in the thirteenth or early in the fourteenth century, when it was held by the de Braoses. The curtain wall was protected on the north-west angle by a semi-circular turret, and a large western tower was added outside the west curtain wall and built on to a rock which had not been a part of the original defences. The south tower of the gatehouse stands almost to its full height, and much of the curtain wall to the north has survived to its battlements. Approaching the castle from the north is the recommended route, by passing through the golf course, but climbing to it from the south gives a graphic idea why, for all the impressiveness of its defensive site, the stronghold succumbed not to man's weapons of attack, but to sand.

Penrhyn Castle

Penrhyn (Gwynedd)
1m (1.6km) E of Bangor on A5122, Open: standard hours,
Admission charge, National Trust

The builder of Penrhyn Castle must have thought he was
Edward I – at *least*. Presumably he would have allied himself
more closely with the Norman usurpers, judging by the architectural and decorative style which George Hay Dawkins Pennant
chose for the property which had come his way through inheritance in the early 1820s. A megalomaniac aggrandisement was
instituted which gradually overcame the Gothic villa, designed
by Samuel Wyatt in the 1780s, and which in its turn had sub-
stantially modernised the medieval building, the home of
Gwilym ap Gruffudd, whose fortified manor house reflected his
considerable status in Gwynedd, as a descendant of Ednyfed
Fychan, a seneschal to Llywelyn ap Iorwerth.

The principal feature of Gwilym's Penrhyn was its tower, which was, according to the fifteenth-century poet, Rhys Goch Eryri (*fl.* 1385–1448), comparable to the Eagle Tower of Caernarfon Castle, an exaggeration which was a literary device characteristic of poets to the medieval gentry. Gwilym's first wife was a Tudor, of Penmynydd in Anglesey, later renowned as the home of the ancestors of the royal Tudor dynasty. After her death, his marriage to Joan, the daughter of Sir William Stanley of Horton in Cheshire, connected him with one of the most powerful families of the north-west and established a continuity of influence and prestige. It was not until the early eighteenth century that the Penrhyn estate lost hold of its integrity and connection with Gwynedd, and was sold to John and Henry Pennant, sons of Edward Pennant of Clarendon, Jamaica.

In the 1810s Richard Fenton, during his tours in Wales undertaken between 1804–13, described his visit to Penrhyn in these words: 'Out of the Hall you ascend the old Tower by a Corkscrew staircase of stone, from the Top of which you have a delightful prospect. There is, Lady Penrhyn told me, an authority under the Great Seal ... for the then Proprietor to build that Tower, or rather to give the House a castellated form, for no man could crenell his house without the royal permission.'

Thomas Pennant, the naturalist and antiquary (1726–98), also makes reference to the crenellated character of his distant kinsman's house: 'the hall is preserved and finished in a plain but beautiful manner; and the front is made uniform by the addition of another tower. The top is embattled.'

These were the improvements made to the medieval house by Samuel Wyatt for Richard Pennant (1739–1808) who brought about enormous improvements to the Penrhyn estate, not only by his agricultural innovations, but by his entrepreneurial skills in developing the industry which the natural resources of his acres possessed in abundance – slate.

Penrhyn Castle, as conceived, erected and furnished by George Hay Dawkins, had therefore a long and distinguished Welsh ancestry, allied through marriage with a great deal of English wealth, much of which came from Jamaican sugar plantations, the property of Richard Pennant, and inherited from his father. These considerable means were augmented by rich pickings from the Slave Trade, and by Richard's own exploitation of the slate quarries of Nantffrancon, which were, along with those of neighbouring Dinorwig, the largest in the world, and frightening in their aspect and impact.

The Reverend William Bingley's account of his visit in the early 1800s conveys something of the awesome nature of the site: 'Here I found several immense openings . . . as rude as imagination can paint, that had been formed in getting the slate. On first surveying them, a degree of surprise is excited, how such yawning chasms could have been formed by any but the immediate operations of Nature.' The scene which seemed so spectacular to Bingley bore no relation to the crippling toll that it exacted from the quarrymen. Pennant's wealth, already based on Sugar and Slaves, was further augmented by Slate, which was to yield the greatest fortune, one which eventually passed to his great-nephew, George Hay Dawkins, who added the name Pennant in 1808, when this vast inheritance came his way. It was not until 1820 that he commissioned Thomas Hopper (1776–1856), a particularly versatile architect who could turn his style to satisfy the most demanding of his clients' whims. For a man of fifty-six this was an act of considerable optimism; he must have realised that the completion of such an enterprise would not be achieved until he was in his seventies. In fact, work at Penrhyn was eventually finished in 1844. Dawkins Pennant had died four years previously.

Before Hopper undertook his commission at Penrhyn, he had already had experience of the Norman Revival style in his work for the 2nd earl of Gosford at Gosford Castle, in Co. Armagh. By the time it had been completed, Penrhyn represented the apogee of castellated domestic architecture in Wales. Such commanding presence did little to convince the German Prince Pückler-Muskau, who on being told during his visit in the late 1820s that the inspiration behind Penrhyn was the Norman castle at Rochester, remarked that 'What could then be accomplished by a mighty monarch, is now executed, as a plaything – only with increased size, magnificence and expense – by a simple country gentleman, whose father very likely sold cheeses. So do times change!' Little did he know!

Dawkins Pennant was succeeded by his son-in-law, Edward Gordon Douglas (1800–86) who took the name of Pennant. He was M.P. for Caernarfonshire before being raised to the peerage in 1866, assuming the title Baron Penrhyn of Llandegai. His son, George Sholto, the 2nd Lord Penrhyn, for all his wide academic and intellectual interests had little knowledge of people. His ignominious treatment of the slate quarrymen created an irreconcilable rift between 'the rich man in his castle / the poor man at his gate' which the Normanesque sternness of the gateway to Penrhyn, built for his ancestor earlier in the century, exemplified all too effectively. The lock-out strikes of 1897 and 1900 will always represent the worst aspects of landowning management, rarely, if ever, paralleled in other great estates which yielded such enormous wealth so selectively distributed. It is little wonder that it has been interpreted as a nineteenth-century form of Edwardian aggression.

In 1951, Lady Janet Harper, née Pelham, the grand-daughter of the 3rd Baron Penrhyn, whose mother had married the 6th earl of Yarborough, inherited vast estates in North Wales from her mother's brother, the 4th Baron Penrhyn. Lady Janet, assuming the name Douglas Pennant, made over the castle and much of its contents in lieu of death duties to H.M. Treasury, which transferred them to the National Trust. It was the first major built property to be conveyed to the National Trust, followed in 1952 by Powis Castle.

Nobody visiting Penrhyn can come away from this 'stately, massive and stupendous creation' in a state of indifference. The response over the years has been one of either amazement or revulsion. As the years go by, irrespective of their interests and political commitments, visitors will regard this gargantuan creation with awe and admiration. It is the world of Citizen Kane. Had Penrhyn been on the market at the relevant time, William Randolph Hearst would surely have chosen Hopper's grandiloquent display of virtuosity in Gwynedd, rather than St Donat's Castle in Glamorgan, and not only for its cyclopean dimensions, but for its healthily lengthy ancestry.

Through a series of legal wranglings, part of the Penrhyn estate, though not the house itself, eventually became the property of John Williams, Lord Keeper of the Great Seal, and later

Archbishop of York, whose monument rests in the church of Llandegai, and whose ancestors were a branch of the Gruffudd family. Their seat, Cochwillan, barely two miles away, is one of the best surviving examples of a medieval hall house in the whole of Wales.

As slate was the major source of the wealth which created this leviathan, Penrhyn is virtually an advertisement for this material which was essential in providing roofing material for the proliferation of houses built for the frenetic needs of the Industrial Revolution, not only in Wales, but in the relentlessly expanding streets of Liverpool and Manchester, to mention only two of the contributors to the extraordinary force that transformed the face of the British Isles. With the expansion of a new social class, and the provision of a skeletal educational structure for the ensuing generation, Penrhyn's product also became an essential material for writing-slates and blackboards. The increasing popularity of billiards in working men's clubs and institutes further increased the sales of slate, essential for the even surfaces of the tables.

At Penrhyn as is only fitting, the entire billiards table is made of slate. There is also the famous slate bed, weighing well over a ton, probably carved by a monumental mason, more customarily engaged in fashioning and decorating the slate gravestones of Gwynedd. At one time, and very appropriately, there used to hang in the slate bedroom, Henry Hawkins' awesome depiction of *The Penrhyn Slate Quarry* in the early 1830s.

It was about this time that the thirteen-year-old Princess Victoria, only a few years later to become Queen, wrote vividly about her visit to the scene:

> It was very curious to see the men split the slate, and others cut it while others hung suspended by ropes and cut the slate; others again drove wedges into a piece of rock and in that manner would split off a block. The little carts about a dozen at a time rolled down a railway by themselves.

The splitting referred to was divided, according to size, into categories called Queens, Empresses, Duchesses, Countesses and Ladies. What irony, when one considers that an average of 150 men were wounded, and seven or eight killed every year, in order to extract such precision of size.

Hawkins' picture was moved from the slate bedroom to the passage from the breakfast room during a major rehanging of the pictures in 1990, so that the distinguished collection of Old Masters, acquired by Edward Douglas-Pennant (1800–86) the 1st Baron Penrhyn of Llandegai, could be seen to the best possible advantage.

Penrhyn is recognised for miles around by its keep, inspired reputedly by that of the castle of Rochester, the town where Thomas Hopper was born. The resemblance between Rochester and Hedingham, in Essex, is pronounced, and both could have been fused into Hopper's landmark. The views from the castle are expansive and spectacular, encompassing the Menai Strait and Beaumaris, and the formidable Snowdonia range. But prominent in another way are the deep cuts into the nearer hills of Cae Braich y Cefn, which made such an impact that Prince Pückler-Muskau was moved to record his impressions:

I reached the fearfully magnificent scene of operations. It was like a subterranean world! Above the blasted walls of slate, smooth as a mirror and several hundred feet high, scarcely enough of the blue heaven was visible to enable me to distinguish mid-day from twilight . . . The perpendicular sides were hung with men, who look like dark birds, striking the rock with their long picks, and throwing down masses of slate which fell with a sharp and clattering sound.

Today the scene is one of scars and silence.

As early as 1845, that is very soon after the house was completed, Louisa Costello in *The Falls, Lakes and Mountains of North Wales*, remarked that 'To wander through the wondrous halls of Penrhyn is like struggling along in a bewildered dream occasioned by having studied some elaborate work on the early buildings of the Saxons and Normans.' Today visitors are bewildered by the *reality* of such elaborate work, mostly associated with the extravagances of a fictional world created at

inordinate expense by great moguls of the film industry. Whatever the motives of its builder, or the ancestry of the style that
the architect chose to execute his client's wishes, Penrhyn is a
unique edifice, etched firmly into the memories of everyone who
has visited it.

Picton (Pembrokeshire)

*Off A40 between Canaston Bridge and Haverfordwest, at the Rhos,
Open: July–September, Sunday & Thursday afternoons, Admission
charge, Picton Castle Trust*

The original earth-and-timber Norman stronghold belonging
to William de Picton stood to the east of the present castle which
was built between 1295–1308 by Sir John Wogan, justiciar of
Ireland, and described in 1302 as 'lord of Pykton'. Along with
Chirk, Penhow and Powis, Picton has long maintained its claim
to have been uninterruptedly inhabited since the Middle Ages,
and during the last 500 years it has been the property of one
family only. The male line came to an end with the death early
in the fifteenth century of another John Wogan, whose daughter
married Owain Dwnn of Kidwelly. In 1491 their grand-daughter
became the wife of Thomas ap Philip of Cilsant, a prosperous
West Wales landowner, and the castle has remained in the
hands of that family who later adopted the surname Philipps,
with its idiosyncratic spelling.

During the Owain Glyndŵr uprising, Picton was captured
by French mercenaries who had landed at Milford in support
of the Welsh cause, and the castle saw further action in the
Civil War, when it changed hands twice during 1645, submitting
first to the Royalists in April, and then, after a three-week siege,
to the Parliamentarians in September.

The Philipps family were renowned throughout the seventeenth and eighteenth centuries for their political and social
involvement not only in Pembrokeshire, but in the whole of
West Wales. One of them, Sir John Philipps was a pioneer in
charity education, and was a founding member of the Society
for Promoting Christian Knowledge.

Picton reputedly bears a resemblance to a group of Irish

thirteenth-century castles, including Carlow and Ferns. It is unusual in that it has no courtyard, but consists of a rectangular block with two drum towers on each of the long sides; one of the short sides has two towers but placed so closely together that they resemble a gatehouse. The singular drum tower on the west side was removed in the early nineteenth century and a large castellated four-storey addition was made.

A great deal of the curtain wall was taken down at the end of the seventeenth century as part of a 'modernisation' programme, which also involved building a terrace to give access to the house at first-floor level. The interior is very much in the eighteenth-century taste, and the hall, that hub of castle life in the Middle Ages, is now an elegant reception room decorated with classically inspired plasterwork. On the balustraded gallery is a Snetzler organ, one of two in Wales, the other having been recently acquired by the National Museum of Wales at Cardiff.

Powis, Y Castell Coch (Powys)
.5m (.8km) W of Welshpool, Open: Spring to Autumn, Wednesday –Sunday, Admission charge, National Trust

Commanding long balustraded terraces decorated with sculpture, and containing everything that would delight the most erudite plantsman as well as the reluctant weekend gardener, Powis epitomises peace and civilisation. (Powis refers to the castle and the family, Powys to the county.) Even the soft rose colour of the limestone, which gives it its Welsh name Y Castell Coch (the Red Castle: not, of course, to be confused with Gilbert de Clare's Castell Coch in Glamorgan, restored by the 3rd marquess of Bute and William Burges in the late nineteenth century), is at variance with the usual image of a castle as being grey and menacing, and belies its ancestry as a genuine fortress. Of that ancestry there is no doubt. What is now its attraction: its magnificent situation on a ridge above the wide fertile valley of the Severn, was in times of political discord and territorial envy, its vulnerability as well as its strength. Its rock was its salvation in a region of generously sweeping plains which were a welcoming prospect to English invaders, rather than a daunting challenge. Powys, which was as extensive as it was fruitful, reached 'from the summit of Pumlumon to the gates of Chester, from Bangor Iscoed to the forested frontier of Meirionydd', according to a twelfth-century court poet. The riches of the region were very much envied by the Princes of Gwynedd, whose aggressive spirit motivated the Princes of Powys to ally themselves with the Crown.

Powis, the stronghold of Gruffudd ap Gwenwynwyn, was destroyed by Llywelyn ap Gruffudd in 1275. Two years later, by the Treaty of Aberconwy, Llywelyn's power was severely curtailed. It not only forced him to make amends for his previous refusal to do homage to the king, but limited the title of Prince of Wales to his lifetime. Gruffudd ap Gwenwynwyn's recompense was to be rewarded by Edward I with the barony of de la Pole, which, most probably, gave the name Welshpool to the Welsh settlement of Y Trallwng. It also initiated the ambitious building programme in masonry of his border stronghold, inherited in 1286 by his son Owain, who styled himself Baron de la Pole. Owain's daughter, Hawys Gadarn (the Firm or the Hardy, for reasons that have not been fully explained) married a John de Cherelton, or John Charlton. Both husband and wife were represented in the Jesse window which they donated to St Mary's Church, Shrewsbury. Their descendants owned Powis until the middle of the sixteenth century, when the male line became extinct.

In 1587, the castle was bought by Sir Edward Herbert, son of the 1st earl of Pembroke (of the second creation), and the evolution and development of the castle from medieval fortress to grand house belongs to this dynastic involvement.

The plan of the medieval castle is clearly discernible, and its compactness is a fascinating contrast to the extensive acres of another border fortress, Chirk, twenty-five miles (40km) away. Powis was a Welsh castle, and private, whereas Chirk was English and seigneurial, built from the beginning in the tradition of the great concentric style of the Edwardian fortress. Chirk has a vast inner bailey, now its delightful Oxbridge quadrangle; Powis, on the other hand, has no more than a small courtyard which the visitor sees only through the windows of the long

Powis Castle

gallery, which dates from the possession of the castle by Sir Edward Herbert, and represents the only part of his extensive modernisation to have survived.

Sir Edward's son was created the 1st Baron Powis in 1629, but it is to his grandson, the 2nd baron, who embarked on an ambitious scheme of improvement, that the castle owes its present appearance. This building programme was initiated to repair the damage done in the Civil War, when Powis fell to Parliament in a night attack in October 1644. Despite tenacious resistance, Sir Thomas Myddelton took the castle, and with it Lord Powis, his brother, two sons, and eighty officers and men. The extensive works which followed were not confined to making good the havoc caused by the onslaught, but were an expression of the increasing feeling of security which followed the Restoration.

The first of the two most outstanding and memorable features of this period is the Great Staircase, prudently 'behind barriers', thereby not only safeguarding its preservation, but allowing it to be admired from the landing and from the ground floor, without interference. It is a work of unabashed exuberance, unrivalled in Wales, and worthy of comparison with some of the greatest English examples of that style. Just over the border, in Shropshire, Longnor Hall, built in the 1670s, and displaying the most advanced architectural and decorative tastes, might well have had a considerable influence. Longnor was well in advance of its time, so that the Lord Powis would have had no reservations about emulating its enlightened sophistication.

It might well have been his recent succession to the title, through the death of the 2nd Lord Powis in 1667, that gave the impetus to create from what is essentially a passage from one level to the next a work of sculptural delight, dramatic in its sweeping boldness. This element of bravura is seen in its climax in the State Bedroom, the most theatrical room in the castle and probably in any British country house. Its bed is placed behind a proscenium arch, with a centrally placed cartouche bearing the initials CR though there is no evidence that Charles II ever slept here. Separating the bed from the room itself are ornamental rails, whose balustrading is almost identical to that of the Great Staircase, reputedly designed by William Winde, who was, presumably, responsible for those in this, the most 'public' of private places.

Both ornate displays of social prestige must have given the 3rd Baron Powis great satisfaction when he was created earl of Powis in 1674 and marquess of Powis in 1687. The gateway and most of the range of the outer ward belong to the same period.

As supporters of James II, the Herberts abandoned Powis in 1688, and on the death of the exiled marquess in 1696, William III gave the castle to his nephew, William van Nasau-Zuylestein, who was created earl of Rochford.

He inspired one of Europe's great gardens. The four terraces at Powis have been compared to the Hanging Gardens of Babylon and have given the place its mark of distinction ever since they were designed. Thomas Pennant, the eighteenth-century naturalist and traveller, however, was not impressed by them as they 'are to be descended to by terraces below terraces, a laborious flight of steps'. He clearly did not begin to appreciate the taste of the Italian Renaissance which had inspired them, even if their designs were executed by a Dutchman. The expert advice of 'Capability' Brown's disciple, William Emes, that they should be erased altogether, would no doubt have pleased Pennant.

In 1722 the 2nd marquess of Powis was allowed by George I to return to Powis, from which Lord Rochford had 'carried away all that he thought worth taking of the pictures and furniture as well as the family records'. This Powis reinstatement resulted in another phase of decorative taste, exemplified in the Blue Drawing Room.

Twenty years or so later, when the marquisate became extinct, an earldom was given to a distant relative, whose daughter married Clive of India's son, who in 1804, became the earl of Powis of the third creation. It is this alliance that accounts for the splendid museum devoted to Clive memorabilia in the former ballroom.

Although Robert Smirke (1781–1817), the architect of a great number of public buildings, among them the British Museum, was responsible for major repairs at Powis, the most prominent feature of the castle is the work of G.F. Bodley, who was not only commissioned to enlarge the east tower, but also to convert the medieval hall into a dining room, a challenge which would have defied the expertise of any architect. The fact that he did not succeed in no way reflects his inability, but accentuates the impossibility of the task assigned to him. Few castles have rooms of such irregular shapes; its plan was a problem which confronted subsequent generations who were concerned about making it a comfortable as well as a stately home. Today that quirkiness is its charm. In 1952, it was bequeathed to the National Trust.

Raglan (Monmouthshire)

7m (11.2km) SW of Monmouth, just off A40 or A449, Open: standard hours, Admission charge, Cadw

It is tempting to define Raglan Castle as unique, but every castle is unique in so far that each was built to be as defensively effective as the period, the terrain and the resources of the builder would allow. What sets Raglan apart from the Norman castles in Wales, or those of the Welsh princes, or the Edwardian fortresses is the reason for its existence. Although it might well stand on the site of a Norman stronghold, its appearance in the mid-fifteenth century seems to have been a matter of choice rather than necessity. It was an expression of pride and prestige rather than a statement of hostility. Even in its ruined state it has a magnetic appeal and its remains offer tantalising glimpses of the structural and decorative transitions which it underwent from its beginnings. They were grand for the simple reason that the builders of Raglan aspired to grandeur. The subsequent history of the castle was a continuation of that principle of aggrandisement, as each new generation not only indulged in domestic comforts, but applied architectural awareness and knowledge with panache to the ever-expanding empire of the Herbert family. It is a magnificent display of status and spectacle; one could not be divorced from the other.

The builder was William ap Thomas who had fought in the French wars and who made judicious marriages, first to Elizabeth Bluet, who brought him the property of Raglan, and then to Gwladys, the daughter of Dafydd Gam. Both led to consider-

Raglan Castle

able social advancement, resulting in his being knighted by
Henry VI in 1423. This recognition introduced him to a higher
sphere of achievement and influence which included the stewardship of the lordship of Usk and Caerleon. By 1435, the
Blue Knight, as he was called, by virtue of the colour of his
coat-of-arms, was in a position to show Gwent and the whole
of South Wales the measure of his success. Raglan Castle was
built to convey precisely that. The Yellow Tower of Gwent,
Twr Melyn Gwent, as it was to be known by later generations,
was the beginning of a castle which ultimately became part-
fortress and part-palace, a hybrid that has no parallel anywhere
in Wales.

It was an enormously strong hexagonal building rising to
five storeys, and built on the site of the Norman motte which
would have been one of William FitzOsbern's footholds during
his advance westwards, and held by one of his vassals. Although
it was built in the tower-keep tradition, the date of its construction puts it into the category of the tower house, where domestic
comfort and social display was as important as the sterner

considerations of defence. Precautions on this latter front were taken not only by the provision of a moat, cross-shaped arrow slits, and the machicolations under the battlements, but by far more 'modern' devices, such as the round gun ports. The self-contained Yellow Tower, built well after the aggressiveness of the Edwardian conquest, and the uncertainties caused later by the Owain Glyndŵr rebellion, indicates that there were still threats to a rich man's property. Symbolically, William ap Thomas's creation might convey chivalric ideals; in practical terms it showed its builder's concern about the constant threat of marauders.

Its polygonal forms brings to mind the towers of Edward I's great administrative fortress at Caernarfon, but closer in terms of time and place was the tower which Richard Beauchamp, earl of Warwick from 1423–39, built for himself at Cardiff Castle. Both were expressions of power and, as such, would have appealed greatly to William ap Thomas, though he would have found in Beauchamp's single tower a scale which was easier to emulate, and, indeed to supersede. The hexagonal form of the Yellow Tower was to influence subsequent builders at Raglan, for all the towers and projections are polygonal.

On his death in 1445, William ap Thomas was succeeded by his son, another William, who adopted the name Herbert, rather than what would have been the Welsh form of William ap William. William Herbert, like his father, was a soldier, and was knighted by Henry VI in 1449. A powerful Yorkist supporter during the Wars of the Roses, he reaped considerable privileges and honours for his support of Edward IV. In 1462 he was created Baron Herbert; he received also the town, castle and lordship of Pembroke, together with several castles on the Welsh Marches. In 1468 he became earl of Pembroke in recognition of his success in ousting the Lancastrians from their hold of Harlech Castle. A year later he was defeated at the Battle of Edgecote, and beheaded soon afterwards.

In just over twenty years, William Herbert, at extravagant expense, had expanded and embellished Raglan, making it a place of palatial splendour, which had a distinctly French character, as a result of the time that both father and son had spent abroad on military campaigns.

The area which had probably formed the original Norman bailey had been partly developed by William ap Thomas, by the formation of the Fountain Court, so called because of the adornment of 'a pleasant marble fountain'. To this his son added another court, entered by the Great Gatehouse. Though dwarfed by the Yellow Tower, its twin semi-hexagonal towers are still awesomely defensive, having retained their original height and their machicolations. From the inside of this new court, called the Pitched Stone Court, the appearance of the gatehouse is understandably far less aggressive, and above the entrance passage, the generous fenestration suggests that there might have been a succession of apartments, or a long gallery here. The combination of the courts of father and son produced an expansive enclosure, defended by the angularly placed kitchen tower and closet tower at the north-west and north-east ends.

The earl of Pembroke's great pride and joy on which he had lavished such exorbitant sums of money to realise his ambitious plans and to satisfy his aesthetic appetites, passed, through the marriage of his grand-daughter Elizabeth, to Charles Somerset (1460–1526) who was, through his wife, styled Baron Herbert. Further privileges culminated in his being created earl of Worcester.

It was William Somerset (1526–89) the 3rd earl of Worcester who was responsible for the next major change at Raglan, by developing the hall range which had, in a minor way, occupied part of the Fountain Court, but which was now to divide that area from the Pitched Stone Court. It is the best surviving structure at Raglan which exemplifies the castle's architectural and social evolution. A spectacularly expansive oriel window lights the dais end, the most socially important area of the great hall, whose status is further indicated by the ornate stone shield bearing the arms of the 3rd earl as a Knight of the Garter. The doorways leading to the service rooms, including the buttery and the pantry, stand traditionally at the opposite end of the hall, and the area between the porch in the Pitched Stone Court and the doorway leading into the Fountain Court would have been screened to form a passage. Tantalisingly small evidence, by way of chimney breast supports and the basic structure of a large window at the semi-hexagonal end, indicate the importance of the long gallery on the first floor. It well deserved the adjective, for it was 126ft long (38.5m), with half its length built over the chapel and the porch in the hall.

A description of Raglan's garden in the time of William ap Thomas refers to 'orchards full of apple trees and plums and figs, and cherries and grapes, and French plums and pears and nuts, and every fruit that is sweet and delicious'. The 3rd earl developed the garden with his customary flair, and formalised large areas on the west side of the Fountain Court with terraces leading down to the valley. The external lay-out of the castle in consequence must have matched the splendours of the interiors.

By the time of his death, the 3rd earl had given Wales a palace of unparalleled splendour, which his son Edward was to improve still further with the addition of a moat walk, with its surrounding wall providing niches for the display of statues of the Roman emperors. He seems to have embodied the spirit of the Renaissance by virtue of the range of his skills and interests. Reputedly a man of action, 'the best horseman and tilter of his time', he was also deeply involved with the arts, and particularly with acting, music and literature. The composer William Byrd and the poet Edmund Spenser were both recipients of his patronage.

At the outbreak of the Civil War, Raglan was garrisoned for the king by Henry, the 5th earl, who was created marquis of Worcester, in recognition of the vast sums of money that he had contributed to the royal cause. He entertained the king at Raglan on two extended visits in July and August and again in September 1645. It was while playing bowls at Raglan in that September that Charles I heard of the surrender of Bridgwater and Bristol, news that prompted his immediate departure from Raglan, to which he never returned.

In 1646, the castle was defended for thirteen weeks against a force of Parliamentarians supervised during the final stages by Sir Thomas Fairfax (1612–71), Parliamentary commander-in-chief. Life was grim for the marquis who 'had to dine in his withdrawing-room to the accompaniment of musket balls coming in through the windows'. In spite of the enormous sums which the marquis had spent in his attempts to withstand Cromwellian attack, during which he displayed 'the utmost skill, gallantry and resolution against every effort of the Roundheads', he eventually gave way, when 'heavy cannon, which included mortars firing twelve inch shells breached the walls'. Raglan was surrendered on terms in August 1646. The marquis was taken prisoner and died soon afterwards. His grandson, the 3rd marquis of Worcester, recovered possession of Raglan after the Restoration of King Charles II in 1660, but devoted his energies to developing and rebuilding Badminton House which had been in the family since the early part of the seventeenth century. He was made duke of Beaufort in 1682. It was the 10th duke who put Raglan into the guardianship of the Ministry of Works in 1938. Today it is maintained with great care by Cadw.

Rhuddlan (Flintshire)
Castle signposted in the middle of the town. Small car park. Footpath to Twthill. Open: standard hours, Admission charge, Cadw

Rhuddlan is generally linked with Flint because they were the first two castles built by Edward I in his Welsh campaign of 1277. Nevertheless, there are many geographical as well as architectural differences which set them apart. Unlike Flint, Rhuddlan was by no means a virgin site for defensive operation, nor did it possess the necessary requirements for an effective military location: navigable tidal access, which Flint, by virtue of its position on the Dee estuary, could boast.

Water, however, did play a significant part in the origins of Rhuddlan and its importance as a fording point, an advantage which, in the days when national boundaries were arbitrarily defined, was territorially crucial. As a result, it was an area to which both English and Welsh laid claim. If Offa's Dyke, the boundary named after the Saxon King Offa of Mercia (757–96), was an attempt to clarify the demarcation, it did not do away with the traditional hostility, and in 796, the English, fighting beyond the new frontier, won a battle at Rhuddlan

Rhuddlan Castle

and eventually gained control over Englefield, in Welsh called Tegeingl, named after the Celtic tribe Deceangli.

By 1063 it was back in Welsh hands and the seat of Gruffudd ap Llywelyn, King of Gwynedd and Powys, whose plundering of the English territories south-eastwards as far as Oswestry was brought to a stop by King Harold who overran Gruffudd's men and burned his property at Rhuddlan in 1063, only three years before he himself was to suffer defeat by William the Conqueror.

With the Norman Conquest, Hugh d'Avranches was granted lands on the North Wales and English border and given the title earl of Chester, with the express purpose that he should extend Norman territorial supremacy westwards. He chose as his lieutenant Robert 'of Rhuddlan', a relation, who according to Domesday Book (1086) had power over the whole of North Wales beyond the river Clwyd, on payment of £40 rent a year. Robert's motte-and-bailey, thrown up in 1073 was firm evidence of his right to exert such power. Its impact on the region must have been formidable, and over 900 years later, the mound known as Twt-hill, a very short distance from the castle, still has a compelling presence in its now bucolic riverside setting.

It gave rise to a borough of eighteen burgesses, a church and even a mint.

The stone castle we visit today was built by Edward, rather than strengthening his father's hillside castle at Dyserth a few miles to the east. In order to take full advantage of his fleet, which included twenty-five ships of the Cinque Ports, Edward concentrated his strongholds in places with direct access to tidal waters. Where this was not possible, as at Rhuddlan, he constructed a canal from the coast, which was made navigable up to the very foundations of the new fortress. It was an enormous engineering operation, involving on average a work force of sixty-six men working six days a week over a period of three years. This major enterprise was supervised by the master *fossator* William of Boston, and considered of such importance that the king himself was present during most of the autumn of 1277 at Rhuddlan. It was the first of Master James's three concentric castles in Wales, though it does not have the uniformity of design that is evident at Harlech and even more conspicuous at Beaumaris. Aberystwyth, which was also built in 1277 under the direction of Edward's brother Edmund, was also concentric and like Rhuddlan had a diamond-shaped inner ward, which unlike Rhuddlan, was repeated in its outer counterpart. Nevertheless, there is no evidence to suggest that Master James played any part in its design.

The outer curtain walls at Rhuddlan follow those of the inner ward on only three sides, each not only protected by a dry moat revetted in stone, but strengthened by turrets and amply provided with loop-holes. The outer ward on the fourth side is almost a triangle, with a square tower at the apex in order to command the canal and the entrance from it into the castle dock and dock gate. This is called Gillot's Tower, probably named after Gillot de Challons, a mason who was later to work at Conwy.

In order to appreciate the importance of water in the military strategy of the site, we must imagine how, at the time of the castle's construction, the Clwyd would have lapped against the outer western curtain wall, thereby creating the necessity for a river postern gate. Further to the north, the Town Gate, another of the four original entrances – the other two being the Friary and the Dock Gates – was reached by a wooden bridge across the natural dingle which separated the castle from the medieval town.

The inner ward was protected by a forbidding twin-towered gatehouse at the west and the east. Both were of four storeys, and in general appearance they strikingly mirror one another, an optical impact which Master James was to repeat at Beaumaris where the less military, and more palatial north and south gatehouses, had they been completed, would have created an even more dramatic effect. The north and south sides of Rhuddlan were protected by single towers, the arrangement of the latter bearing a striking resemblance to the gatehouses. Its windowless ground floor could only be entered by means of a trap door from the storey above and is reminiscent of a number of Norman castles in South Wales where this particular disposition was introduced by William Marshall at Pembroke. The northern tower follows a different arrangement, allowing direct access from the inner ward into a semi-basement.

In the general atmosphere of tranquillity at Rhuddlan today it is difficult to understand that the spaces between these grey walls would have been considerably smaller and would have echoed with voices and clangour. Now there are only footings, foundations and roof traces to remind us that there would have been timber-framed buildings erected against the sides of the courtyard. These would have fulfilled functions ranging from basic practicalities necessary for the efficient running of a garrison to considerations of domestic comfort and to the even more demanding requirements of royalty which resulted in considerable expense being incurred between 1283–86 on a private chapel and other apartments for Queen Eleanor, thereby giving her an independent establishment from that of the king who had his own hall and chamber. Among the buildings which once stood in the outer ward were the stables, the smithy and the granary. Between them, in one of the gatehouses, was the residence of the constable whose rôle was also that of the commanding officer of the garrison.

Edward I had high aspirations for the importance of Rhuddlan as a fortified settlement which would have asserted his presence even more forcefully, and in 1281, he applied to Rome for papal authority to transfer the see of St Asaph, a few miles away, to Rhuddlan. For all his claims for the newly gained prestige of the town, it was never walled in stone, and the cathedral has remained, in spite of the later efforts of Robert Dudley, earl of Leicester, to remove it to Denbigh, in its original position in the main street of the small hillside town of St Asaph.

The revolt of Madog ap Llywelyn in 1294 had little effect on Rhuddlan and, although considerable damage was done to the town a little over a hundred years later during the uprising of Owain Glyndŵr, the castle remained unscathed, and underwent no other form of hostility until the Civil War in 1642–48 when it was held for the king by Colonel Gilbert Byron, described by Archbishop Williams, the great Royalist supporter, as 'lately married and very indulgent to his lady'.

The siege of Rhuddlan began in May 1646; by July, Byron had surrendered to General Thomas Mytton, the Parliamentarian commander-in-chief. After it was disgarrisoned, the fortress was demolished and soon afterwards became a quarry for robbing on a massive scale.

In 1944 the owner of the castle, Admiral Rowley-Conwy, gave the ruins and the neighbouring Twthill to the then Ministry of Works, and a programme of clearing and strengthening was undertaken in 1947 which has proceeded ever since, now under the supervision of Cadw.

A descendant of the donor, Lord Langford, is constable of the castle, a tradition that stems back to the beginning of the fifteenth century when his ancestor Henry de Conwy held that office. Lord Langford's home, Bodrhyddan a mile away, is open to the public on Tuesday and Thursday afternoons throughout July and August.

Very prominent from the castle is the massive statement of Bodelwyddan Castle, not a miraculously preserved white-washed medieval military stronghold, but a nineteenth-century romantic interpretation, designed by J.A. Hansom (of cab fame) and now housing the Victorian displays of the National Portrait Gallery.

Ruthin, Rhuthun (Denbighshre)
Off Castle Street in town. Limited remains in grounds of Ruthin Castle Hotel.

This prominent hillside site in the Vale of Clwyd indicates that there have been defences here dating from early times. Begun in 1277, the present castle whose remains are submerged in a country house built in the 1820s was, like its exact contemporaries, Flint and Rhuddlan, part of Edward I's building programme of his first Welsh campaign. It was then granted to and held by not an Englishman, but the king's Welsh ally, Dafydd, the brother of Llywelyn ap Gruffudd from whom Edward had won it in that same year.

The history of the stronghold had up until then been one of gain and loss. By tradition, Ruthin had been regarded as the administrative centre of the *cantref* of Dyffryn Clwyd, but by the Treaty of Woodstock (1247), Henry III, as a mere titbit for his vast territorial appetite, had taken possession of it, along with the *cantrefi* of Rhos, Rhufoniog and Tegeingl. By 1256, however, Llywelyn had recovered Ruthin only to lose it again in 1277 and, more ignominiously, to see it granted to his volatile brother who, because of a family feud, had fled to England and fought with Edward's army.

Having been given in addition to Ruthin the castles of Denbigh and Caergwrle by the king, Dafydd changed his allegiance dramatically, and on Palm Sunday of 1282 made a night raid from Caergwrle on the three English castles of Flint, Hawarden and Rhuddlan. The dire consequences of that assault resulted in Edward's second Welsh campaign. Dafydd made Castell y Bere his stronghold of last resort for a short time before taking up the desperate life of a fugitive. He was eventually brought to face the king at Shrewsbury, where on the 3rd October 1283, he met his fate as a traitor.

After Dafydd's undignified end, Edward granted the *cantref* of Dyffryn Clwyd to Reginald de Grey, whose descendant, also Reginald, brought about the Welsh uprising of 1400 by raiding the lands of his neighbour Owain Glyndŵr at Glyndyfrdwy. The attack on Owain's property resulted in a retaliatory assault on de Grey's castle at Ruthin and on the town itself. Within days the revolt escalated to such an extent that Denbigh, Flint, Hawarden, Holt and Rhuddlan were attacked and set on fire.

During the Civil War Ruthin was put under considerable pressure, not only because of the inhabitants' objection to supplying the Royalist troops with accommodation and sustenance, but because many of them were conscripted to fight for the king's cause. At the end of hostilities, the castle was completely wrecked.

The Edwardian castle would have been a dual-ward stronghold, one approximating to a pentagon, entered through a twin-towered gatehouse; the other was in the form of a rectangle. A rock-cut ditch separated them.

The country house which utilised so much of the masonry is now a hotel, having been between 1920–63 a private clinic. Its red sandstone walls make a great impact from miles away. From the garden of Nantclwyd House in Castle Street (occasionally open), it is possible to appreciate not only the original defensive limits of the castle, but many of the medieval burgage plots.

Skenfrith, Ynysgynwraidd (Monmouthshire)
On B4521 10m (16km) NE of Abergavenny. Open access,
Admission free, Cadw/NT (Guidebook from Post Office)

Along with Grosmont and White Castle, Skenfrith forms the Gwent Trilateral, or Three Castles, because they were originally built as one defensive scheme, probably by William FitzOsbern, the builder of Chepstow. All three were of earth-and-timber, which were replaced with masonry defences in the thirteenth century by Hubert de Burgh. Each castle has its own distinctive features, and what characterises Skenfrith is the free-standing round keep which was built not on the previous motte, as at Tretower and Bronllys, both in Powys, but on ground level, with the mound being piled around its base as the building was being erected. Originally the entry to the keep was at first-floor level, with access to the basement through a trap door. Steps built into the semi-circular projection led to the upper floor, where a large fireplace suggests that this might have been

Skenfrith Castle

Hubert de Burgh's private chamber. A hoard or wooden fighting platform projecting from the highest level of the building added further protection, a device also seen at the great cylindrical keep at Pembroke, built by de Burgh's ally, William Marshall.

The remainder of the castle consisted of a quadrilateral enclosure, with semi-circular towers at each corner, their arrow slits providing covering cross-fire to the whole area surrounding the castle. None of the towers had living quarters; these were built against the west curtain wall, but survive only to basement level. The entry to the castle was through an arched doorway in the curtain wall, not unlike William Marshall's simple gate at Chepstow, except that William Marshall's was protected by the siting of a tower one side of it and the river cliff on the other.

With the exception of the semi-circular tower in the middle of the west curtain wall, added in the late thirteenth century, Hubert du Burgh's castle at Skenfrith was built between 1219–32, when he fell from royal favour and was forced to surrender the Trilateral. The medieval historian, Matthew Paris, on recording de Burgh's misfortune, mentions that these castles were the most prized of his possessions, on which he had spent vast sums of money.

In 1267 they were granted by Henry III to his younger son, Edmund Crouchback, earl of Lancaster, but at Skenfrith no changes of any scale were made to detract from de Burgh's original fortress which owes a great deal to the ideas he gathered fighting in France against King Philip Augustus. The concept of the curtained enclosure with the corner towers was to be developed and perfected almost fifty years later by Master James of St George in his Edwardian masterpieces in North Wales.

The walls of Skenfrith still rise to their original height in most places, and the mural walk gives the visitor not only an idea of the military importance of the site, washed as it is by the river Monnow which also filled the moat, now dry, but a wonderful view of the rich Gwent countryside. The parish church of St Bridget is for the most part contemporary with the castle and would in the Middle Ages have been at the centre of a small borough, which never developed into a trading town, probably because of its close proximity to Grosmont, which could boast a twice-weekly market. The church contains the handsome tomb of John Morgan (d. 1557), the last governor of the Three Castles, and steward to the Duchy of Lancaster, and his wife Anne (d. 1564), together with four sons and four daughters.

Skenfrith is the corruption of the Welsh *Ynys* (island or river meadow) of *Cynwraidd*, or *Cynfraidd*, a sixth-century chieftain.

St Donat's (Vale of Glamorgan)
3m (4.8km) SW of Cowbridge, Open: Sunday afternoons in July and August, Admission charge, Atlantic College

The twelfth-century castle of St Donat's which belonged to the Norman family of de Halwein or de Hawey was much altered soon after 1298 when the heiress, Joan, married Peter de

St Donat's Castle

Stratelinges, whose surname may originate from Strätligen in Switzerland. He was a relation of Sir Otto Granson (or Grandison), a close friend of Edward I who supported him as the first justiciar of North Wales 'to keep that land'. St Donat's followed the concentric plan typical of the Edwardian fortresses which owed architectural distinction to the military genius of the king's master mason, James of St George. Outwardly the castle has retained a great deal of its defensive character, provided by the strong curtain walls and the rock-cut ditch.

The Stradling dynasty, which lasted for over 400 years, brought about the gradual transformation from fortified building to comfortable country seat befitting the status of a prominent gentry family who, generation after generation, exerted considerable influence on the county of Glamorgan. John Leland in the late 1530s noted that in the 'space betwixt the castelle and the Severn is a parke of fallow dere. There is a nother park of redde deere more by northe west from the castelle. The parkes booth and the castelle long to Stradeling a gentilman of very fair landes in that countery.'

Much of the improvement of the sixteenth century which included a long gallery, an essential feature of any great Elizabethan house, was the work of Sir Edward Stradling, a scholar and bibliophile who collected a magnificent library. He promoted the publication of a Welsh Grammar by Dr Sion Dafydd Rhys in 1592, and wrote an extended study of the Norman conquest of Glamorgan. His embellishments to the gardens, as well as to the estate itself, exemplified the ideas and ideals of a Renaissance man.

The Stradling family were ardent supporters of the king during the Civil War. With the death of Sir Thomas Stradling in 1738, St Donat's underwent a period of deep decline, but it regained something of its former stature when Dr John Nicholl Carne of Merthyr Mawr bought the property in 1862. In 1901, it was sold to Morgan Stuart Williams (1846–1909) of Aberpergwm, near Glyn-neath, whose long and distinguished ancestry was celebrated by the Welsh bards. The coal that was mined on the Aberpergwm estate from the late seventeenth century brought great wealth, but by the beginning of the twentieth century, it had almost engulfed the house, a catastrophe that forced the owner to seek a less polluted area for a home. This he found at St Donat's Castle, which he restored with the help of Thomas Garner and, after Garner's death in 1906, G.F. Bodley. The castle passed to Godfrey Williams on his father's death in 1909, but by 1922 it was on the market, and again, three years later, when it was bought by William Randolph Hearst, the fabulously rich American newspaper tycoon, who was the inspiration of Orson Welles' *Citizen Kane*. Reconstruction and additions on a gigantic scale followed, including the removal of the prior's lodging from Bradenstoke priory in Wiltshire, together with the guest house and the tithe barn to St Donat's. By the late 1930s Hearst was forced through crippling debts, accelerated by the Depression, to relinquish his hold on the Welsh medieval castle on which he had spent ten times more than the purchase price. It was supposedly bought for his mistress, Marion Davies, and her few visits there prompted lavish hospitality when stars from the film world and prominent politicians were entertained in great style in the most splendid surroundings designed by Sir Charles Allom, who had recently redecorated Buckingham Palace, and who had strong antiquarian interests.

In the early 1960s the castle became a school, later to be called Atlantic College, the property of the United World College of the Atlantic. It is the home in late summer of the annual Vale of Glamorgan Music Festival, for which the grounds in general and the Bradenstoke Hall in particular, make the most suitable background.

Swansea, Abertawe (Swansea)
Castle Street, Swansea, Views from exterior only, Cadw

Henry I granted Gower in or soon after 1106, on the assassination of its owner, Hywel ap Goronwy, to Henry de Beaumont, earl of Warwick, who was also referred to as Henry de Newburgh, after le Neubourg in central Normandy. By 1116, Warwick had established Swansea as a *caput* of his new lordship of Gower, a gesture which might have motivated Gruffudd ap Rhys of Deheubarth's attack in the same year, which proved to be unsuccessful.

Nothing remains of the motte-and-bailey of Henry de Beaumont, whose descendants ruled over Swansea until 1184, when it came under the control of the de Braose family, who held it for almost the whole of the thirteenth century. In 1217 Rhys Gryg destroyed Swansea Castle and all the other strongholds in the lordship, and it was soon after that year that John de Braose rebuilt Swansea in stone, of which there are no remnants. Further developments took place in the late thirteenth century and it is this 'new' castle whose all-too-scanty remains we see today, dwarfed by the multi-storeyed building in the background. Samuel and Nathaniel Buck's East View of Swansea, 1748, depicts substantial portions of the castle, as well as a prominent motte.

Swansea Castle lost a great deal of its military and social importance when the de Braose family decided to live at Oystermouth Castle further west along the bay, and gradual dismantling took place, leaving what remained of the buildings to be put to a variety of uses, including a debtors' prison.

The existence of a highly organised and beautifully decorated arcaded parapet running along the upper walls of the south block suggests that there were features of equal splendour in other parts of the castle. There is such a striking similarity between the parapet and some of the ornamental masonry at the bishop's palace at St David's and at the summer residence at Lamphey, that it is tempting to attribute its design to the same builder, Henry de Gower, bishop from 1328–47.

Unfortunately, the castle has not been treated sensitively by urban development, but glimpses of its former dignity are very rewarding.

Tenby, Dinbych Y Pysgod (Pembrokeshire)
Few remains, Open access, Admission free, Local Authority

Leland in the 1530s described 'Tinbigh' as the town 'which stondith on a main rokke, but not veri hy, and the Severn Se so gulfeth in about hit, that at the ful se almost a third part of the toune is inclosid with water'.

The resemblance between the name Tinbigh and the land-locked Denbigh in Clwyd is immediately recognisable, as both stem from the same two Welsh roots: *din* (fort) and *bych* (small).

Tenby, from an early date, was referred to a Dinbych-y-pysgod (The Little Fort of the Fishes), the name it bears to this day for Welsh-speakers. In a ninth-century poem, praises were made to its fortified antecedents, though not the building whose sparse remains we see today:

> A splendid fort stands on the wide sea
> A sturdy fortress, sea-encircled.

The visitor to Tenby today, like Leland, feels that he is almost surrounded by sea since its position on a headland suggests all the characteristics of a defensive site, with the presence of the castle on the furthest tip of the promontory taking on the rôle of the keep, the final precautionary measure.

Scanty though the built evidence may be, the compensation provided by the castle's site is considerable, and the speculation about its defensive history is further aroused by the remains of the town walls, and in particular, the Five Arches, near which is a stone referring to the rebuilding of the medieval structure in order to contend with the threat of the Spanish Armada.

Tomen Y Rhodwydd (Denbighshire)
On A525 Wrexham–Ruthin, take B5431 towards Llanarmon yn Iâl. Soon after turning lay-by on L. Admission: permission from neighbouring farmer, Local Authority

Acknowledged as being among the finest earthwork castles in Wales, the motte-and-bailey of Tomen y Rhodwydd was thrown up by Owain Gwynedd (d. 1170) in 1149 as part of his strategy to annex the *cwmwd* of Iâl. Only two years previously, Owain's brother Cadwaladr had built a new castle at Cynfael, near Tywyn. The fact that both new strongholds lay on the borders of Gwynedd was no mere coincidence.

Tomen y Rhodwydd was powerfully sited commanding, not only the entrance to Nant-y-Garth, leading to the Vale of Clwyd, but that of Bwlch yr Oernant, which led to Powys, three of whose *cymydau*, Edeirnion, Cyfeiliog and Arwystli, became easy prey for Owain from his new base. It was also a vantage point from which he could move eastwards in order to gain control over Tegeingl, the much prized region east of the river Clwyd, with its coastal plain extending along the Welsh banks of the Dee estuary. The death of Ranulf, earl of Chester in 1153 facilitated such an objective and Owain concentrated his attention and energy in that direction. By 1167 he could boast that his hold over Gwynedd extended from Anglesey to the banks of the Dee.

King John strengthened Tomen y Rhodwydd in 1212 during his campaign against Llywelyn ap Iorwerth. With its deep ditches and banks, the military importance of the site is still obvious, in spite of its agricultural surroundings.

Tretower Castle

Tretower, Tretŵr (Powys)
*3m (4.8km) NW of Crickhowell. After 1.8m (2.9km) on A40
towards Brecon, take A479. Property clearly signposted. Open:
standard hours, Admission charge, Cadw (Excellent
audio-presentation)*

The fascination of Tretŵr lies in the fact that the medieval
castle and the fortified manor house stand side by side, and
although the place derives its name from the original Norman
fortification, it is the feeling of the continuity of human settlement from times of vigilance and defence to the more pastoral
and spacious days of security and peace that makes a visit to
Tretower Castle and Court a unique experience.

At the end of the eleventh century one of Bernard de Neufmarché's supporters, Picard, threw up a motte-and-bailey here
at a spot which could command the northward valley route,
and westwards along the more open countryside towards the

steeply inclined pass of Bwlch. Nearby the Rhiangoll flows southwards to meet the river Usk. The military importance of this flood plain was recognised by the Romans, as indicated by their fort, Pen-y-Gaer (The End or Head of the Fort) which commanded the route between Abergavenny and Brecon.

In the middle of the twelfth century Picard's son, Roger, replaced the timber structure on the motte with a shell keep – Cardiff is the only other example in Wales – comprising a gatehouse, a first-floor hall and a solar with a kitchen below. The domestic quarters are distinguished by the high quality of the sculpted Romanesque decoration surrounding windows and doorways, a rarity in secular ornament.

Major changes were made early in the thirteenth century when the Picard of the day introduced one of the most recent innovations of defensive building, the cylindrical tower which still dominates the surrounding countryside. Bronllys, a few miles away, could boast a similar construction, and further afield there were examples at Caldicot and Skenfrith (Gwent) and, most powerfully of all, at Pembroke (Dyfed). The new great tower consisted of a basement and three storeys, with a first-floor entry by external steps. Such an improvement or modernisation involved sacrificing the domestic accommodation of the shell keep. The outer walls were kept and, with the blocking up of their windows, formed an extra measure of defence. Roger Picard's other addition was the surrounding of the bailey with stone walls, defended by rounded corner towers. Today this enclosure is a farmyard, with a complex of agricultural buildings.

The great tower was last prepared for serious defence during the time of the Owain Glyndŵr uprising, although it had ceased to be used as a residence a hundred years previously when the family, finding that it was neither comfortable nor convenient, started work on the Court only a few hundred yards away. The north range dates from that period, and was built by a Picard heiress who had married Ralph Bluet of Raglan. A descendant of theirs in about 1420 sold both Tretower and Raglan to the thrustful and ambitious Sir William ap Thomas whose wife, Gwladys, the daughter of Sir Dafydd Gam of Brecon, had been previously married to Sir Roger Vaughan, by

Tretower Court

whom she had a son, also Sir Roger Vaughan. Her son by William ap Thomas called himself William Herbert, and was later created earl of Pembroke. Herbert gave Tretower to his half-brother, Vaughan who, no doubt seeing the transformation taking place at Herbert's Raglan, set to work on a building programme at Tretower, which was to last from 1457–71 when, as a Yorkist, he was executed in Chepstow Castle by Jasper Tudor after the Battle of Tewkesbury.

The aggrandising of Tretower Court was completed by his son, Sir Thomas, and it was probably the insecurity brought about by the protracted and unpredictable nature of the Wars of the Roses that accounted for his building the gatehouse and enclosing the courtyard with a battlemented wall-walk. In the 1630s Sir Charles Vaughan, an uncle of the Metaphysical poet Henry Vaughan 'The Silurist', refenestrated the west wing and added a covered passage along the south wall.

The Vaughan family sold Tretower in the late eighteenth century, and by the early part of this century the west range was the only section of this once impressive gentleman's residence that was inhabited; the rest became virtually farm buildings.

The Court was purchased in 1928 by local subscription, with grant aid from the Pilgrim Trust. Work of restoration and conservation was begun immediately by the then Ministry of Works. In 1947 the castle also came into state guardianship. Sensitive restoration by Cadw is still in progress. Tretower during the summer months is a wonderful setting for performances of period plays. Several films with historical backgrounds have been made here.

Usk (Monmouthshire)
In the town, Open: by appointment, Admission charge, Private ownership

The importance of the site had been recognised by the Romans who, in following the river Usk southwards, built forts at Abergavenny (*Gobannium*) and at Usk (*Burrium*) before establishing the centre of their control over South Wales at Caerleon (*Isca*). The Normans, led by William FitzOsbern, used Usk for their own purposes and raised an earthwork here soon after 1066.

The rectangular keep represents the first phase of the construction of Usk in stone and was characteristic of the time. This dates from the period of de Clare's tenure of the castle and lordship of Usk, which lasted from 1115–74. It was almost certainly 'the new castle on the Usk' which was visited by Henry II in 1172 on his way to London from Ireland, spending Easter at Pembroke and calling at Laugharne and Cardiff on the same journey. This three-storey keep still stands to its original height, though, with each successive period of stability, windows became more numerous. Like all such buildings, the entry was at first-floor level with an unlit basement level reached by a trap door. This was the access arrangement to be found also in the successor to the rectangular keep, the cylindrical keep, which represented the most advanced military thinking of the late twelfth century. It was far less susceptible to mining and battering as it had no right-hand corners. The earliest of them in Wales was built by William Marshall at Pembroke. In size and in its powerful presence, it was not to be matched by any other in the country. It was completed soon after his marriage to Isabella de Clare, the 'Maid of Striguil' (an old Welsh form for Chepstow) and the heiress not only of Chepstow, but of Pembroke and also Usk. Marshall had won for himself a considerable reputation for his soldierly prowess and acumen, and his military experience in Anjou had made him very aware of the most recent offensive and defensive building techniques. As a result each one of the Welsh strongholds that came into his possession was gradually transformed to implement the most sophisticated forms of castle construction.

A curtain wall was built around the earlier lay-out of Usk and to the original rectangular keep were added four round towers at four of the angles of the octagonal enclosure. Of these only the Garrison Tower survives. An integral part of the curtain wall, it bears a strong resemblance to the keep at Caldicot. It was considered to be a separate defensive unit, reached at first-floor level. William died in 1219, to be succeeded by his eldest son, another William, who in turn was succeeded by his brother Richard. It was during his tenure that Usk experienced its first major upheaval, because of his quarrel with Henry III which led to a great deal of regional discontent and more particularly to the king's attempt to lay siege to Usk in 1233. He did not succeed.

One acquisition of the castle in the 1260s by Gilbert de Clare (1243–95), who had vast estates in South Wales, resulted in substantial improvements which were continued by his sister, Elizabeth de Burgh, after his death in 1314. In 1368, the castle became the property through marriage of the earls of March who held it for thirty years. It was during this time that the gatehouse was built; it is still inhabited.

It is a tribute to the defensive effectiveness of the castle that it was capable of counteracting Owain Glyndwr's attack in 1405, during which 300 Welshmen were taken prisoner and later murdered by the English.

An episode associated with the period when William ap Thomas held the stewardship of Usk and Caerleon under the duke of York in the 1420s relates how this ambitious builder of Raglan Castle supported a particular candidate as a new prior at Goldcliff. He provided him with a force of eighty men who not only broke into the priory but seized the other contender and incarcerated him at Usk Castle, where he was told by William ap Thomas that unless he abandoned his plans for the priorate, 'he would make him, with violence, even if he were on the high altar of the priory'.

His son, Sir William Herbert, built lodgings against the inner side of the inner ward, though only their foundations remain. He died in 1469, a year after he was created earl of Pembroke, and the castle was abandoned. By 1536 it was in ruins.

Usk is by no means the best known of Welsh castles, but what survives represents major trends in the development of military architecture. It is now privately owned, and the gardens are occasionally open to the public.

Weobley (Swansea)

B4295 to Llanrhidian. At Oldwalls, take R to Llanmadoc, sign to castle soon afterwards. Open: standard hours, Admission charge (pay at farm), Cadw

Although called a castle, it is more precisely described in a document of 1410 as a *manerium batellatum*, a fortified manor house. Its principal means of defence was the nature of the site itself, one which is 'as formidable as any that either of the two Llywelyn princes or Edward I himself might have chosen. Weobley is the only fortified building on the north coast of Gower and, given its elevated position towards the end of the peninsula, above Llanrhidian marshes, it has unparalleled views across the Llwchwr estuary towards the now built-up and industrialised areas of Burry Port and Llanelli which are in sharp contrast to the hinterland behind them and to the peaceful surroundings of this part of the peninsula.

The name associated with the beginnings of Weobley is David de la Bere, holder of the lordship of Gower, and with it the castles of Swansea, Oystermouth and Loughor. Work was started here towards the end of the thirteenth century and the accommodation was arranged around a small courtyard, entered through a simple gatehouse, to the right of which is a

Weobley Castle

square tower which represents the earliest part of the complex. The little that remains suggests that it was a building of considerable strength, and it is interesting to speculate whether it was devised as a tower capable of its own independent defence. The most striking accommodation of the main building is the hall which, like the other main rooms, was on the first floor, with the kitchen below it. It is lit by a splendid cusped-headed window, beside which a door leads to a guest chamber and to a polygonal latrine tower. At the dais end of the hall, there is easy access to the solar, with a cellar below, both additions of the early fourteenth century.

Weobley was a victim of severe damage during the Owain Glyndŵr uprising of the first decade of the fifteenth century, and was later described as having been 'destroyed by the Welsh'. It recovered some of its earlier strength and dignity when it came into the possession of Sir Rhys ap Thomas, who had received honours, gifts and privileges from Henry VII for his support in gaining the crown from Richard III at Bosworth in 1485. Compared with Carew, which he also owned, Weobley was modest in scale, but with his customary swagger, he embellished part of the courtyard with an entrance porch on the south of the hall. He initiated a similar but much grander scheme at Carew. Sir Rhys's grandson, Rhys ap Gruffudd was executed for treason in the reign of Henry VIII, and Weobley reverted to the Crown.

In the late sixteenth century Weobley became the possession of the Herbert family who had been lords of Gower since the fifteenth century and whose heirs, the Somersets, were to become earls and marquesses of Worcester and, since 1682, dukes of Beaufort. Weobley, however, was probably too inaccessible and too small for serious family interest, and its social status declined dramatically. It is tempting to compare it with two other fortified manor houses in Wales: Beaupré and Tretower. Both, for different reasons, are 'grander', but neither has what Weobley possesses in abundance: a wonderful view.

White Castle (Monmouthshire)
Llantilio Crossenny. B4233 Abergavenny–Monmouth road. 6m (9.6km) E of Abergavenny. Open: standard hours, Admission charge, Cadw

One of the Gwent Trilateral, built by William FitzOsbern to retain hold of the area established at Chepstow, the castle at Llantilio Crossenny, like those at Skenfrith and Grosmont, was an earth-and-timber stronghold. Although all three were granted to Hubert de Burgh by King John in 1201, the White Castle did not undergo the same defensive changes that were applied to its fellow castles until much later.

The refortification of the White Castle in masonry dating from the twelfth century, took full advantage of the defensive nature of the original site. It comprised a curtain wall safeguarding an almost oval-shaped enclosure, with a rectangular keep at its southern end. Only its foundations remain, as it was demolished in the thirteenth century when the curtain wall was reinforced with six round towers, one of which accommodated the chapel. Two were placed together at the narrowest end of the enclosure, forming an assertively bold gatehouse, enough to deter the most resolute assailant. This strong military aspect

White Castle

is unmistakable even today, situated as it is in the peaceful countryside of Gwent.

A curtain wall incorporating four towers was also built around the outer ward, which was now entered by a gatehouse. These additions were initiated by Edmund Crouchback, earl of Lancaster, and represented major defensive precautions against possible attacks from Llywelyn ap Gruffudd whose increasing intrusion into South Wales indicated a major danger alert. The vestiges of buildings erected against the walls of the enclosure or inner ward suggest quarters essential to the needs of a garrison, rather than the accommodation befitting someone of noble rank. The White Castle was never put to the test, and with Llywelyn's death in 1282 and Edward I's hold on Wales tightening, it gradually lost its strategic significance as a border stronghold, and its dauntingly deep and broad moats became breeding places for swans.

There is no doubt that the fortress was called such because of the white plaster that coated the walls, although it is interesting to note that the pre-Conquest ruler of the area was Gwyn – a personal name meaning 'blessed', 'pure' and 'fair' as well as 'white' – ap Gwaethfoed. His stronghold, therefore, might well have been known as Castell Gwyn – Gwyn's Castle, but also, literally, White Castle; an interesting coincidence, but probably of no historical significance, because there are enough remains to prove that the white-plastering of certain Welsh castles was a distinctive badge of English presence and authority, as can be seen at Cricieth and at Conwy.

South of White Castle is Hen Gwrt (Old Court), a moated site once reputedly owned by Dafydd Gam who distinguished himself at Agincourt. This might account for it becoming the property of the Herberts of Raglan whose forebear, William ap Thomas, was Dafydd's son-in-law. As it occupied part of Raglan's deer park, the original medieval buildings might well have been adapted and improved to serve as a hunting lodge, although there are no remains of either building phase.

The 'tilio' in the village name is an anglicisation of Teilo, to whom the large twelfth-century parish church is dedicated, as indeed was Llandaff cathedral, whose bishops once owned Hen Gwrt. Crossenny is traditionally thought to be Croes Ynyr (Cross of Ynyr), referring to a battle when Ynyr defeated the Saxons.

Appendices

Appendix I

Genealogies

WELSH SURNAMES
Welsh personal names were mainly based on a patronymic system and a man's family identity was immediately apparent: Dafydd ab Owain being Dafydd, son of Owain, Ieuan ap Rhys, Ieuan, son of Rhys. In time ab Owain and ab Einon become Bowen and Beynon (Binyon is a variant), and ap Rhys and ap Hywel become Prys, or Price, and Powell. The origin of an English-sounding surname like Palin can be traced back to ap Heilyn.

People were often identified by their physical attributes. Genealogical tables are scattered with names such as Rhys Gryg (the Hoarse), Merfyn Frych (the Freckled) or Idwal Foel (the Bald). More common was the use of adjectives such as *fychan* (small) becoming eventually Vaughan, *goch* (red-head) giving Gough, and *llwyd* (grey-haired) becoming Lloyd or Floyd.

With the gradual requirements of law and bureaucracy the *ab* or *ap* was dropped, so that Llywelyn ap Gruffudd became Llywelyn Griffith whose son would be named Dafydd Llywelyn and his son, in time, Ieuan Davies or David. Such a system resulted in the present proliferation of surnames such as Davies, Evans, Jones, Griffiths, Howells, Price, Rees, Thomas and Williams.

THE DYNASTY OF GWYNEDD

RHODRI MAWR (d.878)

CYNAN (d.c.1060) = Ragnhildr of Dublin

GRUFFUDD ap CYNAN (d.1137)

Gwenllian = Gruffudd ap Rhys ap Tewdwr

Susannah = Madog ap Maredudd

Cadwallon (d.1132)

Cadwaladr (d.1172)

DAFYDD (Son of Christina)

Others

OWAIN GWYNEDD (d.1170) = 1. Gwladus / 2. Christina

Iorwerth Drwyndwn (Son of Gwladus) = Marared dau of Madog ap Maredudd of Powys

Others

LLYWELYN (The Great) (d.1240) = Joan dau of King John

Tangwystl

GRUFFUDD (d.1244)

Dafydd (d.1246) = Isabel de Braose

Gwenllian (d.1281) = William de Lacy

Helen = John Earl of Chester

Gwladus Ddu = 1. Reginald de Braose / 2. Ralph Mortimer

Margaret = 1. John de Braose / 2. Walter Clifford

LLYWELYN (The Last) (d.1282) = Eleanor de Montfort

Rhodri

Dafydd (d.1283) = Elizabeth Ferrers

Gwladus (d.1261) = Rhys ap Mechyll

Owain Goch (d.c.1282)

THE DYNASTY OF DEHEUBARTH

RHODRI MAWR (d.878)

CADELL (d.909?)

HYWEL DDA (d.950?)

RHYS ap TEWDWR = Gwladus daughter of Rhiwallon ap Cynfyn

Hywel

Nest = Gerald of Windsor (d.c.1136)

Angharad = William de Barri

Giraldus Cambrensis
Gerald of Wales
Gerallt Gymro
(c.1146–†223)

GRUFFUDD (d.1137) = Gwenllian daughter of GRUFFUDD ap CYNAN

Anarawd

Cadell

RHYS The 'Lord Rhys' (d.1197) = Gwenllian daughter of Madog ap Maredudd

Gruffudd
(d.1201)
=
Matilda
daughter of
William de
Braose

Maredudd
Ddall
(d.1239)

Rhys Gryg
(d.1234)

Maelgwn
(d.1231)

Hywel Sais

Gwenllian
(d.1236)
=
Ednyfed
Fychan

THE DYNASTY OF POWYS

Cynfyn ap Gwrstan
=
Angharad dau of Maredudd ab Owain

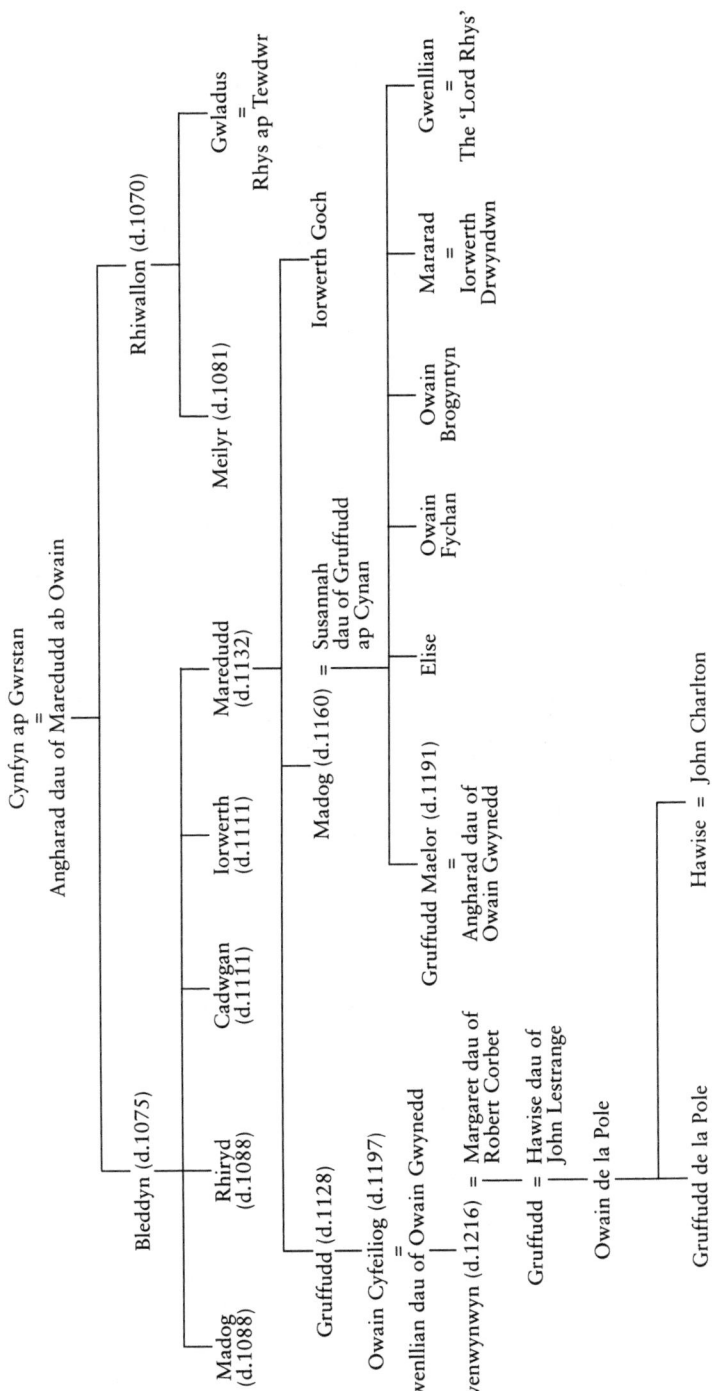

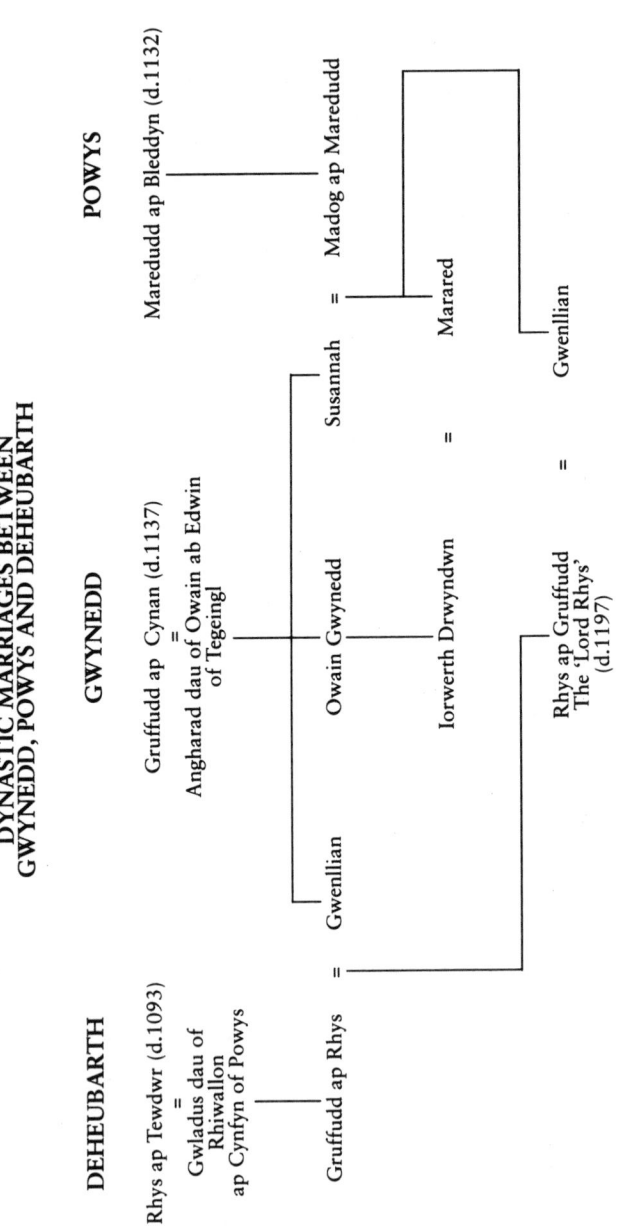

DYNASTIC MARRIAGES BETWEEN
GWYNEDD, POWYS AND DEHEUBARTH

DEHEUBARTH

Rhys ap Tewdwr (d.1093)
=
Gwladus dau of
Rhiwallon
ap Cynfyn of Powys

Gruffudd ap Rhys

GWYNEDD

Gruffudd ap Cynan (d.1137)
=
Angharad dau of Owain ab Edwin
of Tegeingl

Gwenllian   Owain Gwynedd   Susannah

Iorwerth Drwyndwn

Rhys ap Gruffudd
The 'Lord Rhys'
(d.1197)

POWYS

Maredudd ap Bleddyn (d.1132)

Madog ap Maredudd

Marared

Gwenllian

ENGLISH & WELSH CONNECTIONS BETWEEN
THE TIME OF KING JOHN AND EDWARD I

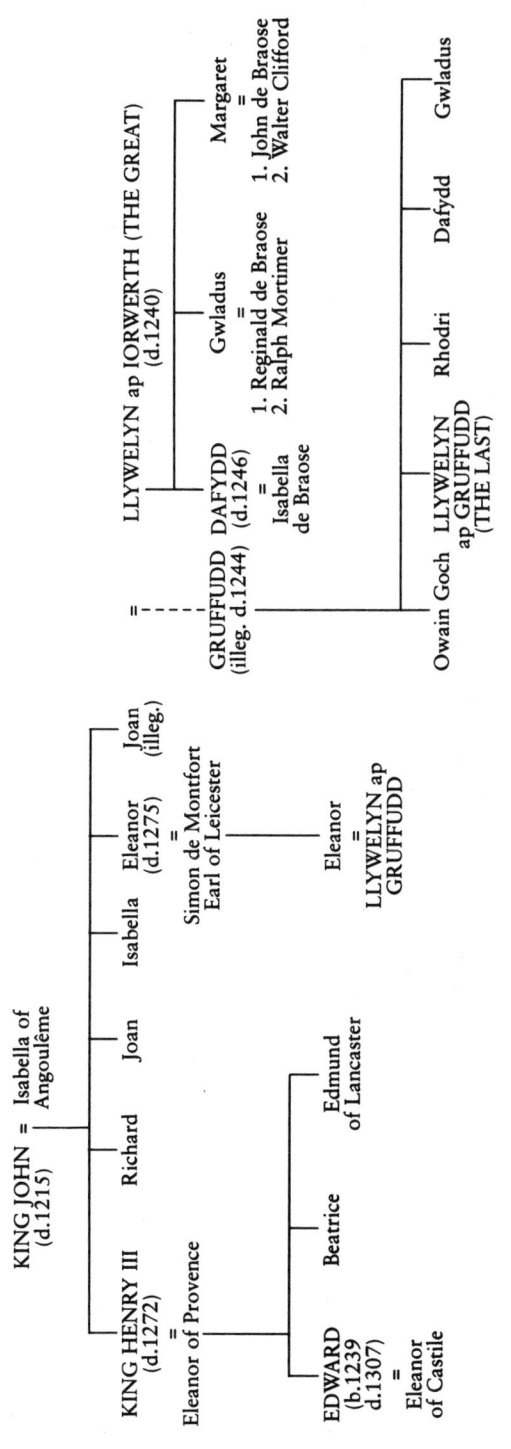

THE ORIGINS OF THE TUDOR DYNASTY

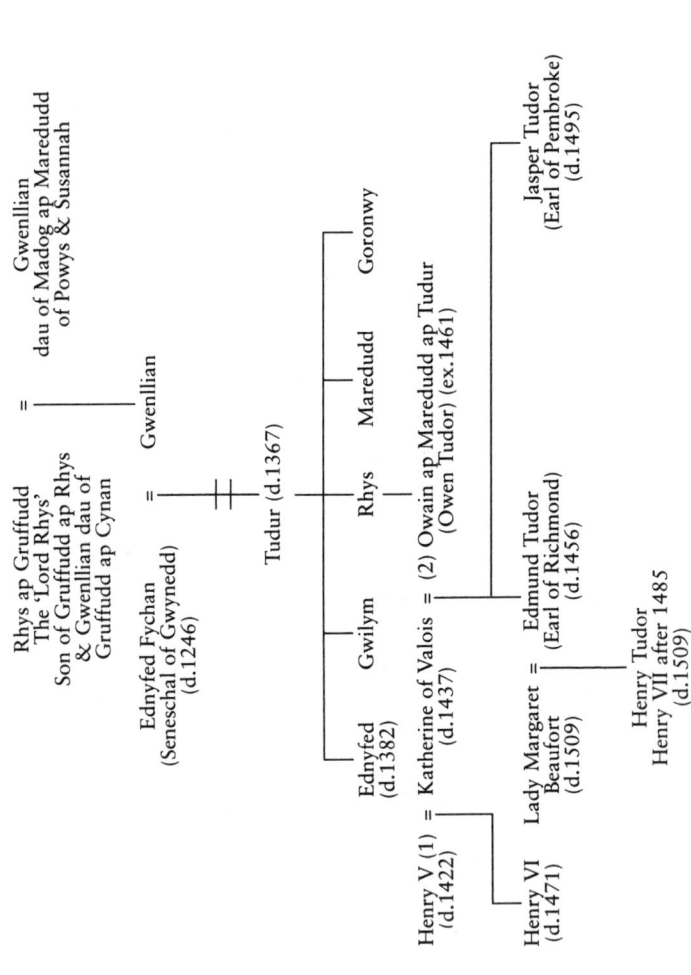

Appendix II

Who, What, When and Where

ABERCONWY, TREATY OF, 1277
After a succession of refusals on the part of Llywelyn ap Gruffudd to do homage to Edward, he was ordered to pay a fine of £50,000, an enormous sum, for his disobedience. Having travelled to Rhuddlan to swear fealty to the king, he later that year was forced to present himself in London at the Christmas court where he did homage to his sovereign. The burning irony was that in spite of the humiliating circumstances of the Treaty which deprived him of his overlordship and those lands which he had gained outside Gwynedd, he was still addressed as Prince of Wales. It represented a complete change of fortune after the Treaty of Montgomery.

BRUT Y TYWYSOGYON
'The Chronicle of the Princes' begins in 682 with the death of Cadwaladr Fendigaid 'the Blessed' and ends with the death of Llywelyn ap Gruffudd in 1282. The entries were based on the records kept by monks since the eighth century, and were translations of a lost Latin text.

CADW
Cadw – which means 'to keep or preserve' – has been an executive agency since 1984, inheriting its role from the Ministry of Public Buildings and Works, later the Department of the Environment. Since its inception Cadw's aims have been to protect, conserve and promote an appreciation of the buildings which are the heritage of Wales.

CANTREF, Cantrefi (pl)

An early Welsh administrative centre. Made up of *can(t)* (a hundred) and *tref*, which has a variety of meanings, including 'home', 'settlement', and latterly, 'town', hence the smallest form of settlement, as in the English 'hundred'.

COMMOTE

See Cwmwd.

CWMWD, Cymydau (pl)

A commote. A subdivision of the Welsh administrative centre, the *cantref*.

CYWYDD

An uncomplicated metre, made up of rhyming couplets of seven-syllable lines. Each pair of rhymes, however, required one stressed and one unstressed syllable. In Iolo Goch's poem to Owain Glyndŵr's Court at Sycharth, we read of

Siopau glân glwys cynnwys cain
Siop lawndeg fel Siêp Lúndain
'Attractive shops with lovely contents
Stocked as well as London's Cheapside.'

DAFYDD ap GRUFFUDD (d. 1283)

The youngest of four sons of Gruffudd, the illegitimate son of Llywelyn ap Iorwerth, 'the Great', Dafydd was a dangerously fickle personality on whose shoulders can be placed blame for a great deal of the tragic events of 1282. Like his brothers, he was given a share in the territories of their uncle, Dafydd, Llywelyn's rightful heir, when he died in 1246 without a son to succeed him. Although the arrangement received the blessing of Henry III a year later, the situation was fraught with tensions from the outset. It was not until 1255 that two of the brothers, Owain and Dafydd attempted to oust their brother Llywelyn from the position of supremacy over Gwynedd which he had claimed as his own. They failed, and after a battle at Bryn Derwin, Llywelyn imprisoned both his rebellious brothers, Owain for over twenty years during which time he was incarcerated at Dolbadarn, while Dafydd found himself a free man within months, probably because Llywelyn recognised in him a powerful ally in the quest to gain independence from the English Crown. In 1263, however, Dafydd defected to the court of Henry III, a gesture all too characteristic of his self-interest.

By the Treaty of Montgomery of 1267, the king recognised Llywelyn as Prince of Wales, an accolade which spurred him to assert his authority in a manner to which rival princes took exception. Plans were set in motion to assassinate Llywelyn and his brother, Dafydd was among the conspirators. When the plot was discovered, he sought refuge in England and sided with the king, being granted the *cantrefi* of Rhufoniog and Dyffryn Clwyd after Edward's 1277 offensive against his brother. In addition, he was given royal aid to build a castle at Caergwrle, at what was probably an established defensive site. The king's gift also included the hilltop fortress of Denbigh.

This recognition of his contribution to Edward's victory over Llywelyn was not enough for Dafydd who began to harbour a resentment which was to gain such momentum that it resulted in a complete change of allegiance. On Palm Sunday, 1282, from his castle at Caergwrle, he descended on the three nearest English strongholds within his grasp: the king's own castles at Flint and Rhuddlan and the baronial establishment at Hawarden.

However fractured the relationship between Dafydd and Llywelyn, the elder brother was honour-bound to support what now seems a pathetically miscalculated assault.

Dafydd fled first to Llywelyn ap Iorwerth's castle at Bere. When it fell to the English army, he led the life of a fugitive for several months before being captured and taken to Shrewsbury where he was hanged, drawn and quartered, a new form of punishment for treason devised by Edward I himself.

DAFYDD ap LLYWELYN (d. 1246)

If the traditional Welsh custom had been followed, Dafydd would have shared his father's inheritance with his older half-brother Gruffudd, born out of wedlock. But in order to maintain the strength of Gwynedd in the hold of one leader, Llywelyn ap Iorwerth had sought to make Dafydd his sole heir, and in 1238 he summoned the native princes of Wales to Ystrad Fflur (Strata Florida) where they gave Dafydd their fealty.

On his father's death, Dafydd saw that his position was far from stable, for Henry III was quick to realise that the young Welshman had inherited little of his father's strength, determination and gift of diplomacy. He therefore took full advantage of the opportunity to reassert his authority in Gwynedd, which he had not been allowed to exercise during the last decades of Llywelyn ap Iorwerth's life. In the meantime, Gruffudd, the bitterly discontented half-brother, had the support of several Welsh leaders who were sympathetic to his claim to his share of his father's inheritance.

Because of his threat to the stability of Dafydd's régime, Henry took Gruffudd and his eldest son Owain hostage and incarcerated them in the Tower of London. Gruffudd's attempt to escape in 1244 ended in his death. Two years later, Dafydd himself died unexpectedly but through natural causes in his *llys* at Aber. As he had no sons, his heirs were, ironically, the sons of his half-brother, the illegitimate Gruffudd.

EISTEDDFOD

Session, or Meeting, based on the verb *eistedd* – 'to sit'. The first eisteddfod held in Cardigan in 1176 bears no relation to the present one, which in spite of its Gorsedd of Bards of the Island of Britain, presided over by the Arch Druid, is a romantic invention of the late eighteenth century, by today considerably refined. The Royal National Eisteddfod of Wales, a competitive assembly involving all the art forms, is conducted completely in Welsh and takes place during the first full week in August, alternating between North and South Wales. The festival has been the starting point for many internationally celebrated singers, such as Bryn Terfel. It should not be confused with the International Eisteddfod held at Llangollen every year.

FENTON, RICHARD (1747–1821)

Born in St David's where he was educated at the cathedral school, and called to the Bar in 1783, it was as a traveller and antiquarian that he is best known. A contemporary regarded him as a man 'of indefatigable industry, of a fine poetical fancy' who possessed 'the best information of any subject'. His *Tours in Wales 1804–1813* are full of fascinating facts and descriptions.

GERALD OF WALES (c. 1146–1223)

Born in Manorbier in Pembrokeshire, which he described so lovingly, Gerald or Gerallt has provided posterity with the most fascinating and stimulating glimpses of a wide range of life in medieval Wales, encompassing the most vivid descriptions not only of the countryside and its buildings but of the social habits of the inhabitants. His education began under his uncle, David FitzGerald, Bishop of St David's, after which he went to the Benedictine abbey of St Peter at Gloucester before finishing his studies at the University of Paris.

In 1188 he undertook his journey through Wales with Archbishop Baldwin as a five-week recruiting mission for the third crusade. The experience resulted in his two most widely read works, his *Itinerary Through Wales* (1191) and the *Description of Wales* (1194). They are immeasurably valuable both as literature and as history, for nowhere else do we get such a directly honest and intimate portrait of life in Wales at the end of the twelfth century where the people were not fond of 'towns, villages or castles. They do not erect sumptuous palaces nor lofty stone buildings, but content themselves with small huts made of boughs of trees twisted together'. Able to converse in French, Latin and Greek, as well as in English, he described himself as 'from the princes of Wales and from the barons of the Marches'. His knowledge of the Welsh language was nevertheless probably very scant, although in the course of the years he identified himself more and more with Wales, venting considerable resentment against the native princes who by their traditional territorial wranglings had deprived the country of its unity and pride.

In spite of several visits to Rome to make a case for his worthiness, his great ambition to be Bishop of St David's was never realised. Like Owain Glyndŵr, over two hundred years later, he attempted to make St David's independent of Canterbury. The Church in Wales did not achieve such autonomy until 1921.

GRUFFUDD ap CYNAN (c. 1055–1137)

The first Welsh ruler to be the subject of a biography, Gruffudd is traditionally thought to have been born in Ireland of half-Welsh and half-Irish–Scandinavian ancestry. In 1081, after an unsuccessful first attempt six years previously to gain his legitimate inheritance, he succeeded in overcoming the usurper, Trahaearn ap Caradog in the battle of Mynydd Carn. (His grand-daughter married Owain Gwynedd and was the grandmother of Llywelyn ap Iorwerth 'the Great'.)

Soon afterwards, he was betrayed by one of his own followers and captured by the Normans who imprisoned him in Chester for twelve years – though the biography also states a period of sixteen years. During his incarceration, the Normans built castles at Degannwy, Bangor, Caernarfon and Aberlleiniog on the island of Anglesey. After his release, he found himself under further threat from the Normans in 1098, and once again escaped to Ireland, to return only a year later, when he established himself as King of Gwynedd which, according to his biography, written in Latin:

> Gruffudd governed for many years successfully and powerfully with moderation and peace, and enjoyed neighbourly relations in accord with the kings nearest to him, namely Henry king of England, Murcadh king of Ireland, and the king of the islands of Denmark; and he was known and prominent both in the kingdoms far from him and in those near him. Then every kind of good increased in Gwynedd and the people began to build churches in every part therein, sow woods and plant them, cultivate orchards and gardens, and surround them with fences and ditches, construct walled buildings and live on the fruits of the earth after the fashion of the men of Rome. Gruffudd also built large churches in his own major courts, and held his courts and feasts always honourably. Furthermore, Gwynedd glittered then with lime-washed churches, like the firmament with stars.

JAMES of St GEORGE (c. 1235–1308)

He is often referred to as Master James, because he was master of Edward I's ambitious state enterprise in Wales from 1277. His genius as a military engineer was seen at its most inventive and innovative during the second Welsh campaign, starting in 1283, with his fortified towns as well as his castles at Conwy and Caernarfon, his rock-perched concentric fortress at Harlech and, lastly, after 1294, his almost perfect concentric creation of Beaumaris on the level marshland on the eastern end of the Menai Strait. The four of them are unsurpassed as examples of European medieval defensive architecture.

Before being brought to Wales, James had been in the service of Edward I's cousin, Count Philip of Savoy, on the French, Swiss and Italian border. His extensive domain included St Georges d'Espéranches, near Lyon, whose construction James had directed, and from which he took his 'trade name' as Master James of St George. Edward had stayed there in 1273 on his way back to England from the crusades.

To a greater or less degree, Master James supervised work not only on these castles, but on the strongholds of the first Welsh campaign of 1277, at Aberystwyth, Builth, Flint and Rhuddlan. The seigneurial castles of Chirk, Denbigh, Hawarden, Holt and Ruthin also received attention from his expert eye, as did the refortification of the Welsh castles of Castell y Bere and Cricieth, as well as Caergwrle (referred to in the English records as Hope).

Between 1290–93 he was Constable of Harlech, having the gatehouse as his domestic quarters. His stature in the eyes of the king had also resulted in his being granted the manor of Mostyn, near his first castle at Flint.

LELAND, JOHN (c. 1506–52)

After the universities of Cambridge and Oxford and finally Paris, Leland took holy orders. Soon afterwards Henry VIII made him his library keeper which led to his appointment as 'King's antiquary', a post that had not existed before that, nor ever afterwards. His extensive tour through England and Wales which took almost a decade, was intended to lead to an authori-

244 · Appendix II

tative survey amounting to the *History and Antiquities of this Nation*. The work never appeared, but his preparatory notes and diary entries are probably just as engaging to a modern reader.

LLYWELYN ap GRUFFUDD (d. 1282)

Although Llywelyn ap Gruffudd inherited many of the qualities of leadership of his grandfather, Llywelyn ap Iorwerth 'the Great', they were consistently negated by actions of impetuous truculence which eventually fractured the spirit of national unity which his ancestor had created.

Henry III's involvement in the Baron's War, during which Llywelyn supported Simon de Montfort, deflected the king's eagle-eyed scrutiny away from Wales. Llywelyn was quick to extend his authority and, although the perennially assailable Powys Wenwynwyn succumbed, Deheubarth was under constant attack and under threat of being completely overrun.

In the Treaty of Montgomery, 1267, Henry acknowledged Llywelyn's bid for the title of 'Prince of Wales' for himself and for his heirs. It was granted in return for homage. This, however, was a condition which Llywelyn was to find extremely difficult to honour. His refusal to attend the coronation of Henry III's son, Edward I, was an act of blatant defiance against a new monarch who had already been for twenty years, and in his own right, lord of all Ireland. Edward also held the earldom of Chester, the duchy of Gascony and of the Channel Islands. Furthermore he had complete control over the king's land in Wales. Whatever terms of mutual understanding Henry III had established with Llywelyn ap Gruffudd, they were inadequate to satisfy his son's demands of the Welsh prince.

The relationship between Llywelyn and Henry was further complicated by the unpredictable behaviour of Llywelyn's brother, Dafydd, whose shift of allegiance between the English court and Wales led, in 1282, to his assault on the three English castles of Flint, Hawarden and Rhuddlan. Although the two brothers were at the time on opposite sides, Llywelyn had no choice but to support his brother's anti-English venom. The incidents of that Palm Sunday in 1282 set off every alarm for the recommencement of hostilities between Edward and the

Welsh. Llywelyn was killed in a skirmish near Builth on 11th December 1282. With the execution of his brother Dafydd in the following year, the hope of Wales as an independent nation seemed at an end.

One of the court poets, Gruffudd ab yr Ynad Goch (*fl.* 1280), in one of the most poignant and despairing elegies in Welsh Literature, expressed the inconsolable bereavement of an entire people.

LLYWELYN ap IORWERTH (d. 1240)

Llywelyn the Great, son of Iorwerth Drwyndwn (Broken Nose), was born in Dolwyddelan in 1173, though not in the present castle which belongs to a later date. Iorwerth's physical imperfection traditionally disqualified him from assuming the mantle of kingship, so his younger brother, Dafydd, was considered worthier of the rôle, a situation which was fiercely disputed by Llywelyn who defeated his uncle in 1194 near Conwy, thereby getting a firm foothold in Gwynedd which, by 1200, he controlled completely.

Llywelyn's powerful position now concerned King John, but by 1205 relationships had softened sufficiently for the prospect of a marriage between the self-styled Prince of Gwynedd and Joan, the king's natural daughter to become a reality. By 1211, tensions of pride and possession had become all too obvious, resulting in loss and recovery of territory. The king's involvement with Magna Carta in 1215 gave Llywelyn free rein to extend his authority, resulting in his being able to take Carmarthen, Cardigan and Montgomery, as well as Shrewsbury, an achievement which King John's son, Henry III, was to acknowledge in the Treaty of Worcester of 1218, when Llywelyn's preeminence in Wales was recognised, though it carried with it no titular distinction. The 'Great' was undoubtedly a more valuable mark of public and national esteem.

He did his best to establish good relations with the Norman barons of the Marches by arranging the felicitous marriage of each of his children. Dafydd maried Isabel de Braose, Gwenllian William de Lacy, Helen became the wife of John, son of Ranulf the earl of Chester. On the death of Gwladus Ddu's first husband, Reginald de Braose, she married Ralph Mortimer, and

Margaret also married a member of the de Braose family, John, before taking Walter Clifford as her second husband.

Such close ties with the de Braose family did not stop Llywelyn hanging William de Braose, his son's father-in-law, in 1230 for committing adultery with his wife Joan. Sometime after 1230 he took the title of Prince of Aberffraw and Lord of Eryri, but in effect he was leader of most of native Wales – *Pura Wallia*.

On his death in 1240 at Aberconwy, he was buried in its abbey, which Edward I removed to Maenan over forty years later when he built his castle and fortified town at Conwy.

THE MABINOGI or *MABINOGION*
These medieval tales survive complete in two manuscripts, *Llyfr Gwyn Rhydderch* (The White Book of Rhydderch) at the National Library of Wales, Aberystwyth, and in *Llyfr Coch Hergest* (The Red Book of Hergest) at Jesus College, Oxford. *Mabinogi* originally meant 'youth', and later 'a tale of youth', before ending up meaning 'a tale' or 'a story'. *Pedair Cainc y Mabinogi* (the Four Branches of the Mabinogi) consisted of 'Pwyll Prince of Dyfed', 'Branwen daughter of Llŷr', 'Manawydan son of Llŷr' and 'Math son of Mathonwy'. The collection also consisted of four independent native tales, 'The Dream of Macsen Wledig', 'Lludd and Llefelys', 'Culhwch and Olwen' and 'The Dream of Rhonabwy', and lastly the Three Romances, namely, 'The Lady of the Fountain', 'Peredur son of Efrawg' and 'Geraint son of Erbin'. In Lady Charlotte Guest's translation (1838–49), the tales were called *The Mabinogion*, the title used in subsequent translations by Gwyn Jones and Thomas Jones (1949) and by Jeffrey Gantz (1976).

MONTGOMERY, TREATY OF, 1267
Henry III was the first English king to recognise a Welsh ruler as Prince of Wales. Llywelyn ap Gruffudd was now not only the holder of that title, which would also be that of his successors, but overlord of the other Welsh rulers who would do homage to him, while Llywelyn himself would do homage to the king.

OWAIN GLYNDŴR (c. 1354–1416)

As a member of the dynasty of northern Powys on his father's side, Owain Glyndŵr could claim descent from Madog ap Maredudd, the last King of Powys. From his mother, Elen, who was also of royal descent through the Princes of Deheubarth, he inherited lands in Ceredigion.

The estates associated with Owain, however, are the lordships of Cynllaith and Glyndyfrdwy (the Glen of the Water of the Dee), between Llangollen and Corwen, from which he took the name that gave him his heroic nature: Owain Glyndŵr – 'of the Glen of the Water'. In the lordship of Cynllaith, on the other side of the Berwyn Mountains, was Sycharth, the family's principal residence, described at length in Iolo Goch's *cywydd*, *Llys Owain Glyndŵr yn Sycharth* (Owain Glyndŵr's Court at Sycharth).

He was the embodiment of Border gentry with whom he mingled freely as a man of authority and property. After several years at the Inns of Court, Owain served as a soldier in the retinues of Henry of Lancaster who, as Henry IV, was to be a bitter adversary, and the earl of Arundel, his powerful neighbour at Chirk, as well as in the armies of Richard II in the Scottish campaign.

His marriage to Margaret, daughter of Sir David Hanmer of Maelor Seisnig (English Maelor) in Flintshire, and one of the most distinguished lawyers of his day, further advanced his political as well as his social standing as a Marcher gentleman. One of his daughters, Alice, married John Scudamore of Herefordshire.

Owain's social achievements did not help him in his dealings with his neighbour, Reginald de Grey, lord of Ruthin, and a great friend of Henry of Lancaster, now King Henry IV. A dispute between them over land took on unforeseen dimensions, and within a year their rancour had become a cause for open hostility. De Grey's adherence to Henry blocked every possible avenue of approach by which Owain might make his own case known to the king. Eventually, he rebelled against such English intransigence with the might and ferocity of a Welshman who could claim to be an heir to the two Llywelyns. Assuming the arms of the two princes – the four lions of Gwynedd – and with the staunch support of his brothers-in-law and other followers who proclaimed him Prince of Wales, Owain launched his revolt against the aggressive autonomy of England.

His aspirations soared, and his zeal excited the imagination of students, the fervour of his fellow Welshmen and the interest of magnates whose widespread influence gave considerable impetus to the campaign. Parliaments were held at Machynlleth and at Harlech, and a coronation witnessed by envoys of Scotland, France and Castile recognised Owain, by the Grace of God, Prince of Wales.

Wales would become independent, with a Welsh Church that would no longer be subservient to Canterbury, with Welsh-speaking clerics and with all the Welsh Church revenues going to Welsh causes. His plans also included the establishing of two universities, in the north and south, with the aim of training young Welshmen to serve their country.

By the end of 1406, the dream had ended and the ambitions been brought to ground. The reality now facing Owain was all too bitter: the heroic leader had become the disillusioned idealist and probably the embittered fugitive. By 1412 he had disappeared from the face of Wales, nor was there any indication of where else he might have found his refuge. Traditionally, his resting place is in the Golden Valley at Monnington Straddel, part of the Scudamore estates.

The nation's despair at the grievous loss of a heroic saviour was not expressed in elegies. There was no equivalent of Gruffudd ab yr Ynad Goch, the poet who had represented the nation's sore bereavement at the loss of Llywelyn ap Gruffudd in 1282.

The reason was obvious to every true Welshman. Owain was not dead, nor could he die. In that assurance of perennial hope, he became a figure of idolatry. He had made his nation acutely aware of its individuality, but he also made its people enemies of the neighbouring English. For someone who had lived with relaxed equality and equanimity on the very border of the two cultures, he could not have foreseen that the dispute between him and Reginald de Grey would have resulted in such Anglo-Welsh suspicion, if not hostility, and in such a crisis of national identity among the Welsh people themselves.

OWAIN GWYNEDD (c. 1100–70)

Owain, the son of Gruffudd ap Cynan, was called Owain Gwynedd to distinguish him from another Owain ap Gruffudd, prince of Powys and a poet who was also known as Owain Cyfeiliog (c. 1130–97). He was a staunch ally of his nephew, Rhys ap Gruffudd, the Lord Rhys, in his attempt to debilitate the grip of the Marcher lords, thereby strengthening the military muscle of both Gwynedd and Deheubarth. Like Rhys, he considered it politically expedient to pay homage to Henry II soon after his succession in 1154, though such a gesture of subservience in no way diminished his energetic and imaginative influence on Gwynedd, let alone his resolve to retain his authority over his much prized territory.

The capture of the king's stronghold at Rhuddlan in 1165 by Owain, with the help of his brother Cadwaladr and Rhys ap Gruffudd, gave him control from the Dyfi (Dovey) on the west to the Dee on the east. His death in 1170 was recorded in the *Brut*.

At the close of that year, in the month of November, died Owain Gwynedd ap Gruffudd ap Cynan, prince of Gwynedd, a man of great renown and of infinite prudence and nobility, the bulwark and strength of Wales, unconquered from his youth, after victories beyond number, without ever having refused to a man the request that was made to him. After taking penance and holy confession and repentance and the communion of the virtues of the Body of Christ and extreme unction his soul departed to the mercy of God.

PENNANT, THOMAS (1726–98)

Pennant was an avid traveller who combined natural enthusiasm and curiosity with considerable knowledge as a naturalist. His accounts of visits to historic places and buildings are sources of constant fascination and amusement, if not always for their accuracy, certainly for the irony which divides his description of certain sites from today's reality. Occasionally, and happily, circumstances have favoured certain places which are now growing in prosperity, a sight that Pennant would not recognise.

His *Tours in Wales* appeared in 1778, followed by *A Journey in Snowdonia* in 1781 and a considerable contribution to both volumes are the illustrations of Moses Griffith (1747–1819), Pennant's man servant whose worth as an artist was quickly recognised so that he became a constant travelling companion, recording visually much of what Pennant was busily writing.

RHUDDLAN, STATUTE OF
See Wales, Statute of

RHYS ap GRUFFUDD (1132–97)
Known as 'Yr Arglwydd Rhys' (the 'Lord Rhys'), he was the youngest of four sons born to Gruffudd, the son of Rhys ap Tewdwr, and to Gwenllian, the daughter of Gruffudd ap Cynan. Rhys's grandparents represented the heads of the dynasties of Deheubarth and Gwynedd. At the age of thirteen he joined his brothers in the South Wales rebellion against the Normans, and their lands and castles in that region.

One by one Rhys's brothers were killed or severely injured in battle, leaving him in sole and undisputed charge of Deheubarth from 1155, a year after the succession of Henry II, to whom Rhys eventually paid guarded homage. This acknowledgement of the monarch's superiority also involved Rhys's agreement to surrender the title of 'king'. The Chronicles from then onwards refer to him as Yr Arglwydd Rhys.

The death of his illustrious uncle, Owain Gwynedd, in 1170 strengthened his power over the whole of Wales. He now built new and up-to-date castles, not only at the ancient capital of Dinefwr, but at Cardigan, where in 1176, in his castle of 'stone and mortar' he held an '*eisteddfod*', though the assembly bore no close resemblance to the competitive festivals which take place today. The original gathering of poets and musicians at Rhys ap Gruffudd's court could well have been the result of an idea borrowed and adapted from the court entertainment which would have been well known to Henry II's queen, Eleanor of Aquitaine, and which, because of the period of diplomatic agreement between the king and Rhys, might well have infiltrated into Welsh awareness. Traditionally, Rhys ap Gruffudd's festival was 'proclaimed' a year before the event itself (as it still is today); with the proclamation went out invitations to the poets and musicians of the four countries of Britain.

Rhys was a patron not only of the arts of music and poetry, but of religious foundations. He rebuilt the present Ystrad Fflur (Strata Florida), after defeating its Norman founder, and established the Premonstratensians at their only Welsh abbey, Talyllychau (The Head of the Lakes) now known as Talley, and still enveloped in pastoral peace.

He died in 1197, having resumed, during the last years of his life, his assaults on his Norman neighbours. His daughter Gwenllian married Ednyfed Fychan, from whose eldest son, Goronwy, Henry Tudor was descended. His younger son Gruffudd was the ancestor of Rhys ap Thomas, the South-West Wales magnate whose support ensured that Henry Tudor became Henry VII, and established a dynasty which produced two of Britain's most renowned monarchs: Henry VIII and Queen Elizabeth I.

RHYS ap TEWDWR (d. 1093)

Rhys ap Tewdwr, like Gruffudd ap Cynan (d. 1137) could claim descent from Rhodri Mawr (the Great) (d. 878); Rhys from Rhodri's son, Cadell, who on his father's death became ruler of Deheubarth, and Gruffudd from another son, Anarawd who at the same time had become ruler of Gwynedd. Both Rhys and Gruffudd found their inherited territorial rights challenged by rival princes, but their victory at Mynydd Carn on the Preseli Mountains in 1087 reaffirmed their undisputed control over Deheubarth and Gwynedd.

In that year, William the Conqueror visited South Wales and, according to the *Brut*, 'William the Bastard, king of the Saxons and the French and the Britons, came on a pilgrimage to Menevia to offer prayers.' His visit resulted in a meeting with Rhys ap Tewdwr who did William homage and agreed to make an annual payment of £40 to the king, who could now regard Rhys as his vassal, an agreement which made for stability and security in Deheubarth, now finding itself free from Norman intrusion. This state of independence, though bought at a cost, came to an end in 1093 with Rhys's death, while defending Brycheiniog against the Normans under Bernard Neufmarché.

The result was a sudden and almost total submission of South Wales to the might of the invaders.

Rhys's daughter was the great beauty, Nest, whose marriage to Gerald of Windsor was one of the first examples of Norman –Welsh conjugal alliances. Their daughter, Angharad, married William de Barri, whose youngest son (c. 1146–1223) was to achieve renown as Gerald of Wales (q.v.).

RHYS ap THOMAS (1449–1525)

By the time of his death Sir Rhys had accumulated a number of honours each one indicating some facet of a lifetime of action and achievement. His most notable contribution to posterity was his unswerving support of Henry Tudor, earl of Richmond, in his bid to gain the Crown of England from Richard III at the Battle of Bosworth field on the 22nd August 1485. (He is referred to in Shakespeare's *Richard III* as 'Rice ap Thomas with a valiant crew'.) It was an act of national significance as well as one of personal loyalty, and rewarded by his being knighted on the very spot of the victory. Such recognition led to his being considered the representative in West Wales not only of Henry VII but of his son, Henry VIII as well.

As a result, a number of the castles of the region came under his control, giving him plenty of opportunity to exercise bardic patronage, and in several cases to make substantial architectural improvements, particularly at Carew, where the embellishments were elaborate and where, on St George's Day, 1507 he held a great tournament to celebrate his admission to the Order of the Garter in 1505. A banner across the gateway depicted St George and St David in fraternal embrace, a gesture which unambiguously showed that the traditional enmity between the Welsh and the English had been halted by the succession of a Tudor king.

Rhys was no mere upstart who had made the most of his opportunities. Lewis Glyn Cothi (*fl.* 1447–86) pointed out in a *cywydd* that whereas Henry Tudor was descended from Goronwy, Rhys was descended from Gruffudd, both sons of Ednyfed Fychan, seneschal to Llywelyn the Great.

Through his parents' estates in South-West Wales, he was a man not only of property but of persuasion, capable of enlisting the support of the squirearchy behind Henry Tudor, earl of Richmond who, as far as the Welsh bards were concerned, was *Mab Darogan* (the Son of Prophecy), the embodiment of the saviour-hero who would free his fellow-countrymen from English aggression.

After the Dissolution of the Monasteries, the tomb of Sir Rhys was removed from Greyfriars monastery at Carmarthen to the church of St Peter's in the town.

WALES, STATUTE OF (*Statutum Walliae*), 1284

Also called the Statute of Rhuddlan, this document unambiguously affirmed Edward's annexation of Wales, which was now divided into shires, according to the custom which already existed in England. Each was to have its sheriff (shire reeve). The royal lands were now divided in three:

The Principality of North Wales now comprised Anglesey, Caernarfonshire and Merioneth.
That of South Wales was made of the shires of Cardigan and Carmarthen.
Third came Flint, a Welsh extension of the earldom of Chester.

What remained was divided into *cantrefi*. In matters of civil cases, the Welsh were allowed to keep the laws of Hywel Dda. The native system of partible inheritance, gavelkind, could continue, though the right of an illegitimate son to inherit his father's property was now abolished. Provision was made for entailment through a female descendant, if the male line failed.

The whole programme of castle building was a conspicuous indication of the king's undisputed right to put his plans into immediate and effective operation.

WOODSTOCK, TREATY OF, 1247

In April, 1247, Henry III, who had already exerted a firm grip on the people of Wales, was able to take full advantage of the uncertainty in Gwynedd caused by the death of Llywelyn ap Iorwerth's son, Dafydd, without an heir. His illegitimate brother Gruffudd's four sons, each staking his claim, could be a disruptive influence as far as the king was concerned. Rather than exercising their own authority within Gwynedd, they were now expected to submit to that of the English Crown. Owain and Llywelyn, the two elder brothers, were given the west regions of Gwynedd, whereas the east was taken by Henry, who asserted himself also at Montgomery, Builth, Carmarthen and Cardigan. The rulers of other parts of Wales were now expected to do homage to the king himself, rather than to the Princes of Gwynedd.

WORCESTER, TREATY OF, 1218

Henry III recognised Llywelyn ap Iorwerth as Wales's undisputed leader, a position of authority which he enjoyed until his death in 1240, thus creating a period of unity lasting almost a quarter of a century.

Appendix III
A Castle Building Glossary

APSE A semi-circular or polygonal recess.

ARROW-LOOP See Loop-hole.

ASHLAR Stone with flat and smooth surface cut to rectangular shape.

BAILEY An enclosure, originally defended by palisades, a fence of pales (hence, 'beyond the pale' referring to King John's dominion in Ireland which was demarcated with pales). The bailey – or ward – was defended by a ditch and could take a variety of shapes. The palisade was later replaced by masonry.

BALLISTA A powerful version of a bow, capable of aiming stones as well as heavy arrows. There is a good reconstruction at Caerphilly.

BARBICAN An additional external protective construction to safeguard the principal fortified entrance to a castle. The one at Beaumaris is a strikingly good example.

BARTIZAN A small turret, sometimes battlemented, jutting out from the corner of a tower.

BASTIDE A town built in conjunction with a castle to form a fortified unit. Introduced into Wales by Edward I at Flint in 1277.

BASTION An earthwork or stone platform, designed and sited to provide flanking fire.

BATTER The sloping base or plinth of a building, offering further protection by its extra thickness.

BATTLEMENT A parapet with alternating crenels or crenelles (openings) and merlons (solid masonry).

BRATTICE A temporary defended timber platform, assembled quickly according to need, which could be used outside the battlements in order to cover dead ground at the foot of towers and walls. Bretasch (or bretache) is an alternative word, which can refer to a free-standing tower in wood. The brattice is based on the same principle as the hoard or hourd. There is a good reconstruction above the main entrance to Castell Coch, the marquess of Bute's nineteenth-century reconstruction of a thirteenth-century castle.

BURGAGE A plot of town land available in return for annual rent.

BUTTERY A storeroom for drink, placed between the hall and the kitchen, often next to the pantry. The 'bouteilerie' or 'bottlery' was presided over by the 'bottler'.

CAPITAL The top part of a column, normally ornamented.

CASTELLATION The battlements and turrets of a castle.

CONSTABLE A key position held by the man who undertook the responsibilities of the smooth running as well as the defence of the castle in the absence of its owner.

CORBEL A stone bracket jutting out from the wall in order to support a parapet or gallery.

CRENEL The open part of a battlemented parapet, the solid parts being called merlons. Before a lord could embattle or fortify his residence, a licence to crenellate was needed from the king.

CUPOLA A small domed turret on a roof.

CURTAIN WALL The outer wall of the castle connecting its towers and gatehouse, thereby creating a fortified enclosure. Enceinte is an alternative word.

D-ENDED TOWER A semi-circular tower.

DAIS The raised level of the hall of a medieval castle and subsequent dwellings up until the end of the Tudor period. The dais end refers to the place of honour where the lord's table was placed.

DEAD GROUND The most difficult area to cover without putting the defenders to great risk.

DONJON The great tower or keep and the most assertive part of the castle before the development of the powerful gatehouse, as at Harlech. *Dungeon* might be a derivative, referring to the castle's subterranean cells which were always placed at the base of the donjon.

DRAWBRIDGE A hinged bridge spanning the ditch or moat leading to the principal castle entrance. It was raised not only to block the entrance but to deprive the enemy of a crossing point.

DRUM TOWERS Circular towers placed strategically along the curtain wall, and so called because of their resemblance to the drum-shape.

EARTHWORKS The earliest castles were defences devised from a system of ditches and mounds or mottes, further protected with palisades. Those that have survived are still formidable in the sense of power which they impart.

FLÈCHE A slender spire (Fr. *flèche*: arrow).

GARDEROBE Though mostly used to refer to a privy, it could have had another function, as its name suggests – a place for the safekeeping of expensive garments and other valuables. As such, it could be the ancestor of the modern wardrobe.

HALL The central non-military part of the castle, fulfilling an administrative and legal as well as a domestic role. The hall in most cases occupied the floor above the storage basement and was entered by external stairs.

HEARTH The hall was heated by means of a central hearth with a ventilation louver above it. Because of the constant risk of unwanted fire, a cover or *couvre-feu* was placed over the hearth when the company retired. A bell was rung to signify the time of such a ritual, an observance which gave rise to the *curfew*.

HOARDS, HOURDS A temporary wooden fighting gallery erected outside the battlements for additional defence. See Brattice.

HOMAGE The medieval ritual by which a vassal formally acknowledged his allegiance to his lord, in return for lands or favours.

KEEP The most heavily defended building within the castle complex. Also called a donjon. Originally square or rectangular, they became cylindrical, and therefore less likely to be weakened by battering.

LICENCE A castle built without royal licence could be forfeited, a principle that was applied equally rigorously to the crenellating of a manor house, thus giving it the appearance of a fortified building. Such strictures were introduced by the Normans, though records of such licences do not survive from the period before King John (1199–1216).

LOOP-HOLE A narrow vertical slit in a wall or in the merlon section of a parapet. It splayed internally thereby giving the defending garrison a wider aim.

MACHICOLATIONS The holes – not unlike murder-holes – in an advantageously placed gallery, or in the parapet itself, through which a variety of missiles could be hurled at the assailant. In principle, not unlike the temporary timber hoard or brattice.

MANGON(EL) A siege engine on the sling principle, loaded with a projectile which was released by a trigger mechanism.

MERLON The solid, masonry section of a battlemented parapet, alternating with the embrasure or crenel (crenelle), and often incorporating arrow-loops.

MOTTE-AND-BAILEY The early type of Norman castle, consisting of a mound (motte) surrounded by a ditch, and an outer area (bailey) protected.

MULLION-AND-TRANSOM WINDOWS Windows divided by mullions (upright posts) and transoms (horizontal posts).

MURAL Refers to anything to do with walls. Hence a mural stair is one built into the thickness of a wall. A murage licence was permission granted to build a wall.

MURDER-HOLES Holes placed strategically above the gatehouse passage or at any similarly assailable point in the castle through which to repel attack.

OGIVAL Adjective of ogee, an S-shaped curve.

ORDER The three Greek orders, Doric, Ionic and Corinthian were augmented by the two Roman orders of Tuscan and Composite. Their decorative elements were often used to embellish the capitals of columns. See Beaupré.

ORIEL WINDOW An important bay window lighting the dais end of a medieval house; it can also refer to a projecting window on an upper storey, supported on corbels.

OUBLIETTE From the French *oublier*, 'to forget'. A vicious form of incarceration whereby a prisoner could be held in a place where he was out of sight and therefore out of mind.

PALISADE A wooden wall used by the Normans as a highly effective method of staking their claim in their conquest.

PANTRY A storeroom for bread – *pain* (French).

PARAPET A battlemented or crenellated protection for a wall-walk.

PORTCULLIS A heavy gate of wood and metal dropped vertically in grooves on both sides of the opening.

PORTE-COCHÈRE A porch or portico wide enough to take a vehicle from which passengers could alight and enter a building under cover.

POSTERN A subsidiary or pedestrian access to the castle, to avoid unnecessary use of the principal entrance.

PUT-LOG HOLES Holes which supported timber scaffolding called put-logs, essential for the maintenance of the higher sections of the castle.

RANGE A wing or section of a building complex.

REVETMENT A masonry supporting wall built facing the sloping side of a deep ditch. A good example is at Rhuddlan.

RINGWORK An oval or circular fortification enclosed by an earthen rampart.

SALLY PORT A quick escape route for a besieged garrison.

SCREENS A wooden partition at the service end of the hall, installed to reduce the draught from the cross passage between the two opposite entrances to the hall. Beyond it were the buttery, pantry and kitchen. The partition eventually became a permanent structure, with a minstrels' gallery above it, an arrangement adopted by Oxbridge colleges and the Inns of Court.

SHELL KEEP A fortification in stone raised on the top of a motte, with various domestic buildings backing onto the circular enclosing wall. Excellent examples at Cardiff and Tretower.

SOLAR A room placed at the dais-end of the hall, to which the lord and his family could retire. It was usually on the first floor and was well lit (hence the name, from the Latin *solarium*), since being the least defended part of the castle, it had a greater expanse of window.

SPYHOLES Holes through which to spy on enemy activity.

TOURELLE A small turret projecting from the upper storey of a building or tower.

TRACERY The decorative work in the upper part of a window, especially one belonging to the solar or to the castle chapel.

TREBUCHET A siege-engine introduced to England in the thirteenth century by Louis of France.

WARD The fortified enclosure of a castle, many of which had both an inner and an outer ward. In principle, similar to the bailey, usually associated with earthwork defences.

Appendix IV

A Welsh Place Name Glossary

abaty — abbey
aber — estuary
afon — river
allt *see* gallt
ar — on
aur — gold, golden

bach/bychan (fach/fychan) — small
bach, bachau (pl) — bend, corner, hook
bae — bay
ban (fan), bannau (pl) — beacon
   Bannau Brycheiniog — Brecon Beacons
bedwen (fedwen), bedw (pl) — birch
   Pant-y-fedwen — Hollow of the birchtree
bedd, beddau (pl) — grave
   Bedd Gelert — Gelert's grave
betws — church, chapel, oratory
   Betws-y-Coed — Church in the wood
blaen, blaenau (pl) — end, source of river, upland
   Blaenavon (Blaenafon)
   Blaenllynfi
   Blaenau Ffestiniog
bod — abode, dwelling
   Bodhyfryd — Beautiful dwelling
   Bodysgallen — Thistle dwelling
   Bodidris — Idris's dwelling
bont *see* pont
braich — arm, ridge
bro (fro) — region, vale
   Bro Morgannwg — Vale of Glamorgan
bron — hillside

bryn, bryniau (pl)	hill
bwlch	pass, gap
Bwlch yr Oernant	(Lit. Pass of the cold brook) Horseshoe Pass
bychan (fechan)	small
Dafydd Fychan	Often applied to describe a person, it developed into the surname Vaughan
cadair, cader	seat, stronghold
Cader Idris	
cae, caeau (pl)	field, enclosure
caer, caerau (pl)	fort, stronghold
canol	middle, centre
capel	meeting house, chapel
carn, carnau (pl)	cairn, rock
carnedd, carneddau/carneddi (pl)	cairn, mountain, mound
carreg, cerrig (pl)	stone, rock
Cerrig y Drudion	Lit. Druid's stones
cartref	home
cartrefle	homestead
cas	castle
Cas-gwent	Chepstow
castell	castle, stronghold
cefn	ridge, back
Cefncoedycymer	
cei	quay
Cei Newydd	Newquay (Dyfed)
celli (gelli)	grove
Y Gelli Aur	Golden grove
ceunant	brook, gorge, ravine
cil, ciliau (pl)	corner, retreat
Cilfynydd	
Cil-y-cwm	
cilfach	corner, nook
Y Gilfach Goch	
clawdd, cloddiau (pl)	dyke, hedge, ditch
Clawdd Offa	Offa's Dyke

clogwyn	cliff, crag
clun	meadow, moor
cnwc	hillock, knoll
coch (goch)	red
	Often used as an epithet, developed into surname Gough
coed	wood, trees
coetir	woodland
coetre	woodland dwelling
coety	wood house
cors	bog, fen
craig, creigiau (pl)	rock
Craig-Cefn-Parc	
crib	crest, summit
Y Grib Goch	
croes	cross, crossroads
crug, crugiau (pl)	knoll, tump
Crughywel	Crickhowell
cwm	valley, combe
Cwm Rhondda	
cwrt	court, yard
cymer, cymerau (pl)	confluence, junction
dan	under
dau, dwy (fem)	two
derwen	oak
din	hillfort
Dinlligwy	
dinas	city, stronghold
Dinas Brân	
diserth	retreat
dôl, dolydd/dolau (pl)	meadow, water meadow
Dolbadarn	
Dolforwyn	
dre *see* tre	
drws	gap, narrow pass, door
Drws-y-coed	
du, ddu (fem)	black

Coed duon	Blackwood
dŵr/dwfr	water
dwy	fem. of *dau* two
dyffryn	valley
eglwys	church
eithin	furze, gorse
erw	acre
esgair	ridge
fach/fechan *see* bach/bychan	
faenor *see* maenor	
fan *see* ban	
faerdref *see* maerdref	
fawr *see* mawr	
felin *see* melin	
foel *see* moel	
fron *see* bron	
ffin	boundary
fforch	fork
ffordd	way, road
ffos	ditch
ffridd, ffriddoedd (pl)	mountain pasture
ffrith, ffrithoedd (pl)	*as above*
ffrwd, ffrydiau (pl)	stream, torrent
ffynnon, ffynhonnau (pl)	spring, well
gaer *see* caer	
gallt	hill, slope
garth	hill, enclosure
garw	rough
gefail	smithy
glan	river-bank
glas	green, blue
glyn	valley, glen
goch *see* coch	
goetre *see* coetre	
gors *see* cors	
graig *see* craig	

grib *see* crib
groes *see* croes
grug — heather
gwaun — moorland
gwern — swamp
gwig — wood
gwyn, gwen (fem) — white, blessed
gwyrdd, gwerdd (fem) — green

hafod/hafoty — summer-dwelling
haul — sun
heli — salt water, sea
  Y Felin Heli — (Port Dinorwic)
helygen, helyg (pl) — willow
hen — old
hendre — winter dwelling, permanent home
heol — road
hir — long

is — below
  Bangor-is-coed
isaf — lower, lowest
isel — low

las *see* glas
lwyd *see* llwyd
llan — church, enclosure, parish; usually followed by saint's name
  Llanfair — Parish of Mary
  Llanbedr — Parish of Peter
  Llantrisant — Parish of three saints
  Llanpumsaint — Parish of five saints
llannerch — clearing, glade
llawr — valley floor
llech — slate, stone
llechwedd — hillside
  Llechwedd Slate Caves

llwch, llychau (pl)	lake cf. Scottish *loch*
Tal-y-llychau	(End of the lakes) abbreviated to Talley (abbey) in Dyfed
llwyd	grey, brown Gave way to the surname Lloyd
llwyn	grove, bush
Llwyn-hendy	
Llwyn-y-groes	
llyn, llynnoedd (pl)	lake
Llyn y Fan Fach	Small lake on the peak, beacon
Llyn y Fan Fawr	Large lake on the peak, beacon
llys	court, hall
maen, meini (pl)	stone
maenol/maenor	chieftain's domain
Vaynol	
Vaynor	
maerdre (f), maerdrefi (pl)	chief's demesne, settlement connected to chief's court
Vardre Clydach	
Llantwit Vardre	
maes, meysydd (pl)	field
mawr	big
meini *see* **maen**	
melin	mill
melindre (f)	mill village
Felindre or	
Velindre	
melyn	yellow
moel	bare
moelfryn	e.g. bare hill, seen in the anglicisation of Celtic origins into Malvern
morfa	marsh, sea fen
mur, muriau (pl)	wall

mwyn	ore, mine
mynachlog	monastery
Mynachlog Ddu (Dyfed)	
mynydd	mountain
Mynydd-Isaf	
nant, nentydd/nannau (pl)	brook
Nantgaredig	
Nantglyn	
newydd	new
ochr	side
odyn	kiln
ogof	cave
Dan-yr-Ogof Caves	
onnen, onn/ynn (pl)	ash tree
pandy	fulling-mill
Ton-y-Pandy	
Rhyd-y-Pandy	
pant	hollow, valley
Pantglas	
parc	park, field
pen	head, end, top
Pen-y-bont ar Ogwr	Bridgend (Glam.)
Penpont	cf. Penpont (Dumfries & Galloway)
penmaen	promontory
Penmaenmawr	
penrhyn	promontory
pentir	promontory
Pentir	cf. Pentire (Cornwall)
pentre (f)	village
Pentre'r felin	
Pentre-ty-gwyn	
pistyll	well, spout
plas, plasau (pl)	mansion, country house
Plas Newydd	
pont, pontydd (pl)	bridge

Pontardawe
Pontnewydd
Bontnewydd
porth   gateway, harbour
   Porthmadog
   Porthcawl
pwll   pit, pool
   Pwll-glas
   Pwllheli

rhaeadr   waterfall
   Rhayadr
   Llanrhaeadr-ym-Mochnant
rhandir   region, allotment
   Rhandirmwyn
rhiw   hill, slope
   Rhiwlas
rhos   moorland
   Rhostryfan
   Rhosneigr
rhyd   ford
   Rhydaman
   Rhyd-y-fro
   Rhyd-ddu

sarn, sarnau (pl)   causeway
   Talsarn
   Talsarnau

tafarn, tafarnau (pl)   tavern
   Tafarnau-bach
tair *see* tri
tal   end
tan   under
   Plas Tan-y-bwlch
teg   fair
tir   land, territory
tomen   mound
   Tomen y Rhodwydd

ton	grassland
traeth	strand, beach
trallwng	wet land
Y Trallwng	(Welshpool)
traws	cross
Trawscoed	
tre (f)	homestead, settlement, town
Y Drenewydd	Newtown
tri, tair (fem)	three
troed	foot
Troed-y-rhiw	
tros	over
trum	ridge
trwyn	point, cape
	cf. Troon (Strathclyde), Treen (Cornwall)
tŵr	tower
twyn	knoll, hillock
tŷ, tai (pl)	house
tyddyn/ty'n	small-holding
Ty'n y Coed	
uchaf	upper, higher
uchel	high
uwch	above, over
waun *see* gwaun	
wen *see* gwyn, gwen (fem)	
wern *see* gwern	
y/yr/'r	the
yn	in
ynys	island, river meadow
ysbyty	hospital, hospice
Ysbyty Ifan	
Ysbyty Ystwyth	
ystrad	wide valley, strath
Ystrad Fflur	Strata Florida
Ystradgynlais	cf. Strathaven (Strathclyde)

Bibliography

AVENT, RICHARD, *Castles of the Princes of Gwynedd*, H.M.S.O., 1983.

BELL, DAVID, *The Artist in Wales*, Harrap & Co, 1957.

BELL, H.I., *The Development of Welsh Poetry*, O.U.P., 1936.

BOTTOMLEY, FRANK, *The Castle Explorer's Guide*, Bracken Books, 1979.

BRADNEY, J.A., *A History of Monmouthshire* (Vol. 1, Parts 1 & 2), London, 1907.

BROWN, R. ALLEN, *Castles from the Air*, C.U.P., 1989.

BURNHAM, HELEN, *Clwyd and Powys: A Guide to Ancient and Historic Wales*, H.M.S.O., 1995.

CARR, A.D., *Medieval Wales*, St Martin's Press, 1995.

CREW, PETER (with CHRIS MUSSON), *Snowdonia from the Air*, R.C.A.M./Snowdonia National Park Authority, 1996.

DAVIES, ELWYN (ed.), *A Gazetteer of Welsh Place Names*, U.W.P., 1958.

DAVIES, JOHN, *A History of Wales*, Penguin, 1990.

DAVIES, JOHN, *The Making of Wales*, Cadw, 1996.

DAVIES, R.R., *The Age of Conquest*, O.U.P., 1987.

DAVIES, R.R., *Owain Glyndŵr*, O.U.P., 1996.

DAVIES, V. EIRWEN, *Gruffudd ap Cynan*, U.W.P., 1959.

EVANS, D. SIMON (ed.), *A Medieval Prince of Wales: The Life of Gruffudd ap Cynan*, Llanerch Enterprises, 1990.

FENTON, RICHARD, *Tours in Wales 1804–1813*, ed. John Fisher, London: Bedford Press, 1917.

FOX, CYRIL, *Ancient Monuments in South Wales and Monmouthshire*, H.M.S.O., 1954.

FORDE-JOHNSTON, JAMES, *A Guide to the Castles of England and Wales*, Constable, 1981.

GAUNT, PETER, *A Nation Under Siege: The Civil War in Wales, 1642–48*, Cadw, 1991.

GIROUARD, MARK, *Victorian Country Houses*, revised and enlarged edition, B.C.A., 1979.

HARRIS, NATHANIEL, *Castles of England, Scotland and Wales*, George Philips, 1991.

HASLAM, RICHARD, *Powys: Buildings of Wales*, Penguin/U.W.P., 1989.

HERBERT, TREVOR (ed.), with GARETH ELWYN JONES, *Edward I and Wales*, University of Wales Press, 1988.

H.M.S.O., *Anglesey*, 1937, reprinted 1968.

H.M.S.O., *Caernarfon*, East, 1956; Central, 1960; West, 1964.

H.M.S.O., *Glamorgan: An Inventory of the Ancient Monuments: The Early Castles*, 1991.

HUBBARD, EDWARD, *Clwyd: Buildings of Wales*, Penguin/U.W.P., 1986.

HUGHES, GWILYM REES (ed.) with A.O.H. JARMAN, *A Guide to Welsh Literature*, Vol. 1, Christopher Davies, 1976.

HUGHES, QUENTIN, *Military Architecture*, Beaufort Publishing Ltd, 1991.

HUMPHRIES, P.H., *Castles of Edward I in Wales*, H.M.S.O., 1983.

HYDE, RALPH, *A Prospect of Britain: The Town Panoramas of Samuel and Nathaniel Buck*, Pavilion, 1994.

JARMAN, A.O.H. (ed.) with GWILYN REES HUGHES, *A Guide to Welsh Literature*, Vol. 1, Christopher Davies, 1976.

JENKINS, A.D. FRASER, *The Romantic Traveller in Wales*, National Museum of Wales, 1970.

JONES, GWYN (trans.) with THOMAS JONES, *The Mabinogion*, J.M. Dent, 1949.

JONES, THOMAS (trans,) with GWYN JONES, *The Mabinogion.*

JONES, THOMAS (trans. and notes), *Brut y Tywysogyon: The Chronicle of the Princes*, O.U.P., 1955.

JOYNER, PAUL, *Samuel Hieronymus Grimm*, National Library of Wales, 1983.

KERR, NIGEL & MARY, *A Guide to Medieval Sites in Britain*, Diamond Books, 1992.

KIGHTLY, CHARLES, *Chieftains and Princes*, Cadw, 1996.

KING, D.J.C., *The Castle in England and Wales*, Routledge, 1988.

LELAND, JOHN, *Itinerary in England and Wales 1536–39*, ed. Lucy Toulmin Smith, S. Illinois University Press, 1994.

LYNCH, FRANCES, *Gwynedd: A Guide to Ancient and Historic Wales*, H.M.S.O., 1995.

MATARASSO, FRANCOIS, *The English Castle*, Cassell, 1995.

MILES, DILLWYN, *Castles of Pembrokeshire*, Pembrokeshire Coast National Park Authority, n.d.

MOORE, DONALD, *The Artist and the Castle*, Exhibition Catalogue, National Library of Wales, 1974.

MOORE, DONALD, *The Earliest Views of Glamorgan*, Glamorgan Archive Service, 1983.

MORGAN, RAY with ELLIS PETERS, *Strongholds and Sanctuaries*.

MORGAN, T.J. & PRYS, *Welsh Surnames*, University of Wales Press, 1985.

MORRIS, JOHN E., *The Welsh Wars of Edward I*, O.U.P., 1901. Fac. reprinted 1994, Llanerch Publishers.

MUSSON, CHRIS, *Wales from the Air*, R.C.A.M., n.d.

MUSSON, CHRIS with PETER CREW, *Snowdonia from the Air*, R.C.A.M./Snowdonia National Park Authority, 1996.

NEWMAN, JOHN, *Glamorgan: Buildings in Wales*, Penguin/U.W.P., 1995.

PENNANT, THOMAS, *A Tour in Wales* (2 vols), London, 1784.

PETERS, ELLIS & MORGAN, ROY, *Strongholds and Sanctuaries (The Borderland of England and Wales)*, Alan Sutton, 1993.

PLATT, COLIN, *The Castles in Medieval England and Wales*, Secker & Warburg, 1982.

REES, DAVID, *Sir Rhys ap Thomas*, Gomer, 1992.

REES, DAVID, *The Son of Prophecy*, Black Raven Press, 1985.

REES, SIAN, *Dyfed: A Guide to Ancient and Historic Wales*, H.M.S.O., 1992.

ROBINSON, D.M. (ed.), *A Mirror of Medieval Wales*, Cadw, 1988.

ROBINSON, D.M. (ed.) with ROGER THOMAS, *Wales: Castles and Historic Places*, Cadw/W.T.B., 1990.

ROBINSON, DAVID, *Heritage in Wales*, Cadw, 1989.

RODERICK, A.J. (ed.), *Wales Through the Ages*, Vol. 1, Christopher Davies, 1959, Vol. 2, Christopher Davies, 1960.

SANCHA, SHEILA, *The Castle Story*, Harper Collins, 1991.

SMITH, PETER, *Houses of the Welsh Countryside*, H.M.S.O., 1975.

SODEN, R.W., *A Guide to Welsh Parish Churches*, Gomer, 1984.

SORRELL, ALAN, *British Castles*, Batsford, 1973.

SORRELL, M. (ed.), *Reconstructing the Past*, B.C.A., 1981.

SOULSBY, IAN, *The Towns of Medieval Wales*, Phillimore, 1983.

STEPHENSON, DAVID, *The Last Prince of Wales*, Barracuda Books, Buckingham, 1983.

TAYLOR, A.J., *The King's Works in Wales 1277–1330*, H.M.S.O., 1974.

THOMAS, ROGER, *Castles in Wales*, A.A./W.T.B., 1990.

THOMAS, ROGER with D.M. ROBINSON, *Wales: Castles & Historic Places*, Cadw/W.T.B., 1990.

THOMPSON, M.W., *The Decline of the Castle*, C.U.P., 1987.

THOMPSON, M.W., *The Rise of the Castle*, C.U.P., 1991.

TUCKER, NORMAN, *North Wales in the Civil Wars*, Bridge Books, Wrexham, 1992.

WALKER, DAVID, *Medieval Wales*, C.U.P., 1990.

WHITTLE, ELISABETH, *Glamorgan and Gwent: A Guide to Ancient and Historic Wales*, H.M.S.O., 1992.

WILLIAMS, GLANMOR, 'The Middle Ages' in *Ancient Monuments of Wales*, H.M.S.O., 1973.

WILLIAMS, GLANMOR, *Owain Glyndŵr*, O.U.P., 1993.

WILLIAMS, GWYN A., *When Was Wales?*, Penguin, 1985.

BACKGROUND READING

Edith Pargeter's sequence of four novels entitled *The Brothers of Gwynedd* are an imaginative and atmospheric evocation of thirteenth-century life in North Wales, and the constant feuds between the native princes among each other as well as against the English throne. The individual titles are: *Sunrise on the West*, *The Dragon of Noonday*, *The Hounds of the Sunset* and *Afterglow and Nightfall*. Originally published by Macmillan between 1974–77, they have been in paperback, published by Headline since 1987. Edith Pargeter also writes under the name of Ellis Peters.